The Role of Franchising on Industry Evolution

Rosalind Beere

The Role of Franchising on Industry Evolution

Assessing the Emergence of Franchising and its Impact on Structural Change

palgrave
macmillan

Rosalind Beere
Dublin, Ireland

ISBN 978-3-319-84077-2   ISBN 978-3-319-49064-9   (eBook)
DOI 10.1007/978-3-319-49064-9

Cover illustration: Cosmo Condina / Alamy Stock Photo

Printed on acid-free paper

This Palgrave Macmillan imprint is published by Springer Nature
The registered company is Springer International Publishing AG
The registered company address is: Gewerbestrasse 11, 6330 Cham, Switzerland

Acknowledgements

This book would not have been possible without the invaluable support of my colleagues, friends, and family. I would also like to thank my mother Helen, my family, and friends, and especially my husband Cian, and children Catherine and Senan for their love and support.

Contents

List of Figures

List of Tables

Introduction

This book focuses on the role of franchising on industry evolution. It explores how franchising can affect an industry, and the empirical evidence presented in this book suggests that franchising can bring an industry from a structural state of fragmentation to one of consolidation. This book offers an insight into why franchising emerges and how it impacts industry evolution (and includes case studies).

The impact of franchising on the structural change of an industry has been defined by contextual drivers which have led to the adoption of franchising. This book investigates two elements of franchising: one being its emergence and the second being its impact on industry. One of the main chapters in this book investigates the emergence of franchising, which is often initiated by changes in the macro-environmental such as government impact, economic and social change, and technology effects. Industry-level context was also important in the adoption of franchising which was mostly driven by (a threat of) national/international competition, national-level developments, expanding industry boundaries, the emergence of new sectors as well as agency factors (entrepreneurs) and customer expectations. All of these factors are important triggers for the introduction and adoption of franchising in an industry and are particularly pertinent as a learning mechanism for the emerging markets where franchising is in its emerging phase.

The book will also look at the impact at industry level which has been neglected as a core element in much of the research to date. Indeed once adopted, the impact of franchising contributes to industry-level structural changes. Specifically, it can expand industry boundaries, encourage the emergence of new sectors, increase competition, create new institutions, and change industry-level relationships. Franchising also increases the franchise system's own internal capabilities (and the capabilities of its franchisees), generate/transform knowledge and information, increase industry capabilities, and protect industry boundaries by erecting barriers to entry as well as preventing state regulation by achieving self-regulation. Finally franchising has the ability to fundamentally transform an industry's structure from one of fragmentation to one of consolidation. Most authors view franchising as a marketing approach or a means of distribution of goods and services. However, this author has recognised that franchising is well suited to 'disorganised' industries which can benefit from its organisational structure. The reason for writing this book is based on a number of theoretical and empirical grounds, including the general neglect of the area in the literature, the potential implications for future research, and potential contribution recognised by academics, practitioners, and policy makers.

The book also contains two industry case studies which are information-rich examples providing empirical evidence and analysis as to why franchising emerges and its impact on industry evolution.

1

Franchising: An Overview

This chapter will provide an overview of the definition of franchising as well as how the franchising system works. The history of franchising is also explored—looking at the origins of franchising and the three stages of development citing examples throughout. Specifically business format franchising will be the main focus of this book, and as such business format franchising as well as its dominance internationally and across multiple industries is discussed in this chapter.

The Origins of Franchising

The word 'franchising' is a French term, which when translated means 'a granting of right' or 'an exemption' (Williamson, 1992). Franchising is a form of business arrangement, which originated from Western Europe in the Middle Ages, at a time when feudal lords initiated the practice of selling the rights to collect taxes and operate markets on their behalf. The first examples of franchising are to be found in mid-nineteenth century Germany where brewers set up contracts with tavern owners to sell their beer exclusively in their taverns (Shane, 2008).

© The Author(s) 2017
R. Beere, *The Role of Franchising on Industry Evolution*,
DOI 10.1007/978-3-319-49064-9_1

In terms of the growth of franchising, it is possible to identify three stages in its development. The first stage dates back to the middle of the nineteenth century in the USA when the Singer Sewing Machine was introduced through a licence/franchising-like arrangement (Hackett, 1976). The Singer Sewing Centre was developed by Isaac Singer in 1858. He encountered two obstacles post invention—a lack of capital to manufacture the machine in large numbers and a need for user training. To address these concerns he began selling the rights to local business people, to both sell and train customers in the use of his machine. This proved successful and the business expanded rapidly as the fees earned from the licence rights helped to fund his manufacturing costs. In the early 1890s another successful franchisor was Coca-Cola. Coca-Cola chose to franchise the rights to bottle its carbonated beverage to a large number of independent businessmen who received exclusive territories in which to distribute the product (Shane, 2008). According to Dant and Grunhagen (2014), whereas the focus of traditional franchising is on the product of the manufacture, in business format franchising, the second variant to develop, the outlet itself is the product. Dant and Grunhagen (2014) refer to business format franchising as the franchisor selling a 'way of doing business' together with a comprehensive package of services, together with an operating manual and other operational supports. Dant and Grunhagen (2014) suggest that the first true business format franchise system was created in the early 1890s by Martha Matilda Harper, who had succeeded in developing a network of over 500 Harper Beauty Shops by the mid-1920s (Plitt, 2000). While Harper Beauty Shops did not make a lasting mark in the USA franchising arena some of the other early business format franchise systems, for example Hertz Car Rentals, A&W Restaurants, Terminix Termite, and Pest Control, that started in the 1920s continue to exist and operate as franchises.

During the second stage of development in the USA during the 1920s and 1930s, similar license/franchise relationships were developed by petrol companies and some wholesalers and retailers (Aydin & Kacker, 1989). The franchising model was quickly copied in several industries, in particular by major motor manufacturers and oil companies (Shane, 2008). Furthermore, Ford and General Motors began to franchise dealerships to independent business people as they did not have sufficient funds to create the necessary retail outlets when they first began to operate. A further development, within the franchising model, occurred in the 1920s, when the major oil companies became pioneers of conversion franchising. In this model, already established independent businesses became franchisees under the umbrella of the franchisor's brand name (Shane, 2008). During this time franchising in retail and service businesses developed in the USA. The earliest retailers to adopt franchising were the Ben Franklin stores and Piggly Wiggly stores; both began to franchise in the 1920s. The earliest fast food franchise was A&W Root Beer, established in the USA in 1924. Howard Johnson was the first to franchise restaurants in the USA in 1935 (Shane, 2008).

The third generation of franchising, namely business format franchising dates back to the late 1940s and early 1950s (Mendelson, 1992). This form of franchising really took off in the USA. In the 1950s and 1960s many of today's large franchise chains were founded such as Tastee-Freez, KFC, McDonald's, and Burger King. The acceleration in franchising during this period can be attributed largely to two factors: first, the rise of television advertising, which made national advertising a viable way to build a brand, as businesses began to gain competitive advantage over rivals by building brands and national chains; and second, the establishment of the US national highway system, which made travel to unfamiliar places more common and created the need to have national brand names as a way to demonstrate quality to customers in various locations (Shane, 2008). However, with the rapid adoption of business format franchising in the 1960s, some problems arose. Fraud became an issue with an increase in franchise operations taking potential franchisees' investment and subsequently shutting down. This activity led to the development of franchising regulation in the 1970s in the USA. The Federal Trade Commission (FTC) initiated its first fraud investigations in 1975. In the same year, the North American Securities Administration drew up draft guidelines for Uniform Franchise Offering Circulars (UFOCs). These have become the standard for disclosing franchise opportunities to franchisees (Shane, 2008).

What is Franchising?

In simple terms, a franchise is a particular form of organisation, in which the development of a business concept and its execution are undertaken by two different legal entities. The US FTC (the US government agency responsible for regulating franchising) provides a legal definition of this arrangement.

> The term 'franchise' means any commercial relationship … whereby a person offers, sells or distributes to any person … goods, commodities, or services which are (1) identified by a trademark, service mark, trade name, advertising or other commercial symbol … or (2) directly or indirectly required or advised to meet the quality standards prescribed by another person where the franchisee operates under a name using the trademark, service mark, trade name, advertising or other commercial symbol. (Federal Trade Commission Rule 436.2, paragraph 6160)

Comparatively, the International Franchise Association defines a franchise operation as 'a contractual relationship between the franchisor and franchisee in which the franchisor offers or is obliged to maintain, a continuing interest in the business of the franchisee in such areas as know-how and training; wherein the franchisee operates under a common trade name, format, or procedure owned by or controlled by the franchisor, and in which the franchisee has made or will make a substantial capital investment in his business from his own resources'. The broad category of franchising is made up of two different business models: product franchising and business format franchising. Product franchising is an arrangement in which one party, a franchisor, develops a trade name and licenses it to another party, a franchisee. The product franchise contractually agrees for the use of the trade name to deliver products or services to end customers for a certain time period, at a certain location. Examples of companies that engage in product franchising are Coca-Cola and Goodyear Tires (Shane, 2008).

In business format franchising, the franchisor develops a brand name and an operating system which will deliver products or services to end customers. The franchisor licenses the franchise to another party, a franchisee, for a certain time period, at a certain location. This form of franchising is most common in industries in which companies need to operate a large number of outlets across a wide variety of geographic locations. According to Shane (2008), business format franchising is an important mechanism for obtaining the financial and human resources that firms need for rapid organisational growth and brand identity, and to gain a necessary competitive advantage (Shane, 2008).

The Franchising System

Franchising has two characteristics that distinguish it from other organisational forms such as joint ventures and strategic alliances. First, franchising typically occurs in businesses where there is a notable service component that must be performed near customers. The result is that service-providing outlets must be replicated and dispersed geographically. The second key characteristic is that, franchise contracts typically reflect a unique allocation of responsibilities, decision rights, and profits, between a centralised principal (the franchisor) and decentralised agents (franchisees). The franchisor sets and enforces chain-wide standards for performance, selects franchisees, approves outlet locations, manages brand image, and coordinates activities such as purchasing, where scale economies are available (Caves & Murphy, 1976).

The franchisor's revenue comes primarily from royalty payments tied to franchisee sales. In some cases franchisor revenue can be substantial when calculating new franchisee partnerships as initial capital payments are made by the franchisee. Apart from paying royalties, in most cases franchisees have a degree of autonomy and are instrumental in establishing their local outlet, setting local policy such as price, hours, and staffing, and managing day-to-day operations in exchange for profits after royalties and other expenses. Franchisors, in general, give detailed guidelines to their franchisees as to how they are to conduct the business, a management system for operating the business, and a shared trade identity. Franchising can also be seen as a pooling of resources and capabilities with the franchisor contributing an initial capital investment, know-how, and experience, and the franchisee contributing the additional capital investment and operating experience. Furthermore, the franchisor tends to provide marketing, training, and purchasing support, as well as product development services for franchisees. This model appears in a multitude of industries such as catering and hotel services, car maintenance, car and truck rental, business services such as accounting and employment agencies, and consumer services such as home cleaning, education, and real estate brokerage.

The Franchising Literature

This section will explore the literature on franchising from its origins and evolution in terms of research output. Franchising has become immensely important and represents a prominent and successful form of organisation in the Irish and global economies. This is particularly evident within the retail sector representing a massive financial contribution to the economy and stakeholders therein. This section reviews the franchising literature in terms of its origins and the major streams of within the franchising literature. The literature will be assessed from two perspectives: first the emergence of franchising and second relating to its impact on industry evolution. It must be noted that franchising research to date has been mainly focused on the reason or decision to franchise at firm level, predominately using transaction cost economic and resource scarcity explanations. There is very little research done to date which relates to the emergence of franchising at industry level or addresses the macro-environmental context for its emergence. Thus there is a substantial gap in the research that this research endeavours to address. The franchising literature has focused a good deal on research relating to entrepreneurship or has been from an entrepreneurial perspective. The significance of agency and the influence of individual entrepreneurs with regard to the emergence of franchising research have mainly been from a quantitative perspective and are thereby limited in offer in-depth insights. This research uses qualitative and more in-depth and inductive methods, thereby adding to the body of research to date. Franchising has rarely been looked at from a strategy lens and this research hopes to address that gap in the research. However, one of the main contributions of this research is to try to fill the fundamental gap in terms of research and literature relating to franchising and its impact on industry as well as the evolution of franchising over time. There is some work on competitive advantage and franchising (Collis & Montgomery, 1995; Truss, 2004) but again this is limited and only from the firm level perspective and not relating to a broader industry level, as this research proposes to do. Pertaining to this gap, one specific paper by Elango and Fried (1997) was uncovered whereby the authors had made a call for research on franchising and industry effects and implications which have still remained unanswered. Furthermore Porter (1980) while looking at industries made the connection between franchising and its ability to overcome industry fragmentation. To date this area remains underexplored.

The Study of Franchising

According to Dant and Grunhagen (2014), even though the USA is thought to be the home of franchising, franchising actually has a long history stretching back to ancient China (Thomas & Seid, 2010). The roots of franchising can also be traced back to feudal times (Purvin, 1994) and the Middle Ages (Dicke, 1992). The term 'franchising' or the Old French term 'franche' means to invest with a 'franchise or privilege' and 'franchising' directly translated means 'a granting of right' or 'an exemption' (Williamson, 1992). Moreover, modern day franchising describes a contractually vested inter-firm business relationship between two legally independent entities involving a grantee (or franchisee) and a grantor (the franchisor), where the franchisee pays the franchisor for rights to sell the franchisor's product or service using franchisor's trademarks and its proprietary business system in a pre-specified location for a pre-specified length of contract. A distinction is usually proposed between the first to develop traditional (or product and trade name) franchising, and the second, business format franchising where the outlet itself is the product, where the franchisor sells a 'way of doing business' (Dant & Grunhagen, 2014).

Commensurate with its economic importance, franchising has captured the attention of a wide array of researchers and has become a very popular form of economic organisation as suggested by Dant and Grunhagen (2014) and for this reason alone, should be of major concern for organisation and management research (Brickley & Dark, 1987; Lafontaine, 1992; Norton, 1988; Rubin, 1978; Shane, 1996). As franchising has increased its visibility and impact on the business landscape, it has attracted the attention of a wide variety of researchers from different academic backgrounds with hundreds of articles in a variety of academic fields, such as economics, finance, management science, law, and marketing, having been published on this topic by the mid-1990s (Elango & Fried, 1997). Despite the rapid adoption of the franchising concept, there is still a lack of understanding and consensus on the theoretical determinant and creation of this organisational form and business strategy (Inma, 2005). Due to several distinct structural properties of franchise systems, it offers ample opportunities to research topics of more general theoretical and managerial interest. For the past four decades, agency theory has been popularly used to explain the foundation of franchising. According to Inma (2005), there is a limitation to using agency theory to explain the fundamental of franchising and a complete understanding of franchising practice may require an explanation involving more than one theory. Drawing together much of this research by juxtaposing the two key theories used to explain franchising—resource scarcity theory and agency theory—the empirical findings are usually centred on three key franchising constructs: franchise initiation, subsequent propensity to franchise, and franchise performance. It has been suggested by a number of scholars that research emphasis needs to shift towards understanding why firms initiate franchising and how franchising impacts different types of organisational performance at firm level. Franchising research needs to be addressed by looking at external factors in terms of industry effects and also the influence of agents or actors within franchise systems themselves. As this is a multi-level, multi-modal study, the literature will be reviewed with this in mind. This research therefore looks to focus on the emergence of franchising and to develop the under-researched aspect of franchising and its impact on industry structure and evolution.

Different Streams of Franchising Literature

This section will review the different streams of franchising literature which includes the perspective of strategic management of which this research is centred and as such franchising is viewed in strategy as an important organisational form (Combs & Ketchen, 1999). From the perspective of entrepreneurship, franchising is a vehicle for attaining business ownership (Shane & Hoy, 1996). From the marketing perspective, franchising is an important distribution channel (Kaufmann & Rangan, 1990) and from the economics viewpoint, franchising is a leading venue for understanding the structure of contracts (Lafontaine, 1992). Whereas an advantage of attracting scholars from many academic disciplines is that a sizable literature has grown up around franchising, a disadvantage is that competing discipline-based paradigms, hidden assumptions, and varying methodological norms make the literature particularly difficult to review and synthesise. Researchers have begun to take stock of this ever-growing research in an attempt to draw appropriate conclusions and guide future inquiry.

Strategy Literature

More specifically, the strategic management literature includes topics such as vertical control without the cost associated with vertical integration (Carney & Gedajlovic, 1991). In this manner, franchising can be viewed as a hybrid organisational form but much of the research is utilising economic or sociological theories and is mostly quantitative in nature. However, the resource-based view of the firm (RBV) has been a leading framework for strategy scholars for the past few decades. Along this line of reasoning, Knott (2003) looks at franchising and stresses the tie between competitive advantage and tacit knowledge in the context of routines. Her logic is that if routines are what make firms flourish, then in a franchising system these routines must be transferred to the franchisees. However, if the routines do not contain tacit knowledge, they are easily transferable and not likely to garner a competitive advantage. Indeed, the prevailing strategy-based theme in terms of franchising is in the study of Agency Theory (an economic theory discussed in depth later in the chapter) which is concerned with principal–agent alignment especially in incentive schemes. The problems that arise in the agency approach are adverse selection, moral hazard, and holdup. In order to minimise the first two issues, firms may choose to franchise operations in order to give the other party a residual claim on excess profits. In this manner, the franchisee can be viewed as a district manager but one that holds the right to earn these profits (Shane, 1998a,1998b; Lafontaine, 1992; Brickley & Dark, 1987). As mentioned, franchising can be viewed as a hybrid organisational form and following on this theme are companies that mix operations whereby some outlets are company owned and others are franchised out. The ability for the franchisor to pick this strategy is derived from the amount of power involved in the relationship between mother firm (franchisor) and franchisee (Michael, 2000). Yin and Zajac (2004) argue that it is not whether companies franchise or not in terms of performance but instead that the right fit is incorporated into the company structure. In other words, since flexibility is a benefit of franchising, firms that need to be more flexible will perform better if they choose franchising whereas a more rigid structure is conducive to more control-oriented firms.

Marketing Literature

In the field of marketing, much of the research is empirical. Srinivasan (2006) studies the link between the dual distribution schema of a firm and its intangible value. According to Srinivasan, the dual distribution consists of firms which own some of their retail locations while also franchising others. Although he focuses on the restaurant industry, the finding that having a dual distribution mechanism of governance increases intangible value is pertinent for numerous industries. In addition, the paper attempts to study industries which are highly fragmented. Dant and Kaufmann (2003) follow the history of Oxenfeldt and Kelly's (1968) argument which was that once the franchisor established itself enough in terms of assets, experience, and cash-flow generation, it would discontinue franchising operations and, instead, only focus on company-run stores. They find that moderators such as sales share, lack of long-term contracts, net conversion gain, and attrition are contributing factors in the ownership redirection theory and the adoption of franchising as suggested by Oxenfeldt and Kelly (1968). Wu (1999) focuses on the pricing of a brand name (i.e., Franchisor) in the motel services industry and asks a question: Are franchised brands valuable? In other words, if franchised and non-franchise systems not only compete but thrive in the same space, how does branding help?

Economics Literature

The economics literature contains many works that reiterate some of the same themes previously discussed, yet from a different, and again often from a more quantitative, angle. Kalnins (2005) is concerned with franchisor–franchisee contracts in the context of development commitments. He finds that the larger the development commitment in the franchise system, the less likely a firm is to survive. Lafontaine and Shaw (2005) revisit the dual distribution schema that many scholars have studied and find that franchisors with high brand name value have higher rates of company ownership. Dnes and Garoupa (2005) focus on externalities in franchise systems. They posit that firms have a trade-off decision between managerial motivation and trying to limit externalities. Furthermore, this trade-off explains which organisational forms firms choose. Windsperger (2002) emphasises the role of intangible assets in franchising with a concentration on property rights. In essence, and after testing the hypothesis, he finds that there is a positive relationship between the amount of intangible knowledge that a franchisor owns and the amount of ownership rights that should be transferred to the franchisee. Following on the rights and contracts approach to franchising, Chaudhuri, Ghosh, and Spell (2001) show that franchisors, due to asymmetry in power and rights, choose more profitable locations for company-owned stores and less profitable ones for franchisees. Dnes (1996) and Lafontaine and Slade (1997) reviewed much of the empirical literature from economics and highlighted agency theory as a motivation for franchising. Elango and Fried (1997) took a broad view by reviewing research on franchising's role politically, economically, and socially, why firms franchise, and how franchise systems are managed. More recently, Combs and Ketchen (2003) employed meta-analysis to test ten commonly studied correlates of franchising.

Entrepreneurship Literature

The entrepreneurship literature takes a different focus on franchising than strategy, marketing, and economics because, at its core, franchising is an entrepreneurial option. Combs, Ketchen, and Hoover (2004) study franchising in the backdrop of strategic groups and find that those restaurant firms that franchise out of resource scarcity had poorer performance than other groups. Hoffman and Preble (2003) studied conversion franchising where franchisors pull independent firms into their system as opposed to only recruiting potential entrepreneurs to commence new operations; therefore conversion franchising has been an ever-increasing phenomenon in that space in recent years. Kaufmann and Dant (1996) look at four topics regarding franchising—(1) innovation, (2) concepts, (3) risk, and (4) multi-unit franchising—in an attempt to explain three key areas of their work, namely traits, processes, and activities.

Within the franchising context, Oxenfeldt and Kelly (1968), Caves and Murphy (1976), and Norton (1988) have argued that entrepreneurs use franchising to gain access to significant resources that are in short supply in the early stages of the development of their chains. These growth-minded but resource-constrained entrepreneurs have two realistic options available for securing external resources: (1) selling equity and (2) selling franchises. Debt options are often not realistic because growing chains are seldom able to furnish requisite collateral to qualify for the level of loans needed, a problem exacerbated by the novelty of many franchise concepts at the time they are introduced (e.g., leak detection, cookies in a mall). Selling equity secures access to only financial capital. Franchising, however, represents an efficient bundled source for all three critical capitals (i.e., financial, managerial, and informational; cf. Norton, 1988). As entrepreneurs, individual franchisees engage in innovation and experimentation to generate more efficient processes and better products (Bradach, 1997). For example, Darr, Argote, and Epple (1995) describe how a franchisee in Pennsylvania solved a problem with pepperoni shifting during the baking of pizza and the entire franchise system benefitted from this innovation. The gain for the franchisor can be increased adaptability to local markets (Kaufmann & Eroglu,

1999), increased chain-wide innovation (Bradach, 1997), and eventually improved performance (Sorenson & Sorensen, 2001). Despite considerable anecdotal evidence, however, no formal examination of the claim that franchising is a vehicle for innovation has yet occurred. One potentially fruitful avenue for future inquiry might be to investigate whether the benefits of franchisee innovation for the franchisor are moderated by the quality of franchisor–franchisee relations. Whereas many innovations developed by franchisees are not communicated to franchisors (Darr et al., 1995), franchisors with good franchisee relations might be better able to identify and implement local adaptations that will benefit the entire chain (Bradach, 1997). According to Combs et al. (2001) today's franchising researchers are leveraging new theories, investigating under-examined aspects of franchising, and exploring contextual factors that shape its use. Chirico, Ireland, and Sirmon (2011) also recognise that many, if not most, franchisors and franchisees are family-run enterprises, and they use this insight to draw implications about franchising from research on family firms. They also assert that entrepreneurship as a discipline is a natural home for franchising research as that, like entrepreneurship, franchising is inherently multidisciplinary. As such entrepreneurship research addresses the diverse activities that entrepreneurs confront, such as opportunity recognition, team building, strategy, marketing, finance, and law—and entrepreneurship researchers come from disciplinary backgrounds that reflect these activities (Busenitz et al., 2003).

In terms of an overview as mentioned the franchising literature still remains fragmented. Moreover, much remains to be done and improvements need to be made in the theory base supporting franchising research. Past research has been too closely tied to theories of agency and power. While helpful, these theories are quite narrow. They have often ignored both the franchisee's perspective and the important knowledge that can be gained and shared from the franchisee's perspective. Adoption of other research methods may also be advantageous. Many important questions cannot be answered without using more fine-grained research methods. The next chapter will look at the franchising research from the emergence perspective and assess the literature and its gaps.

References

Aydin, N., & Kacker, M. (1989). International outlook of U.S. based franchisors. *International Marketing Review, 7*(2), 43–53.

Bradach, J. L. (1997). Using the plural form in the management of restaurant chains. *Administrative Science Quarterly, 42*, 276–303.

Brickley, J. A., & Dark, F. H. (1987). The choice of organizational form: The case of franchising. *Journal of Financial Economics, 18*, 401–420.

Busenitz, L., West, G., Shepherd, D., Nelson, T., Chandler, G., & Zacharakis, A. (2003). Entrepreneurship research in emergence: Past trends and future directions. *Journal of Management, 29*(3), 285–308.

Carney, M., & Gedajlovic, E. (1991). Vertical integration in franchise systems: Agency theory and resource explanations. *Strategic Management Journal, 12*, 607–629.

Caves, R. E., & Murphy, W. R. (1976). Franchising: Firms, markets, and intangible assets. *Southern Economic Journal, 42*, 572–586.

Chaudhuri, A., Ghosh, P., & Spell, C. (2001). A location based theory of franchising. *Journal of Business and Economics Studies, 7*(1), 54–67.

Chirico, F., Ireland, D., & Sirmon, D. (2011). Franchising and the family firm: Creating unique sources of advantage, with F. Chirico and R.D. Ireland. *Entrepreneurship Theory & Practice, 35*(3), 83–501.

Collis, D. J., & Montgomery, C. A. (1995). Competing on resources: Strategy in the 1990s. *Harvard Business Review, 73*(July–August), 118–128.

Combs, J. G., & Ketchen, D. J. (1999). Explaining interfirm cooperation and performance: Toward a reconciliation of predictions from the resource-based view and organizational economics. *Strategic Management Journal, 20*, 867–888.

Combs, J. G., & Ketchen, D. J. (2003). Why do firms use franchising as an entrepreneurial strategy?: A meta-analysis. *Journal of Management, 29*, 443–465.

Combs, J. G., Ketchen Jr., D. J., & Hoover, V. L. (2004). A strategic groups approach to the franchising–performance relationship. *Journal of Business Venturing, 19*(6), 877–897.

Dant, R., & Kaufmann, P. (2003). Structural and strategic dynamics in franchising. *Journal of Retailing, 79*(2), 63–75.

Dant, R. P., & Grunhagen, M. (2014). International franchising research: Some thoughts on the what, where, when and how. *Journal of Marketing Channels, 21*(3), 124–132.

Darr, E. D., Argote, L., & Epple, D. (1995). The acquisition, transfer, and depreciation of knowledge in service organizations: Productivity in franchises. *Management Science, 41*, 1750–1762.

Dnes, A., & Garoupa, N. (2005). Externality and organizational choice in franchising. *Journal of Economics and Business, 57*(2), 139–149.

Dnes, A. W. (1996). The economic analysis of franchise contracts. *Journal of Institutional and Theoretical Economics, 152*, 297–324.

Elango, B., & Fried, V. H. (1997). Franchising research: A literature review and synthesis. *Journal of Small Business Management, 35*, 68–81.

Hackett, D. W. (1976). The international expansion of franchise systems— Status and strategies. *Journal of International Business, 7*(2).

Hoffman, R., & Preble, J. (2003). Convert to compete: Competitive advantage through conversion franchising. *Journal of Small Business Management, 41*(2), 187–204.

Inma, C. (2005). Purposeful franchising: Rethinking of the franchising rationale. *Singapore Management Review, 27*(1), 27–48.

Kalnins, A. (2005). Overestimation and venture survival: An empirical analysis of development commitments in international master franchising ventures. *Journal of Economics & Management Strategy, 14*(4), 933–953.

Kaufmann, P. J., & Dant, R. P. (1996). Multi-unit franchising: Growth and management issues. *Journal of Business Venturing, 11*, 343–358.

Kaufmann, P. J., & Eroglu, S. (1999). Standardization and adaptation in business format franchising. *Journal of Business Venturing, 14*, 69–85.

Kaufmann, P. J., & Rangan, V. K. (1990). A model for managing system conflict during franchise expansion. *Journal of Retailing, 66*, 155–173.

Knott, A. M. (2003). The organizational routines factor market paradox. *Strategic Management Journal, 24*(8), 292–943.

Lafontaine, F. (1992). Agency theory and franchising: Some empirical results. *RAND Journal of Economics, 23*, 263–283.

Lafontaine, F., & Slade, M. E. (1997). Retail contracting: Theory and practice. *The Journal of Industrial Economics, 45*, 1–25.

Mendelson, M. (1992). *Franchising in Europe*. London: Cassell.

Michael, S. C. (2000). Investments to create bargaining power: The case of franchising. *Strategic Management Journal, 21*, 497–514.

Norton, S. W. (1988). Franchising, brand name capital, and the entrepreneurial capacity problem. *Strategic Management Journal, 9*, 105–114.

Oxenfeldt, A. R., & Kelly, A. O. (1968). Will successful franchise systems ultimately become wholly-owned chains? *Journal of Retailing, 44*, 69–83.

Plitt, S. (2000). *The Oxford handbook of international antitrust economics* (Vol. 2). (Eds. R. D. Blair & D. D. Sokol). Oxford, UK: Oxford University Press, 3 Nov 2014.

Porter, M. E. (1980). *Competitive strategy.* New York: Free Press.

Purvin, R. L. (1994). *The franchise fraud.* New York: John Wiley and Sons.

Rubin, P. H. (1978). The theory of the firm and the structure of the franchise contract. *Journal of Law and Economics, 21,* 223–233.

Shane, S. (1996). Hybrid organizational arrangements and their implications for firm growth and survival: A study of new franchisors. *Academy of Management Journal, 39,* 216–234.

Shane, S. (1998a). Explaining the distribution of franchised and company-owned outlets in franchise systems. *Journal of Management, 24,* 717–739.

Shane, S. (1998b). Making new franchise systems work. *Strategic Management Journal, 19,* 697–707.

Shane, S. (2008). *From ice-cream to the internet, using franchising to drive the growth and profits of your company.* Prentice Hall.

Shane, S. A., & Hoy, F. (1996). Franchising: A gateway to cooperative entrepreneurship. *Journal of Business Venturing, 11,* 325–327.

Sorenson, O., & Sorensen, J. B. (2001). Finding the right mix: Franchising, organizational learning, and chain performance. *Strategic Management Journal, 22*(6–7), 713–724.

Srinivasan, R. (2006, July). Dual distribution and intangible firm value: Franchising in restaurant chains. *Journal of Marketing, 70,* 120–135.

Thomas, D., & Seid, M. (2010). *Franchising for dummies.* Canada: Wiley & Sons.

Truss, C. (2004). Who's in the driving seat? Managing human resources in a franchise firm. *Human Resource Management Journal, 14*(4), 57–75.

Williamson, G. (1992). *Franchising in Australia: The practical guide to all the promises and pitfalls.* Australia: Alien & Unwin Pty Ltd.

Windsperger, J. (2002). The structure of ownership rights in franchising: An incomplete contracting view. *European Journal of Law and Economics, 13*(2), 129–142.

Wu, L. (1999). The pricing of a brand name product: Franchising in the motel services industry. *Journal of Business Venturing, 14*(1), 87.

Yin, X., & Zajac, E. (2004). The strategy/governance structure fit relationship: Theory and evidence in franchising arrangements. *The Strategic Management Journal, 25*(4), 365–383.

2

International Context

Franchising International Context

The concept of franchising is well developed and is a popular business strategy in many countries. A mature level of franchising can be found in the USA, Europe, and Australia, while Asia, South America, Central America, and Mexico report rapid growth (Alon & McKee, 1999). However, it is difficult either to measure accurately the scope in one country or to make comparisons between countries due to the varying definitions of franchising and limitations in methods of data collecting.

The USA

US franchise systems are the oldest and most recognisable franchise brand names globally. A recent study commissioned by the International Franchise Association in Washington and conducted by PricewaterhouseCoopers examines the economic impact of franchising

© The Author(s) 2017
R. Beere, *The Role of Franchising on Industry Evolution*,
DOI 10.1007/978-3-319-49064-9_2

in the USA. The main findings are as follows: 'franchised businesses operated 767,483 establishments in the United States in 2012 counting both establishments owned by franchisees and establishments owned by franchisors. They provided 9,797,117 jobs, made $229.1 billion in terms of payroll and produced $624.6 billion output. To indicate economic size, franchise businesses employed the same number of people in 2012 as did all manufacturers of durable goods, such as computers, cars, trucks, and planes.' See Table 2.1 on the Franchise business economic outlook 2007–2012 (PricewaterhouseCoopers 2012 study).

Between 2001 and 2005, the number of business format franchise establishments increased by 5.6 per cent per year, their employment capability increased by 3.7 per cent, and their annual economic output increased by 9.7 per cent. However, growth slowed in 2007/2008 to 2.8 per cent. In 2010 economic output declined by 0.7 per cent, with a net loss of $5.7 billion. In 2012 PricewaterhouseCoopers estimates that output would increase by 2.8 per cent, with a net gain of $23.6 billion.

According to Dant, Grünhagen, and Windsperger (2011), franchising has become the dominant mode of retail entrepreneurship in the USA and globally. Almost 3000 companies manage franchise chains, in more than 80 industries. These companies work with 901,093 franchisees that employ 18 million people. Franchise systems generate $2.1 trillion in sales annually, accounting for approximately 40.9 per cent of all US retail sales. However, despite the widespread reach of franchising, surprisingly few companies succeed at franchising. There are more than 200 new franchise

Table 2.1 Franchise business economic outlook 2007–2012, USA

	2007	2008	2009	2010	2011 (per cent)	2012 (per cent)
Establishments	847,244	883,984	883,292	901,093	−0.1	2.0
Employment (thousands)	9859	9931	9522	9558	−4.1	0.4
Output billion	$802.9	$850.4	$844.7	$868.3	−0.7	2.8

Source: PricewaterhouseCoopers

Table 2.2 Franchising in the US industries by performance

	Establishment	Employment (thousands)	Output (billions)
Automotive	38,340	182	$36.4
Commercial and residential services	57,007	230	$38.2
Quick service restaurants	192,827	3343	$203.6
Retail food	70,722	853	$67.5
Table/full service restaurants	48,609	1066	$64.0
Lodging	31,827	627	$62.7
Real estate	41,630	60	$22.8
Retail products and services	88,312	577	$50.5
Business services	231,669	1420	$189.6
Personal services	100,151	1101	$132.8
Total	901,093	9558	$868.3

Source: PricewaterhouseCoopers

systems established in the USA each year. From that, 25 per cent do not last one year, 75 per cent fail within a decade and only 15 per cent remain operating for anything up to 17 years, with a small percentage lasting beyond 20 years.

US Franchising by Industry

Some industries are better than others when it comes to creating success-ful franchise systems (see Table 2.2).

Half of all franchisors are concentrated in the top ten industries for franchising (see Table 2.3). In some industries such as tax preparation, printing and copying, and specialty food retailing, franchisors account for the majority of all firms. Today franchising occurs in more than 80 different industries.[1] Although the list is long and broad, franchising does

---

[1]Today franchising occurs in more than 80 different industries, including car repair, car sales, book selling, building materials, business services, camera sales, car washes, carpet sales, computer training, chemists, credit agencies, cleaning contractors and domestic cleaning services, data processing, dentistry, dry cleaning, e-commerce, employment agencies, fast food, formal wear rental, greeting cards, grocery sales, hair care, hardware, insurance, music sales, optical care,

Table 2.3 Top ten US industries for franchising in percentage of franchisors

Industry 2012	Percentage of franchisors	Percentage of franchised units
Fast food	18	26.8
Restaurants	7.0	3.8
Automotive products	6.2	5.5
Maintenance and cleaning	5.4	8.2
Building and remodelling	4.9	1.5
Specialty retail	3.8	1.5
Specialty food	3.8	2.0
Health and fitness	3.3	3.5
Child development	3.2	0.7
Lodging	3.1	5.9

Source: Adapted from data contained in R. Bond's Bond's Franchise Guide, 15th annual edition (Oakland, CA: Sourcebook Publications, 2012)

not occur in all industries and there is a high concentration in just a few. One study from the International Franchise Association reports that 18 per cent of all franchise systems are found in fast food (see Table 2.3) and 11 per cent in general retail.

Shane (2012) identified nine characteristics that make an industry appropriate for franchising:

1. Production and distribution occur in limited geographic markets.
2. Physical locations are helpful for serving customers.
3. Local market knowledge is important to performance.
4. Local management discretion is beneficial.
5. Brand name reputation is a valuable competitive advantage.
6. High levels of standardisation and codification of the process are needed for creating and delivering the product or service.
7. The operation is labour intensive.
8. Outlets are not extremely costly or risky to establish.
9. The outlet operator's effort is hard to measure relative to their performance.

---

petrol stations, photo processing, tax preparation, security systems, travel agencies, and weight loss centres.

The UK

The NatWest & British Franchise Association (BFA) survey provides the following comparison. In 2012, after four years of growth, the franchise systems increased total national turnover to £12.4bn, an increase of £600 million (+5 per cent). Since 2007, the number of franchise systems has also grown by 15 per cent, despite a UK GDP growth rate of only 9.4 per cent in the same period. The number of franchise systems operating in the UK has grown to 897, increasing the number of franchise units to 36,900. Total employment by franchise systems is 521,000. Franchising has also helped to drive international trade. Around a third of UK franchisors have units located outside the UK. Additionally, 38 per cent of domestic-only franchises plan to expand abroad (NatWest BFA survey 2012). According to the survey, four out of five franchisees said that being part of the franchise model offers them a competitive advantage over non-franchised competitors, with 89 per cent reporting profitability. They claimed that branding, the appearance of being part of a larger business with standardised products/services, and the perception of quality were the main advantages.

Franchisors also anticipate better prospects for their business than the wider economy performance, with 75 per cent expecting improvements in the coming years of trading. Two-thirds of franchise businesses trading less than two years reportedly made a profit. In the UK, the average franchisee fee is £15,300, and the average start-up investment cost is £46,600. The average management service fee is 11.2 per cent (8.2 per cent in 2008 and 7.5 per cent in 2012), with the average advertising levy at 2.6 per cent (3.9 per cent in 2008 and 1.9 per cent in 2012).

Franchising in Ireland

According to the Irish Franchise Association (survey conducted by Ipsos MRBI for AIB and the Irish Franchise Association 2015) the combined annual turnover of franchise systems (business format franchising) operating in Ireland was estimated at €2.4 billion, representing a significant impact on economic growth and future development. From a general stakeholder perspective, the phenomenon of franchising represents a prominent and successful form of organisation and business activity in the Irish economy. Within the retail sector in particular, it represents a substantial contribution. Since the first franchise was introduced into Ireland in the late 1970s there are more than 270 different franchises operating in 2012. Franchising is almost exclusively a service-oriented business. As Ireland's economy becomes increasingly dominated by services, franchise companies will benefit. According to the Ulster Bank and UCD Smurfit franchise survey 2010, the past 15 years have witnessed significant growth in franchising throughout Ireland, spanning many industries. Moreover, the number of franchise systems has doubled since 1997 (see Table 2.4).

By the 1980s there were fewer than 20 franchise systems operating in Ireland, and in 1983 the Irish Franchise Association was established. The association was set up as an independent body offering franchise information for both franchisors and franchisees. By 1989, 44 franchise systems operated. A decade later in 1998, 140 franchise systems were operating. This represented an increase of ten new franchises each year over the 10-year period. By 2003, over 180 franchises were operating in Ireland. In recent years the franchising of domestic systems has improved significantly. By 2012 the UK had become the dominant source of franchise systems, with the USA diminishing in terms of system origin. As shown in Table 2.4, the continual growth and economic success of franchise systems in Ireland are evident and today there are over 350 systems operating, contributing a combined annual turnover of over €2.5 billion. Over 50 per cent of franchise systems in Ireland operate in the service sector, with over 30 per cent in the retail sector, the minority being mobile

Table 2.4 Irish franchise systems 1989–2012 annual turnover

Year	Franchise systems	Annual turnover (€)
1989	44	80 million
1998	140	450 million
2003	180	1.2 billion
2010	270	2.419 billion
2012	350	2.5 billion[a]

[a]Irish franchise association figures for 2012
Source: based on Bank of Ireland franchise survey data 2006 & Ulster Bank and UCD Smurfit franchising in Ireland survey 2010

or van based. The food and drink industries dominate and account for over 20 per cent of franchise owners. Over 30 per cent of those have held a master franchise for three years or less, indicative of the continued growth in this sector. Overall, there has been a 36 per cent growth in the franchising industry in Ireland, during the last five years. With a failure rate of only 7 per cent, franchising has become one of Ireland's fastest growing sectors.

Indigenous Irish franchises account for nearly 20 per cent of total franchise systems, or 54 out of the total 270 franchise systems. Currently this may seem like a small percentage, but growth is evident in the increase from 14 per cent in 2010. Examining the origin of franchise systems, the UK has overtaken the USA as the dominant source, accounting for over 30 per cent, or 81 franchise systems, of the total market. New entrants, from other countries such as Australia, Spain, and the Far East, have also begun to establish themselves in the Irish market in recent years.

In 2012 the combined annual turnover (see Table 2.5) for franchise systems operating in Ireland was estimated at €2.5 billion, according to the Ulster Bank and UCD Smurfit Franchising in Ireland survey 2010 and recent Irish Franchise Associations figures (2012) combined. This represents a substantial increase since the last survey carried out by Bank of Ireland and McGarry Consulting in 2006. At present there are more than 4086 operating units generating 42,927 full-time jobs (see Table 2.6). In addition to generating employment directly, there is indirect job creation. In a time of economic downturn the franchise sector has increased employment figures every year since 2008 and has positively contributed to the Irish economy in the form of taxation (see Tables 2.5 and 2.6).

In terms of geographical spread of franchise systems, Dublin would appear to be the key location for the sector, with 75 per cent of all franchises having at least one outlet in Dublin city. However, the regional spread of franchise units is quite even with almost 75 per cent of fran-

Table 2.5 Annual turnover for franchise systems in Ireland 1995–2012

	1995	1997	1999	2001	2003	2006	2012
Turnover	0.256	0.397	0.571	1.02bn	1.272bn	2.099bn	2.5bn
% Change	+62	+55	+43	+79	+24	+ 69	+15

Note: Turnover figures do not include sales by the retail symbol groups

Table 2.6 Total employment for franchise systems in Ireland 1995–2012

	1995	1997	1999	2001	2003	2006	2012
Employment	4900	7400	9600	14,400	17,890	25,461	42,927
% Change	+48	+51	+30	+50	+24	+42	+35

Note: Turnover figures do not include sales by the retail symbol groups

chise systems operating outside the capital. Northern Ireland is another stronghold with 58 per cent of all franchise systems in Ireland having at least one outlet located there.

Regarding gender representation across Irish franchise systems, men continue to dominate the Irish franchise business, accounting for 83 per cent of franchisees. Franchising is also a younger person's business. According to the UCD Ulster Bank 2010 report, 87 per cent of franchisees are under 50 years of age. Additionally, 25 per cent of franchisees were self-employed prior to buying their franchise. A further 25 per cent were employed in a large private company, with another 25 per cent employed by a small private company and 20 per cent unemployed. In terms of education, 30 per cent of franchisees hold a Leaving Certificate and a further 40 per cent have higher educational qualifications.

In relation to the cost of a franchise system, the research in 2012 by the Irish Franchise Association showed that the average initial franchisee fee is €24,638. This represents little to no change from the Bank of Ireland 2006 report or the 2010 UCD Ulster Bank report. However, there was a significant difference in terms of the average working capital and total set-up costs. The research found that the average working capital is €21,873, which is significantly reduced when compared to €39,300 in 2006. Similarly, there has been a significant decrease in total set-up costs; they have dropped from an average of €226,000 in 2006 to €124,330, in line with the recent economic downturn. However, the average management services fee charged to franchisees in Ireland has increased from 6.5 per cent in 2006, to 8.1 per cent in 2012. The advertising contribution made by franchisees has decreased from an average of 2.2 per cent in 2006 to 1.9 per cent. Certainly, 25 per cent of franchise owners do not solicit any marketing contribution from their franchisees.

In Ireland, 95 per cent of all franchise owners provide an operating manual for use by the franchisee. All franchisors provide comprehensive training, with 50 per cent providing training on a short-term basis, lasting less than two weeks. There is an increase in franchisors opting for training courses of two weeks to one month (shorter training periods), which are becoming the norm and a move away from training that lasts over one month.

One of the main changes in the retail landscape, and a factor that has affected the locations of franchising outlets, is the significant increase in shopping centres across Ireland. This has presented a mutually attractive proposition for franchisors and retail centre developers alike in helping to manage risk. The brand recognition that is an inherent part of a franchise offers the potential for greater footfall for the developer, while offering the franchisor a certain level of security in location set-up. Ireland's shopping centres now account for an increasing volume and value of retail sales. As such the pervasive presence of franchising is shifting away from the traditional focus on the High/Main Street.

Further evidence of the growing importance of franchising is the recent launch of the Irish National Franchise Centre (NFC). In 2011 The Limerick Institute of Technology (LIT) and the Limerick Chamber of Commerce announced the launch of Europe's first third-level franchising centre. The centre was set up in response to statistics which claim that over 80 per cent of start-up companies fail in the first five years, whereas 80 per cent of franchises succeed in the first five years. Additionally, because of this success rate banks provide a higher level of funding for franchise systems. According to the NFC, it is estimated that within a decade franchising will represent over 50 per cent of the total Irish retail economy and will employ more people in Ireland than all US multinationals combined.

While many franchise businesses have proven to be outstandingly successful, there is no guarantee that failure will not occur. If a franchise involves a proven product or service with a well-recognised brand, combined with hard-working, well-financed franchisees, the chances of success are very high. If on the other hand, the franchisor is under-funded, with a poor business concept that has not been tested properly, and the franchisees are poorly recruited or trained, failure is likely. Shane (2012) identified the transaction cost problems associated with franchising, arising from the delivery of a product or service to end customers by a set of legally independent entities. Several transaction cost problems that are not present in chains of outlets, owned by a single company, arise: free riding, under-investment, and loss of intellectual property. Pressures such as these may account for some of the franchise failures which can be found amongst all the successes. Some failed franchising endeavours include: Bewley's, which withdrew from the franchising concept for its cafes; the 7–11 convenience store chain, which failed to take off despite success in other countries; and KFC, which encountered difficulty establishing a successful entry into Ireland.

However, the statistics show that franchising is a growing and successful business system which continues to contribute to the employment and financial success of many businesses in Ireland, contributing a significant amount to Ireland's economy and future economic growth prospects.

The Asia-Pacific Region

According to Stephen Giles of Norton Rose Australia (Franchising in the Asia-Pacific Region November 2012 Franchise), the Asia-Pacific region has enthusiastically embraced franchising. Indeed many of the developing economies of the Asian region are experiencing the exponential growth of franchising seen in the USA in the 1980s and 1990s.

Population growth and economic development in the Asia-Pacific region are likely to drive high levels of demand for goods and services over the next decades. As has been the case in other Western countries, franchising is fast becoming the preferred means of establishing retail and distribution networks in the region. Indeed in Australia (1100 franchise systems) and New Zealand (460 systems) it is already the dominant means of distribution, with those two countries able to lay claim to the most franchised nations in the world per head of population (source: the World Franchise Council. For more details see 'Go East Young Franchisor: Franchising in the Asia Pacific Region' (Loewinger, Giles and Sakr, American Bar Association Forum on Franchising, October 2011). Franchising in China is in its infancy, yet China still reports currently having 4000 franchise systems. South Korea has 2400 systems and

Indonesia 1475 (source: the World Franchise Council). The phenomenal growth of franchising is illustrated by the fact that there are over 1.5 million franchised outlets in Asia-Pacific (sourced from the World Franchise Council). Most franchise systems in each country are home grown rather than imported.

Early fears that franchise regulation would stifle the growth of franchising in Asia-Pacific have been unfounded. Indeed the specific regulatory frameworks established in many Asian countries have given franchising credibility, and appear to have avoided some of the excesses that led to the regulation of franchising in the USA. In countries like Malaysia and Singapore, governments explicitly encourage franchising through a range of incentives, as they see franchising as an excellent mechanism to educate, train, and empower local people.

There are a variety of models for franchise regulation in Asia. The regulatory environment runs the gamut from no regulation and a quite laissez-faire approach to franchise-specific legislation with stringent registration requirements. There is almost every permutation in between. There are conceptual similarities between most of the regulated markets, with prior disclosure a common element, but the detail as to the nature of disclosure and the other elements of the regulatory framework is remarkably different. No two countries are sufficiently alike to provide any real efficiency for a foreign franchisor, and few of the laws are sufficiently straightforward to obviate the need to obtain specific advice from local counsel on the practical application of the law.

India, Hong Kong, Singapore, New Zealand, the Philippines, Thailand, and Japan have adopted a laissez-faire approach, but they are in the minority. And even in some of these markets, notably New Zealand, the Philippines, and to a lesser extent Japan, industry codes of conduct have become a form of de facto regulation. Other countries have been quite prescriptive, with Australia, China, Indonesia, Malaysia, South Korea, and Vietnam moving well beyond basic prior disclosure to regulating the franchise relationship and other elements in their legislative frameworks. Macau and Taiwan favour a disclosure-only model, whilst Kazakhstan stands alone as having franchise relationship requirements, but no disclosure obligations.

India, Hong Kong, Singapore, and Thailand have no specific franchising regulation and take a minimalist approach to legislative intervention in franchising matters, although India and Thailand have more restrictive foreign investment laws that can significantly impact international franchising. Franchising legislation is under consideration in Thailand. The Philippines and New Zealand have voluntary regimes conditional upon optional membership of the franchise associations, whereas Australia, China, Indonesia, Kazakhstan, Macau, Malaysia, South Korea, Taiwan, and Vietnam have more comprehensive regulatory frameworks. Japan sits in between, with some regulatory requirements as well as having a code of ethics specified by the Japan Franchise Association. There are conceptual similarities among the regulatory regimes, but it is quite striking how each country has taken a different approach to the regulation of the franchise sector.

Nowhere is local counsel input more important than in the Asia-Pacific region. Although there are conceptual similarities with US franchise regulation, the detail can be quite different. It is usually not possible to use a franchisor's US disclosure document, and there are often provisions in a typical US franchise agreement that will need to be modified before that document can be used in the Asia-Pacific region. In some countries, such as Indonesia, the franchise agreement must be in the Indonesian language. Registration requirements exist in China, Malaysia, Indonesia, and South Korea. In countries such as Thailand there can be significant differences between franchising law and franchising practice. In China and South Korea there are quite prescriptive requirements before a franchisor can commence franchising. In Australia certificates concerning the obtaining of legal and business advice must be provided by a franchisee to a franchisor prior to signing the franchise agreement, and there is a mediation-based dispute resolution process that is mandatory once either party to a franchise agreement elects to use it. Malaysia and Australia have cooling-off periods where franchisees can change their mind and receive a refund of monies paid less reasonable costs. China has a very extensive registration and establishment process.

Trademark and intellectual property protection is an important first step for all franchisors contemplating international expansion. Although most countries have taken significant steps to improve their intellectual property regimes, enforcement can remain challenging in some parts of Asia. Perhaps more importantly, it is critical to understand that there are differences between applicable trademark regimes that need to be considered. The most critical distinction is between those countries that adopt a system that grants protection based on 'first to register', and those that base protection on the concept of 'first to use'. Australia, Hong Kong, India, Malaysia, New Zealand, and Singapore have a first-to-use system, whereas China, Indonesia, Japan, Kazakhstan, Macau, the Philippines, South Korea, Taiwan, Thailand, and Vietnam have a first-to-file regime. In first-to-register jurisdictions foreign owners of intellectual property need to more actively protect their intellectual property, as failure to register can be fatal to the use of the trademark in some countries.

There are a variety of laws other than franchise-specific laws that affect franchise arrangements in the Asia-Pacific region. Aside from trademark laws, these include technology transfer laws, competition laws, investment restrictions, laws affecting currency repatriation, tax laws, and dispute resolution laws. There are also a host of bilateral treaties and multilateral conventions that apply. (For more information, see *Fundamentals of International Franchising*, edited by Richard M Asbill and Steven M Goldman, ABA Press, 2001.)

Franchising throughout Asia has significant pitfalls. In many countries the franchise agreement will not be paramount, with franchise relationship laws or, in some cases, direct government intervention possible. Foreign franchisors need to appreciate that the legal systems throughout the Asian region can be fundamentally different not just in sophistication, but in underlying structure too. For example Australia, Hong Kong, Singapore, and New Zealand have legal systems based on the English common law and underpinned by democratic principles and values. Some other countries in the region are not democracies, so the legal system and bureaucracy is an extension of the state. Alternatively, the legal system may be based on the European inquisitorial model and give greater emphasis to substance over form. The judiciary may not always be as independent or unbiased as might be desired, and corruption can be a major problem.

There are numerous logistical challenges to doing business in some parts of Asia, and language, time differences, and personal security concerns can add complexity to the franchise relationship. Currency fluctuations and foreign investment regulations may impact on financial returns. There are political and business challenges, cultural and religious differences, and a raft of legislation and bureaucratic processes that require navigation. Each country is quite different, and it is not possible to take a homogenous approach to the region. Market entry needs to be considered on a country-by-country basis.

Despite these challenges, more and more franchise systems are expanding into the Asian region. There is little doubt that many of the major opportunities for franchising lie in the emerging markets of the Asia-Pacific region. While Europe and North America remain affected by the consequences of the global financial crisis, most of the Asian economies are growing strongly. The demand for goods and services from the increasingly affluent middle classes will fuel strong economic growth for the

An Appetite for Franchising

The Japanese economy has had its problems, but it has embraced franchising since the 1970s. A franchise system may have considered franchising in Australia or New Zealand, countries with a language and legal system similar to that in the USA (Franchising World, March 2007).

Is the Next Step International Franchising?

Should the US, UK, and Irish franchise systems focus more on the Asia-Pacific region for international franchising? Reasons for doing so abound, provided the company is truly ready for international franchising. To be ready means to have a successful operation at home, which is generating enough in cash flow to support the effort, or to have additional investment available to support the foreign investment, and the delayed returns which come from international franchising. If the company is considering master franchising, it must be careful to make the requisite investment in legal documentation, development plans, and support services for master franchisees which are critical to the success of its foreign master franchise programme. A franchise brand alone will not make a franchise successful in most international markets.

Franchise companies must understand the costs and returns which are necessary to make their programmes work in each market and they must be candid in their assessments of the time over which the necessary returns can be generated. The amount of time required to do business in each country can vary dramatically. The time and effort required to obtain permits and licenses needed to conduct business may far exceed the time and cost companies have become accustomed to at home.

English is the principal language or is widely spoken in Australia, New Zealand, the Philippines, Hong Kong, Singapore, Malaysia, and India. Other languages and dialects are common in countries other than Australia and New Zealand, and are dominant in other countries in the region. According to Le Sante, most educated business people speak English throughout the region. Still, a franchise company will need to be able to communicate in the vernacular, and have manuals, advertising, websites, and training materials translated into the local languages, and perhaps local dialects to effectively master a market. Computer software and point of sale (POS) systems will need to function in these languages, and franchise systems will need to identify sources of service and parts for the equipment and computer systems they want their franchisees to use. Regardless of the language spoken, franchise organisations must be acutely aware of the business cultural and political environments within which their franchisees will conduct business.

Corruption is a problem in several countries in the region. According to the Corruption Index published by Transparency International, Myanmar, Bangladesh, Cambodia, Pakistan, Indonesia, and Papua New Guinea were ranked among the most corrupt countries in the world. Also in the top 50 most corrupt countries were Nepal, the Philippines, Laos, and Vietnam. China and India (along with Brazil, Egypt, Mexico, Peru, and Saudi Arabia) were ranked 70th for corruption, whereas New Zealand, Singapore, Australia, Hong Kong, and Japan were ranked among the 15 best countries on the index. The USA was ranked the 20th best.

With the fastest growing economies in the world, the Asia-Pacific is a region no international franchise company can afford to ignore for long.

Local companies have seized the franchising concept and are shaping it to work for their businesses. Franchising is an accepted and often encouraged form of economic development in the region and is likely to continue to grow. The region is very attractive, provided franchise systems evaluate the risks and opportunities in each individual market before committing their resources.

The global market value of franchising was estimated at US$3.79 trillion in 2014. Currently, the global franchising market is dominated by the USA, which accounts for 63 per cent of the total, while Asia as a whole represents only 16 per cent of the global market value. In the next five years, the Asian region is expected to post double-digit growth. By 2019, the number of franchise brands in Asia is expected to exceed that of the USA, EU, Australia, and New Zealand combined. According to an HKTDC survey of 70 international franchisors and 80 Hong Kong and mainland franchisees, 87 per cent of the international franchisors questioned have their eyes on the vast China market. Association of Southeast Asian Nations (ASEAN) member countries are also receiving attention from international franchisors, thanks to their large populations, rising disposable incomes, rapid urbanisation, and increasing awareness of franchising as a business opportunity.

As Asian consumers earn more discretionary income, they increasingly crave the quality, convenience, and service associated with Western brands. Busy urban lifestyles leave people with no choice but to outsource functions traditionally done within the family, such as cleaning, cooking, and education. Sectors such as food and beverages (F&B), as well as personal and commercial services that cater to the needs and lifestyles of the middle-income class, are likely to offer higher potential for franchising in Asia.

Hong Kong, apparently, has the edge in serving the growing franchising business in Asia, including its showcase role, track record of organising exhibitions, world-class supporting services, access to quality franchisees, the availability of industry talent, market sensitivity, and close business connections with different markets in Asia. Industry practitioners are positive about Hong Kong serving as a two-way springboard for Western franchisors looking to gain access to the Asian markets, and for the Asian brands to venture into the global marketplace.

In fact, Hong Kong brands have an advantage and enjoy a privileged status in Asia, particularly in China. Mainland consumers think that Hong Kong brands have a unique appeal and are more similar to their local culture than international brands. Hong Kong as a brand denotes quality, reliability, and style. In fact, many F&B chains in China were created using 'Hong Kong Style' as the core of their brand concepts. A lot of mainland consumers, especially those in second-tier cities, perceive Hong Kong brands and products to be superior to their own.

Franchising in India

A survey by global consultancy firm Ernst & Young (E&Y) sees India as the world's most attractive investment destination. With the opening up of foreign direct investment (FDI) in several sectors, India is today an eye-catching destination for overseas investors. The country's 2014–2015 GDP growth was expected to be 5.4 per cent. 'Franchising in India has witnessed impressive growth of around 30–35 per cent year after year over the last 4–5 years with an estimated turnover of US$4 billion', says Gaurav Marya, President, Franchise India.

As we know, India is a huge market of untapped consumers. Having showed consistent growth with an ever-increasing affluent consumer base, it presents very favourable conditions for a franchisor in a broad range of product and service sectors. Consumer expenditure is estimated to be US$6 trillion by 2025 (indiaretailing). GDP growth is forecast at a minimum of 5 per cent for 2015, corresponding to a value of US$2.4 trillion (E&Y's Attractiveness Survey: India 2014). The service sector contributed 57 per cent to GDP in 2014 and is the second fastest growing service sector in the world with a CAGR of 9 per cent (Finance Government of India Economic Survey 2013–14); the 2014 retail market was estimated at US$490 billion and expected to grow (CAGR) 13 per cent and reach around US$950 billion by 2018 (E&Y).

India is already the third largest retail market in the world and forecast to grow (CAGR) 15 per cent in 2016–2017 (Yes Bank-Assocham). Within the retail sector, food and grocery provides 69 per cent of the total market and is one of the main drivers of this sector. Although this is a large percentage of the market, the general view is that India offers a diverse range of retail investment opportunities across all formats and sectors.

By 2016, Credit Suisse Research Institute's Global Wealth Databook expects wealth in India to more than double to US$8.9 trillion. Not only will incomes increase, but we are seeing a related increase in the spending on non-essential products. India's population as well as becoming wealthier and moving themselves up the consumption curve are also relatively young, with a median age of 25 which will rise to only 37 by 2050.

Forecasts:

- India's consumer class is estimated to grow nearly 12-fold to 583 million by 2025.
- The total number of middle- and upper-income earners will grow over the next two decades by almost 170 million—twice the current population of the Philippines (HSBC 2050 Consumer).
- Analysts predict the middle-class will account for 41 per cent of the population by 2025.
- Consumer spending is predicted to increase about 2.5 times by 2025.
- More than 23 million people are likely to be listed among the world's wealthiest citizens by 2025 (McKinsey).

The fattening middle-class group, with their developing, sophisticated tastes and growing appetite for consuming a wider range of new exciting products, will be the target of international and domestic franchisors. As demand growth rises by 11 per cent by 2016 (PricewaterhouseCoopers) new products and services will be in high demand. We can expect a growing influx of companies to fill these desires and needs. At present, there are over 4000 franchising opportunities in India and the franchise industry was estimated at US$13.4 billion in 2012 and is expected to grow by 6–7 times by 2017, both in value and volume terms. KPMG estimates that over 43,000 franchisee establishments (valued at US$36 billion) may be required by 2017 to meet this demand. With only 2.5 per cent of total retail sales through franchises, opposed to 50 per cent in the USA, the existing lack of franchise development is also a key point for franchisors.

The Indian retail sector is fragmented with unorganised formats providing over 90 per cent of total retail but bulk purchasing and shopping in modern retail formats is a growing trend and as consumers' need for global brands is shifting, footfall towards these more modern formats is increasing. The wider choice and a more exciting, inclusive shopper experience match their developing aspirations and busier lifestyles. Modern retail is considered to be an essential driver and is expected to account for 20 per cent of the market by 2020 (ibef.org).

While all sectors have considerable potential, franchising opportunities of particular interest are

- consumer services,
- food and beverages,
- education and training,
- health, beauty, and wellness.

'India will take over where China is leaving off, becoming the driver of middle-class creation over the next decade. Its contribution to growth in the middle-class will increase sharply and is unlikely to peak even after 2020', predicts Goldman Sachs global chief economist Jim O' Neill. Reports suggest that Indian consumers are some of the most confident in the world. The increase in discretionary spending and availability of credit has put them higher on the consumption curve and enabled them to purchase products that they could not before, or regarded as one-off luxury items.

Due to media and the increased availability of global brands, the Indian consumer has become well exposed to these products. With this exposure has come experimentation and learning. Now the consumer is more open-minded while being a lot more knowledgeable and au fait with brands. However, because of increased brand awareness and choice, Indian consumers are more selective about their purchases. They are not primarily buying a product because of its functional benefit but they are also considering the image, status, and lifestyle it portrays or is associated with the brand. Consequently a franchisor will have to differentiate themselves in ways over a lifestyle or emotional connection.

Firm Capabilities in International Franchising

International franchising is an important mode of entry for domestic enterprises wishing to gain and maintain market share in overseas markets. It is especially important for firms seeking to capitalise on the opportunities available due to the ongoing rapid growth of middle classes in the Asia-Pacific region. Identification and analysis of firm capabilities associated with this mode of entry is therefore timely. Success in the lucrative but extremely challenging markets of the Asia-Pacific is, by no means, a foregone conclusion. The development and deployment of a given set of firm capabilities can facilitate market entry. Research points to some key factors to securing sustainable competitive advantage through global franchising: (a) capabilities in market research; (b) selection of overseas partners and (c) entry mode; (d) franchisee monitoring; (e) implementation of an effective knowledge transfer system; and (f) internalising tacit local knowledge of franchisees. Finally, in order for the franchisor to be successful in a foreign market, it needs to be able to achieve adequate bargaining power and control vis-à-vis the franchisee.

The franchising business model is an exceedingly attractive one for firms seeking to project their brands into new markets, especially the emerging markets of the Asia-Pacific. The use of international franchising as a means to gain entry into foreign markets has seen rapid growth since the 1970s. Indeed, it was reported that as many as 94 per cent of foreign outlets of US companies are operated by means of franchise arrangements (Pharr, 2000, p. 100). Franchising is particularly prominent in certain industries, such as hotels, food retailing, and recreation (Alon, 2004, p. 156). However, it can also be used in financial, legal, architectural, and other professional services to gain access to Asian markets, leveraging off successful international brands.

International franchising is part of the bigger picture of an increasingly globalised economic community in which a rising middle class with increasingly homogenised tastes is transforming the competitive environment for businesses seeking new and sustainable profitability offshore. It is also part of the broader process of industrialisation in which global best practices in business are increasingly penetrating new markets, firms, and consumers across the world (Alon, 2004, pp. 161–164).

Global franchising often presents as a relatively cost-effective means for firms to gain entry and project their brands into the attractive, but often diverse and risky, markets of the Asia-Pacific. The symbiotic relationship in which overseas-based franchisors and local franchisees pool their resources and share both the gains and risks of entry offers a tantalising model for expansion. The local entrepreneur achieves access to sophisticated international business processes, support services, and brand name, while the franchisor is afforded resource-efficient and less risky access to new consumers (Gauzente & Dumoulin, 2010).

However, analysis of the literature and empirical research suggests that success in international franchising is far from certain, and that in order to attain sustainable competitive advantage in international franchising, the franchisor will need to develop a number of key capabilities. Finally and quintessentially for the franchise business model, capability in appropriating the scarce and valuable knowledge systems (including tacit know-how) of both the franchisor and the franchisee and blending them for the benefit of the overall operation and franchise brand will be crucial to establishing competitive advantage in new markets. An appropriate mix of knowledge transfer mechanisms (e.g. franchise manual, training, site visits, mentoring) will be needed. Further, the competitive advantage may be capable of being sustained if the international franchisor achieves relative bargaining power over the franchisee, embeds the tacit knowledge acquired from franchisees into its operations, and selects contractual arrangements and a mode of entry that protects its position vis-à-vis the franchisee, competitors, and new entrants.

Conclusion

This chapter looked at the context of franchising, reviewing the definition of franchising, its evolution, and the international context of franchising in the USA, the UK, and then the Irish context. The next chapter will look at the competing literatures from the franchising and industry evolution fields and present the conceptual model for this study.

References

Alon, I. (2004). Global franchising and development in emerging and transitioning markets. *Journal of Macromarketing, 24*, 156–167.

Alon, I., & McKee, D. (1999). Towards a macro environmental model of international franchising. *Multinational Business Review, 7*(1), 76–82.

Dant, R. P., Grünhagen, M., & Windsperger, J. (2011). Franchising research frontiers for the twenty-first century. *Journal of Retailing, 87*(3), 253–268.

Gauzente, C., & Dumoulin, R. (2010). Franchise as an efficient mode of entry in emerging markets: A discussion from the legitimacy point of view. In S. Singh (Ed.), *Handbook of business practices and growth in emerging markets* (pp. 255–272). Singapore: World Scientific Publishing.

Pharr, J. (2000). Conditions and challenges of global franchising in the new millennium: A research agenda. In S. Hall & D. Martin (Eds.), *Proceedings of the American Society of Business and Behavioral Sciences track section of marketing* (pp. 100–107), Las Vegas, 17–21 February.

3

The Emergence of Franchising

This chapter is theoretical in nature and explores the conditions and environmental context necessary for franchising to emerge. What drives the introduction of franchising? This question is explored with engagement of the franchising literature and literature from the industry evolution field. The reality is that most of the franchising literature relates to the emergence of franchising from the perspective of the firm. The decision to franchise has been a subject of interest for students of the economics of organisations and thus at the level of the firm for many years. Initial and still-insightful works are Caves and Murphy (1976) and Rubin (1978). Lafontaine and Shaw (1998) reviewed much of the empirical literature from economics and highlighted agency theory as a motivation for franchising; further amplification and analysis can be found in Blair and Lafontaine (2005). Most franchising research has been grounded in either resource scarcity theory or agency theory and also transaction cost economics. All three aspects will be addressed in the following section.

© The Author(s) 2017
R. Beere, *The Role of Franchising on Industry Evolution*,
DOI 10.1007/978-3-319-49064-9_3

Literature Relating to the Emergence of Franchising

This section will address the issues relating to why and how franchising emerges both in terms of firm level propensity to adopt franchising and any literature relating to the macro-environmental and industry conditions necessary for its emergence.

Reasons to Franchise

Resource scarcity theory views franchising as a mechanism to ease financial and managerial constraints on growth. The most debated topic in franchising research is the reason a firm chooses to franchise which is related to why franchising emerges rather than a firm choosing to expand through company-owned units. Oxenfeldt and Kelly (1968–1969) proposed a life cycle model of franchising, in which a young company with a limited supply of capital becomes a franchisor in order to use the franchisee's capital to expand. Then as it acquires sufficient capital, the franchisor will later take over the larger units from franchisees. This view has become known as resource scarcity (Carney & Gedajlovic, 1991). Initial empirical support for this view was provided by Hunt (1973), who found an aggregate trend towards company-owned units in the fast food industry. He also found that larger and older units are likely to become company-owned units. Caves and Murphy (1976) also observed a similar trend towards company ownership in restaurants, hotels, and motels. Additional evidence was provided by Anderson (1984), who found that the percentage of units owned by franchisors systematically increased over a period of ten years. Thompson (1994) found that company ownership is less likely to occur when units require high capital investment or when the franchisor is experiencing significant growth, thereby supporting the notion that resource constraints drive the decision towards franchising. The importance of resources for firms in the early stages of growth is also evidenced by new franchisors charging a higher initial fee than older franchisors (Sen, 1993). However, the resource scarcity view does not explain why franchising is used by many businesses who clearly have full access to capital markets (Lafontaine & Kaufmann, 1994).

Agency theory is another much used economic theory to explain the propensity to franchise. Note that resource scarcity and agency theory are not contradictory; a firm must both attract resources (resource scarcity) and align incentives (agency theory). Agency theory views franchising as a mechanism for improving the alignment between firm and outlet-level incentives. Following the theory of efficient capital markets, many researchers hold a different perspective based on organisational economics, particularly agency theory. They argue that the franchisor is able to reduce risk by investing in the entire system and hence has a lower cost of capital than does the franchisee, making capital more available to the franchisor than to the franchisee (Rubin, 1978). Agency theory (Brickley & Dark, 1987; Mathewson & Winter, 1985; Rubin, 1978), which holds that managers (the agents), will tend to shirk in their duty to the firm (the principal) because their compensation is fixed and as a result, high monitoring costs will be incurred by the firm to ensure that its managers act in the firm's best interest. Hence, franchisee-owned units are likely to perform better than company-owned units because the contract between the principal (franchisor) and agent (franchisee) is designed to keep their financial interests closely aligned. Support for the agency theory view was provided by Brickley and Dark (1987), who found that high employee-monitoring costs, low initial investment cost per unit, and high frequency of repeat customers per unit favoured franchising over company-owned units. Further support is provided by Thomas, O'Hara, and Musgrave (1990), who found that high unit sales (which spread monitoring costs over more sales dollars) cause units to be converted from franchised to company-owned status (Dahlstrom & Nygaard, 1999). They found no support for the life cycle theory of franchise development. Thompson (1994) also reported that company ownership of units occurs in urban areas and areas where units tend to be large.

Furthermore, Combs and Castrogiovanni (1994) found no support for the notion of resource scarcity but did find significant support for the agency theory and risk-spreading perspectives. Company-owned units generally seem to offer employees higher wage increases over time than franchise-owned units (Krueger, 1991). However, Shelton (1967) found that franchised units outperformed company-owned units, even though the managers of company-owned units received some incentive compensation. According to franchisors, the high level of motivation of franchisees compared to paid employees is the most important advantage offered by franchising (Lillis, Narayana, & Gilman, 1976). This may be a result of the franchisee having a marginal opportunity cost of labour below that of a hired employee (Caves & Murphy, 1976).

Carney and Gedajlovic (1991) attempted to synthesise the resource scarcity and agency views. Based on a study of franchising patterns in Quebec, they developed a path model of the franchising life cycle that incorporates both theories. Similar findings were reported by Lafontaine (1992), who found that franchising is prevalent when there are incentive problems, but firms also use franchising to grow faster; however, the constraints that franchising must overcome may not always be financial. Thompson (1994) argues that managerial talent may be a scarcer resource than capital for a growing organisation.

In addition to agency theory and resource scarcity theory, Oliver Williamson has discussed franchising in several of his works on transaction cost economics (Williamson, 1985, 1996). Franchising has not been analysed explicitly but it has instead been cited as an example of hybrid governance. Forward integration out of manufacturing into distribution would be implied by hierarchy. Franchising awards greater autonomy than say an organisational hierarchy but places franchisees under added rules and surveillance as compared with markets. Costs control and local adaptations are stronger under franchising than hierarchy. The added autonomy (as compared with hierarchy) and the added restraints (as compared with the market) under which franchisees operate nevertheless come at a cost. If, for example, quality assurance is realised by constraining the franchisee to use materials supplied by the franchisor, and if exceptions to that practice are not permitted because of the potential for abuse that would result, then local opportunities to make 'apparently' cost-effective solutions are prohibited. Similarly, the added local autonomy enjoyed by franchisees may get in the way of some global adjustments (Williamson, 1996). Studies at firm level view franchising as a form of organisation for profit maximisation. While this type of research is common in management journals, much of the underlying theory comes from economics, whereby performance is measured by franchise system sales or unit growth. All these reasons are supported conceptually by Caves and Murphy (1976). In summary, it appears that agency theory, resource scarcity theory, and transaction cost economics offer some explanation as to why firms franchise. However, there are other reasons that have not been extensively examined and this research hopes to address.

International Franchising

Another area of research relating to the emergence of franchising is that of international franchising which can be used as a method of entry into a new market or region for firms who already have indigenous franchise systems and for firms who are new to franchising. Franchising as an organisational form is gaining acceptance in many countries (Preble & Hoffman, 1995). Franchising has spread internationally in two stages. Initially it spread to countries characterised by high per capita income and a developed retail service sector; then to countries characterised by greater diversity in culture, income, and political systems (Welch, 1989). This internationalisation of franchising has been of interest to several researchers, although the research is largely atheoretical. For example, a recent study by Accenture found that one-third of US franchisors had overseas operations. Among the firms without overseas operations as yet, 50 per cent indicated interest in operating overseas within the next five years (Tannenbaum, 1992). While franchisors that are older and/ or have a larger number of units are more likely to operate internationally (Huszagh, Huszagh, & McIntyre, 1992), all types and sizes of franchisors are interested in becoming international franchisors (Aydin & Kacker, 1989).

Hackett (1976) found that the major motive for franchisors to move overseas was a desire to take advantage of markets with great potential and to establish a brand name. Many franchising firms were able to enter overseas markets without any change in their marketing strategy and experienced the same level of profitability as they did at home. International franchising also offers a strategic option for firms who do not franchise domestically. Ayal and Izraeli (1990) claim that for high tech products, an international market expansion through franchising could offer many advantages, including higher value accrued to the product due to the services provided by the franchising system coupled with the scale advantages of franchising. Whitehead (1991) found that international franchising provides an opportunity for firms to establish a presence in countries where the population or per capita spending is not sufficient for a major expansion effort. Both Hackett (1976) and Walker and Etzel (1973) found that legal and governmental red tape were the major barriers to international entry by franchising firms. In contrast, Aydin and Kacker (1989) found that the large US market, the lack of international management expertise, and limited financial resources were reasons that franchisors remained domestic. The importance of perceptions in making this decision is illustrated by Kedia, Ackerman, Bush, and Justis (1994), who found that firms whose managers are favourably predisposed to internationalisation are likely to pursue international opportunities. Research has also explored strategies for international franchising. For example, Chan and Justis (1990) suggested master franchising, joint venturing, licensing, direct investment, or governmental agreements as possible entry strategies for franchises trying to enter the East Asian market. Based on the above review, it may be concluded that international expansion will be pursued by franchisors more vigorously in the future as their domestic markets mature. International franchising could also offer opportunities for firms who are not traditionally franchisors. The major barriers to international franchising are the lack of managerial abilities and legal barriers. Franchisors also need to reach a minimum size in order to cover transaction costs from international activities.

Environmental Context

As mentioned, much of the literature pertaining to the emergence of franchising relates to firm level decision and choices. However, there is some research that looks at the environmental context as important in the emergence of franchising. Some of the franchising literature looks at institutional theory which can help connect some external and environmental factors relating to the emergence of franchising. The application of institutional theory has proven to be especially helpful to this stream of entrepreneurial research. Combs, Michael, and Castrogiovanni (2004) discuss institutional theory and explore how its social influence affects organisational decision-making (Oliver, 1997). According to institutional theory, firms exist in an institutional context defined by rules, norms, values, and taken-for-granted assumptions that guide economic behaviour (Oliver, 1997).

It is in Shane and Foo's (1999) exploration of franchising success that institutional theory played a major role in helping to explain the forces that shape entrepreneurial success, apart from organisational (or entrepreneurial) resources (Ahlstrom & Bruton, 2002). While Shane and Foo's work focused on domestic US franchising, institutional theory, as suggested by Hoskisson, Eden, Lau, and Wright (2000), has also proven to be particularly powerful in examining international related topics. The factors that have been widely acknowledged are that for new organisations, the institutional environment defines and limits entrepreneurial opportunities, and thus affects the rate and size of new venture creation (Aldrich, 1999; Gnyawali & Fogel, 1994; Hwang & Powell, 2005). Other institutional factors in the external environment that impact entrepreneurial development and the start-up phase are favourable market incentives and the availability of capital (Foster, 1986). Therefore inadequate institutional development can complicate new venture development such as the adoption of franchising (Baumol, Litan, & Schramm, 2009) while a more developed institutional environment with overly restrictive regulation can hamper firm's founding (Soto, 2000). Moreover, Barthélemy (2011) asserted that a key tenet of institutional theory is particularly relevant to franchising: that is, decisions are influenced by isomorphic pressures arising from the environment. Overall, findings from Barthélemy's (2011) study suggest that researchers should supplement the popular agency theory with institutional theory to adequately explain franchising decisions by investigating whether institutional theory explains variance in franchising decisions beyond what is explained by agency theory.

Industry Context

As well as a lack of research on the broader environmental influences only three articles actually touch on the emergence of franchising from the perspective of the industry. The impact of franchising at an industry level is looked at by Dant, Grunhagen, and Windsperger (2011) in relation to industry fragmentation, and as mentioned previously Elango and Fried (1997) made a call for franchising and industry effects and implications to be investigated. Furthermore Martin (1988) asked questions such as why does franchising exist and why does franchising exist in certain industries? Martin (1988) addressed the first question when he examined franchising from an industry perspective and found that capital needs, market competition, monitoring costs, and the need to reach minimum efficient scale were reasons to franchise. The second question Martin (1988) asked was why is franchising successful in some industries and not others? From the empirical research he found that from multiple quantitative studies there seems some consensus on the following: first, retail sales, fast food, and customer service franchisees were found to have low closure rates, while beauty and health and automotive and hotels had the highest failure rates (Justis, Castrogiovanni, & Chan, 1992). Second, the longer established the franchise system, the lower the failure rates (Lafontaine & Shaw, 1998). But these findings do not get to the bottom of the issue at hand and further research needs to truly address these fundamental questions.

Literature Relating to the Emergence of Franchising from the Industry Evolution Perspective

This section looks at the industry evolution literature relating to the emergence of a new variant or new organisational form such as franchising. One of the major gaps in the literature is the lack of attention to agency or in fact the influence of entrepreneurship in the evolutionary process. This has only recently been mentioned by Jacobides' (2006) work on industry architecture (looked at in more detail in the next section) and the dynamic capabilities (Augier & Teece, 2008) literature as mentioned previously. This section will review the major contribution of variation, retention and selection (VSR) approach in its ability to help explain the introduction and emergence of new organisational forms such as franchising.

The Evolutionary Approach as Meta-Theory

As seen, the industry evolution literature is complex and can be limited in its ability to study dynamic and emerging new industry processes. Furthermore there is a need to complement empirical analysis across a broad range of industries with the development of theoretical frameworks to explain the mechanisms by which industries evolve. As mentioned it is beneficial for this research to engage with an overarching theory, such as the variation, selection, retention meta-theory (Aldrich & Ruef, 2006) which is reviewed in the following section, in the context of organisational evolution and strategy (Durand, 2006). This connects to the use of longitudinal, multi-modal, multi-level studies recommended by industry evolution scholars (Dosi & Malerba, 2002; Malerba & Orsenigo, 1996) which this research promotes.

The following section defines and explains the relevant evolutionary processes that are applicable to this research and its exploration of the emergence of franchising and its influence on industry dynamics. De Wit and Meyer (2010) look at industry evolution and claim that 'the industry dynamics perspective is often referred to as the industry evolution perspective, due to the strong parallel with biological evolution'. They suggest that as with nature, industry evolution is similar as in both instances the survival of firms or species is dependent on their adaptability to their environment. This perspective is useful in looking at the survival of firms and how those who adopt franchising as an organisational form in order to survive in their industry. However, they caution, 'as the environment changes only those that meet the new demands will not be selected out' (De Wit & Meyer, 2010). According to Aldrich (2006), the evolutionary approach is 'a generic framework for understanding social change' and is an overarching approach for studying the processes through which organisations, populations, and communities emerge and change. This research will adopt this approach, and the benefit of this approach is that it looks at the emergence and evolution of firms and industries at multiple levels many individual theories are limited in their ability to do so. It is applicable at multiple levels and looks at the processes of VSR. The idea that organisational and industry evolution follows a comparable form to biological processes is now accepted by most in the social sciences. Emerging from 'universal Darwinism', the non-scientific understanding of evolution differs greatly between disciplines. Futuyma (1986) looked at evolutionary biology and claimed that evolution as 'merely change, and so is all-pervasive; galaxies, languages, and political systems all evolve'.

Evolutionary Approach: The Generic Processes

This research has found that Darwin's VSR model when applied to evolutionary theory (Aldrich, 1999) can be used to explain how particular forms of organisations come to exist in specific kinds of environments. It is a useful model to use in terms of studying industry evolution and the emergence of a new variant such as franchising. VSR occurs simultaneously rather than sequentially. Variation generates the raw materials for selection, by environment or internal criteria; retention processes preserve the selected variation. As such in terms of the emergence and adoption of franchising, it can be viewed as an organisational variation, a new hybrid organisational system which is robust and adaptive in competitive environmental situations. However, once a variation is identified the retention processes also restrict the kinds of variations that may occur. Competitive struggles as well as cooperative alliances may change the shape of selection criteria. Like many scientific analysis, an evolutionary perspective requires that organisational theorists think carefully about some research design questions: What is the most appropriate unit of analysis—organisations, populations, and communities. Given the importance of emergence as an outcome in evolutionary analysis, how can we define organisations or organisational forms as novel?

Looking at variation as a useful analytic to help understand evolution, any departure from routine or tradition is a variation, and variation may be intentional or blind. Intentional variations occur when people or organisations actively attempt to generate alternatives and seek solutions to problems such as the adoption of franchising as a new organisational form. Variations can result not from intentional responses to adaptation pressures but rather from accidents, chance, luck, conflict, malfeasance, and so on. Variations are the raw materials from which selection processes cull those that are most suitable, given the selection criteria. A crucial feature of an evolutionary framework is that it must consider not only variations within existing organisations but also variations introduced by new organisations such as new entrants into an industry. Most founders intend to reproduce the characteristics of organisations perceived as successful. An example of an intentional environmental variation is the development of a strong new organisation by an outsider to an industry (Aldrich, 1999) or introducing a new organisational governance structure such as franchising.

Selection as an evolutionary process is generated by forces that 'differentially select or selectively eliminate certain type of variations' (Aldrich, 1999). The selection criteria are set by the operation of factors like market forces, competitive pressures, organisational structure, and conformity with norms. Consistent selection pressures usually lead to a high degree of similarities across organisations (Aldrich, 1999) such as many firms adopting a franchise model. Scholars of strategic choice argue that managers can often introduce positive internal selectors first by establishing the strategic direction of an organisation and then by favouring elements of organisational design that are consistent with the logic, scope, goals, and competitive advantage of that strategy (Saloner, Shepard, & Podolny, 2001). The retention mechanism occurs when 'selected variations are preserved, duplicated or reproduced' (Aldrich, 1999). If environmental change is slow, replication is important for survival. Aldrich (1999) claims that at the organisational level the retention or preservation of existing organisational norms takes the form of selected routines, structures, and procedures (Nelson & Winter, 1982). They are efficient as long as an organisation continues to fit the relevant selection criteria (Aldrich, 1999). At the organisation level, the retention mechanism preserves collective and overarching competencies, practices, and technologies (such as franchising), which are shared by many organisations.

According to Aldrich and Ruef (2006), evolutionary theory is an overarching meta-theory applied across multiple levels of analysis; it is open to multiple approaches for explaining particular kinds of changes. The evolutionary approach relates to other theories and perspectives and 'holds out the promise of using these (theories and perspectives) to achieve an integrated understanding, not an integrated theory' (Aldrich & Ruef, 2006). The VSR process of industry evolution helps understand how specific forms of organisations survive and act in particular environments. This approach can be useful in assessing the elements pertinent to the emergence of franchising. Major issues are still under debate with regard to VSR, including the question of what is being selected in evolutionary processes (e.g., routines versus organisations), how novel evolutionary variations can be defined, and what research designs are most appropriate in capturing the indeterminacy of outcomes that is a key feature of evolutionary analysis.

The Study of Franchising and Evolution

As highlighted previously this book explores both the emergence and the evolution of franchising. This section will give a brief overview of the issues with regards to the evolution and industry impact franchising has on the structural change at industry level as well as organisational level. Within the franchising literature there is very little that deals with the impact of franchising at an industry level and also limited academic discussion around issues of franchising and its evolution.

The following section will give a summary of some of the common theoretical links between franchising and industry evolution research, First, one piece of work that helps to unify the two streams of franchising and industry evolution focuses indirectly on the emergence and impact of franchising in terms of industry evolution theory is Aldrich's (2000) work on 'Organisations Evolving' which begins to explore the question of how new organisations emerge and evolve. Aldrich notes that organisational scholars have done an excellent job in explaining how things work in organisations that have been in existence for some time but not how they developed over time. Aldrich also argues that the evolutionary approach can be used as an overarching framework within which the value of other approaches such as ecological, institutional, interpretive, organisational learning, resource dependence, transaction cost economising approach can be recognised and appreciated and this research benefits from this approach.

Second, looking at the use of multi-modal approach which this research has adopted is beneficial in terms of connecting the five theories as this research has done and looks at how transaction cost economics, agency theory, resource dependence theory, neo-institutional theory, and population ecology can help to both explain and connect both franchising and industry evolution perspectives. Pfeffer (1993) looked at whether evolutionary theory could be an overarching framework for studying organisations. This leads to an eclectic theoretical approach that is complex and often difficult to distinguish at first glance. For instance, resource dependency theory is often combined with institutional theory when developing more sophisticated theoretical constructs such as industry architectures (Jacobides et al., 2006), which are shaped also by economic perspectives such as transaction cost economics. Some studies combine ecological and institutional perspectives to examine co-evolutionary issues (Koka, Madhavan, & Prescott, 2006), Added to this, research is now combining such sociological approaches with co-evolutionary perspectives to explore industry evolution in greater detail (Lin, Chen, Sher, & Mei, 2011). So it is beneficial to use a multi-modal approach to address such a complex study such as this one and to help connect and make linkages between franchising and industry evolution theory.

Third, VSR is an evolutionary approach and serves as a meta-theory within which the value of other organisational theories can be recognised and appreciated. VSR is a model promoted in the industry evolution literature and its relevance to explaining the emergence of franchising is undeniable. Therefore franchising can be seen as a new organisational variation which is adopted, selected, and ultimately retained. Furthermore research on co-evolution can also be drawn on to assess why franchising is selected as an organisational variation. Firms may therefore adopt a franchising model to help them achieve a competitive advantage in their industry. This leads to firms' legitimisation, the strengthening, and adoption of franchising, and to the development of this organisational structure across many industry incumbents. Co-evolutionary theory ties in with the organisational structures of franchise systems where there is more than one organisational entity at play in the system and there are multiple organisations within the organisational structure that have multiple levels of inter-relationships and inter-organisational interactions. The section on franchising literature relates to franchising as an inter-organisational system where each of the participating firms is an independent agent—where the franchise system co-evolves as an outcome of organisational activity and the actions of each participating firm (franchisor and franchisee)—and acts as an agent and its actions are reciprocally embedded within each of the firms constituting the franchise system, the industry, and society.

Fourth, another theoretical connection between the franchising and industry evolution literature is the role of agency. Entrepreneurship and the role of entrepreneurs is at the forefront in the emergence of franchising, the area of entrepreneurship pervades the franchising literature as well as the role of entrepreneurs and agency. Even though the area of entrepreneurship and agency is limited in the industry evolution field, there still is some work on industry architecture and dynamic capabilities which notes the role of agency and actor in shaping the evolution of an industry.

Finally research on fragmented industries is important when addressing a study on franchising and industry evolution. The relationship between industry fragmentation, franchising, and industry evolution is important, as Porter (1980) stated that franchising overcomes industry fragmentation, this indicates that franchising might have the potential to alter an industry structure, a suggestion which is at the heart of this research. This research will try to verify if franchising does impact industry structure as Porter suggested. In addition Dess (1987) discusses the key attributes of fragmented industries: the presence of a large number of small and medium-sized firms and the absence of market leaders with the power to shape industry events. These industries have a low four-firm concentration ratio, that is the share of industry sales accounted for by the top four firms. Porter (1980) describes fragmented industries as those that contain all or some of the following: low entry barriers, lack of power of buyers, lack of power of suppliers, lack of economies of scale, lack of economies of scope, and regional issues such as high transportation costs and regulation. Porter (1980) concentrates on manufacturing whereas Brown (2011) focuses on service sector and fragmented structure in the real estate industry in a study relating to franchising and industry fragmentation. Porter (1980) suggests that fragmented industries are characterised as being intensely competitive. Borch and Brastad (2003) suggest that research on the strategic behaviour of companies in fragmented environments has been largely ignored and even Porter (1980) only reluctantly recognises the potential for collective strategy in fragmented industries. Brown (2011) asserts that fragmented industries are fundamentally different in terms of their structure and competitive landscape, yet these industries have been neglected by much of the existing literature. Furthermore fragmented service industries have not received the attention that they deserve something this research will address.

In summary, this research will highlight an evolutionary perspective, beginning with antecedent and founding conditions, negotiating and establishing expectations for creating and distributing joint value, the co-evolution of direction, structure, and practices within the context of the evolution of the constituent firms/agents, industry, and institutional environment. Furthermore, absent from the literature are studies of the evolution of franchise systems, as they co-evolve with the changing strategies of the firm, evolving industry strategic practices, and the changing regulatory and institutional environment. This research hopes to advance the view that organisational forms such as franchise systems need to be understood and should be researched in the context of the adaptation choices of the firm over time. The choice to franchise, in this view, is embedded within the firm's history and strategic portfolio and co-evolves with the firm's strategy, the institutional, organisational, and competitive environment, and with management's strategic intent for the creation of the franchise system.

References

Ahlstrom, D., & Bruton, G. D. (2002). An institutional perspective on the role of culture in shaping strategic actions by technology-focused entrepreneurial firms in China. *Entrepreneurship Theory and Practice, 26*(4), 53–70.

Aldrich, H. (1999). Organizations evolving. London; Thousand Oaks, CA: Sage.

Aldrich, H. (2006). *Organizations and environments.* Englewood Cliffs, NJ: Prentice Hall.

Aldrich, H., & Ruef, M. (2006). *Organizations evolving* (2nd ed.). London: Sage.

Anderson, E. (1984). The growth and performance of franchise systems: Company versus franchisee ownership. *Journal of Economics and Business, 36,* 421–431.

Augier, M., & Teece, D. J. (2008). Strategy as evolution with design: The foundations of dynamic capabilities and the role of managers in the economic system. *Organization Studies, 29*(8/9), 1185.

Ayal, I., & Izraeli, D. (1990). International market expansion for new high tech products through franchising. *Journal of High Technology Management Research, 1,* 167–180.

Aydin, N., & Kacker, M. (1989). International outlook of U.S. based franchisors. *International Marketing Review, 7*(2), 43–53.

Blair, R., & Lafontaine, F. (2005). *The economics of franchising.* New York: Cambridge University Press.

Barthélemy, J. (2011, Jan). Agency and institutional influences on franchising decisions. *Journal of Business Venturing, 26*(1), 93–103.

Baumol, W. J., Litan, R. E., & Schramm, C. J. (2009). *Good capitalism, bad capitalism, and the economics of growth and prosperity.* New Haven, CT: Yale University Press.

Borch, O J, and Brastad, B. (2003). Strategic turnaround in a fragmented industry. *Journal of Small Business and Enterprise Development,* 10(4).

Brickley, J. A., & Dark, F. H. (1987). The choice of organizational form: The case of franchising. *Journal of Financial Economics, 18,* 401–420.

Brown, S. (2011). Does institutional theory explain foreign location choices in fragmented industries? *Journal of International Business Research, 10*(1), 59.

Chan, P., & Justis, R. (1990). Training for franchise management. *Journal of Small Business Management, 29*(3), 87–91.

Carney, M., & Gedajlovic, E. (1991). Vertical integration in franchise systems: Agency theory and resource explanations. *Strategic Management Journal, 12*(8), 607–629.

Caves, R. E., & Murphy, W. R. (1976). Franchising: Firms, markets, and intangible assets. *Southern Economic Journal, 42,* 572–586.

Combs, J. G., & Castrogiovanni, G. J. (1994). Franchisor strategy: A proposed model and empirical test of franchise vs. company ownership. *Journal of Small Business Management, 32,* 37–48.

Combs, J. G., Michael, S. C., & Castrogiovanni, G. J. (2004). Franchising: A review and avenues to greater - theoretical diversity. *Journal of Management, 30*(6), 907–931.

Dahlstrom, R., & Nygaard, A. (1999, May). An empirical investigation of ex post transaction costs in franchised distribution channels transaction. *Journal of Marketing Research, 36*(2), 160–170.

Dant, R., Grunhagen, M., & Windsperger, J. (2011). Franchising research frontiers for the twenty-first century. *Journal of Retailing, 87*(2), 253–268.

De Wit, B., & Meyer, R. (2010). *Strategy: Process, content, context.* Andover: Cengage Learning EMEA.

Dess, G. (1987). Consensus on strategy formulation and organizational performance: Competitors in a fragmented industry. *Strategic Management Journal, 8*, 259–277.

Dosi, G., & Malerba, F. (2002). Interpreting industrial dynamics twenty years after Nelson and winter's evolutionary theory of economic change: A preface. *Industrial and Corporate Change, 11*, 619–622.

Durand, R. (2006). *Organisational evolution and strategic management.* London: Sage.

Elango, B., & Fried, V. H. (1997). Franchising research: A literature review and synthesis. *Journal of Small Business Management, 35*, 68–81.

Foster, R. N. (1986). *Innovation: The attacker's advantage.* New York: Summit Books.

Futuyma, D. J. (1986). *In evolutionary biology.* Sunderland, MA: Sinauer Associates.

Gnyawali, D., & Fogel, D. (1994). Environments for entrepreneurship development: Key dimensions and research implications. *Entrepreneurship: Theory & Practice, 18*(4), 43–62.

Hackett, D. W. (1976). The international expansion of franchise systems: Status and strategies. *Journal of International Business, 7*(2), 101–121.

Hoskisson, R. E., Eden, L., Lau, C. M., & Wright, M. (2000). Strategy in emerging economies. *The Academy of Management Journal, 43*(3), 249–267.

Hunt, S. (1973). The trend toward company-operated units in franchise chains. *Journal of Retailing, 49*(2), 3–12.

Huszagh, S., Huszagh, F., & McIntyre, F. (1992). International franchising in the context of competitive strategy and the theory of the firm. *International Marketing Review, 9*(5), 5–18.

Hwang, H., & Powell, W. W. (2005). Institutions and entrepreneurship. In S. Alvarez, R. Agrawal, & O. Sorenson (Eds.), *Handbook of entrepreneurship research: Interdisciplinary perspectives* (pp. 201–232). New York: Springer.

Jacobides, M. G., & Billinger, S. (2006). Designing the boundaries of the firm: From "Make, Buy, or Ally" to the dynamic benefits of vertical architecture. *Organization Science, 17*(2), 249–261.

Jacobides, M. G., Knudsen, T., & Augier, M. (2006). Benefiting from innovation: Value creation, value appropriation and the role of industry architectures. *Research Policy, 35*(8), 1200–1221.

Justis, R., Castrogiovanni, G., & Chan, P. (1992). Examination of franchise failure rates. In *Franchising: Passport for growth and world of opportunity*. Palm Springs, CA: Society of Franchising.

Kedia, B. L., Ackerman, D. J., Bush, D. E., & Justis, R. T. (1994). Determinants of internationalization of franchise operations. *International Marketing Review, 11*(4), 56–68.

Koka, B., Madhavan, R., & Prescott, J. (2006). The evolution of interfirm networks: Environmental effects on patterns of network change. *Academy of Management Review, 31*(3), 721–737.

Krueger, A. B. (1991). Ownership, agency, and wages: An examination of franchising in the fast food industry. *Quarterly Journal of Economics, 106*, 75–101.

Lafontaine, F. (1992). Agency theory and franchising: Some empirical results. *RAND Journal of Economics, 23*, 263–283.

Lafontaine, F., & Blair, R. D. (2009). The evolution of franchising and franchise contracts: Evidence from the United States. *Entrepreneurial Business Law Journal, 3*(2), 381–434.

Lafontaine, F., & Kaufmann, P. J. (1994). The evolution of ownership patterns in franchise systems. *Journal of Retailing, 70*, 97–113.

Lafontaine, F., & Shaw, K. L. (1998). Franchising growth and franchisor entry and exit in the US market: Myth and reality. *Journal of Business Venturing, 13*, 95–112.

Lillis, C. M., Narayana, C. L., & Gilman, J. L. (1976). Competitive advantage variation over the life cycle of a franchise. *Journal of Marketing, 40*(October), 77–80.

Lin, H. M., Chen, H. M., Sher, P. J., & Mei, H. C. (2011). Inter-network co-evolution: Reversing the fortunes of declining industrial networks. *Long Range Planning, 43*(5–6), 611–638.

Malerba, F., & Orsenigo, L. (1996). The dynamics and evolution of industries. *Industrial Corporate Change, 5*(1), 51–87.

Martin, R. E. (1988). Franchising and risk management. *American Economic Review, 78*, 954–968.

Mathewson, G. F., & Winter, R. A. (1985, October). The economics of franchise contracts. *Journal of Law and Economics, 28*(3), 503–526.

Nelson, R., & Winter, S. (2002). Evolutionary theorizing in economics. *The Journal of Economic Perspectives, 16*(2), 23–46.

Nelson, R. R., & Winter, S. G. (1982). *An evolutionary theory of economic change.* Cambridge: Harvard University Press.

Oliver, C. (1997). Sustainable competitive advantage: Combining institutional and resource-based views. *Strategic Management Journal, 18,* 697–713.

Oxenfeldt, A. R., & Kelly, A. O. (1968). Will successful franchise systems ultimately become wholly-owned chains? *Journal of Retailing, 44,* 69–83.

Pfeffer, J. (1993). Barriers to the advance of organizational science: Paradigm development as a dependent variable. *Academy of Management Review, 18*(4), 599–620.

Porter, M. E. (1980). *Competitive strategy.* New York: Free Press.

Preble, J. F., & Hoffman, R. C. (1995). Franchise systems around the Globe: A status report. *Journal of Small Business Management, 33*(2), 80–88.

Rubin, P. H. (1978). The theory of the firm and the structure of the franchise contract. *Journal of Law and Economics, 21,* 223–233.

Saloner, G., Shepard, A., & Podolny, J. (2001). *Strategic management.* New York: John Wiley & Sons.

Sen, K. C. (1993). The use of initial fees and royalties in business-format franchising. *Managerial and Decision Economics, 14,* 175–190.

Shane, S., & Foo, M.-D. (1999). New firm survival: Institutional explanations for new franchisor mortality. *Management Science, 45,* 142–159.

Shelton, J. (1967). Allocative efficiency vs. "X-Efficiency"—Comment. *American Economic Review, 57*(5), 1252–1258.

Soto, H. D. (2000). *The mystery of capital: Why capitalism triumphs in the West and fails everywhere else.* New York: Basic Books.

Tannenbaum, J. (1992). FTC ensures lawmakers its enforcing franchise rules. *The Wall Street Journal,* January 5, B2.

Thomas, W. L., O'Hara, M. J., & Musgrave, F. W. (1990). The effects of ownership and investment on the performance of franchise systems. *American Economist, 34*(1), 54–61.

Thompson, R. S. (1994). The franchise life cycle and the Penrose effect. *Journal of Economic Behavior and Organization, 24,* 207–218.

Walker, B., & Etzel, M. (1973). The internationialization of U.S. franchise systems: Progress and procedures. *Journal of Marketing, 37,* 38–46.

Welch, L. S. (1989). Diffusion of franchise systems use in international operations. *International Marketing Review, 6*(5), 7–19.

Williamson, O. E. (1985). *The economic institutions of capitalism: Firms, markets, relational contracting.* New York, London: Free Press; Collier: Macmillan.

Williamson, O. E. (1996). *The mechanisms of governance.* New York: Oxford University Press.

4

The Impact of Franchising on Industry Evolution

The emphasis in the previous chapter was on the decision to franchise, albeit with a different slant in terms of industry evolution. However, once franchising is adopted what impact does it have both at firm and industry level? How does franchising alter industry structure? Franchising challenges and changes the prevailing institutional structures of an industry. The answer to this question explores the choice made by franchising firms between the alternative sets of strategies available to them within a certain environment. These strategies are dependent on 'why' some firms choose to adopt franchising and 'what' they want to achieve ('what' impact to make). The industry evolution literature explores the notion of firms co-evolving within their industry or industry architecture whereby firms can change the dynamics of the industry structure by their actions. This question of impact also explores the dynamics of franchising firms over time which is under researched from the franchising literature. The impact of franchising on industries is associated with the embedded contextual drivers behind a firm's decision to franchise. Such impacts can be observed when franchise systems successfully challenge/defend the status quo against the prevailing preferences of other agents and environmental factors (macro-environmental and industry context as well as agency).

© The Author(s) 2017
R. Beere, *The Role of Franchising on Industry Evolution*,
DOI 10.1007/978-3-319-49064-9_4

For example, increasing demand for industry standards and branding creates new variation. As a response to this new variation, new industry entrants appear and begin to adopt franchising to compete with the leading firms and thus retain this new organisational form.

The Impact of Franchising on Industry Structure

Theoretical Perspectives

This section looks at franchising research that relates to the impact of franchising on industry structure. As mentioned at the beginning of this franchising literature review, little or no research has specifically looked at the impact of franchising on industry structure, a gap this research tends to address. Institutional theory, resource dependency theory (RDT), and population ecology will be looked at in terms of their relevance to the impact of franchising on industry evolution.

As mentioned institutional theory has been applied to franchising in terms of its emergence but in addressing the impact or influence of franchising on industry only a some link has been made by Gauzente and Dumoulin (2012) also address the relevance of institutional theory to the field of franchising research. Gauzente et al. (2012) maintain that franchising is one of the most dynamic forms of organisation for retail networks. Conceptualised as a hybrid form by transaction cost theory, franchising outlets are supposed, in the long run, to be bought by franchisors in order to capture residual rents. However, franchising has persisted a long time and still represents one of the favourite means to cover territories. Gauzente et al. (2012) suggest that this persistence of franchising in the organisation of retail networks can be explained by institutional theory and those institutional forces exert their influence at multiple levels forcing firms to promote and perpetuate franchising. Combs et al. (2009) submit that social factors described by institutional theory will enhance understanding. Empirically using a sample of 1300 franchisors active during 1980 through 2000 the authors found evidence that both environmental and internal institutional pressures influenced firms' propensity to franchise, but that responsiveness to internal institutional pressures declined as economic reasons to franchise increased. Overall, social factors appear to actively influence franchising, but their impact is muted by economic factors. The results also suggest that perhaps franchising is itself becoming an institutionalised norm. For researchers, institutional theory promises to be a fruitful avenue for increasing understanding about franchising. For franchisors, results highlight the value of systematic analysis of franchising decisions.

Furthermore, in 1999 Shane and Foo (1999) adopted an institutional perspective to investigate franchising. Empirically they examined 1292 new franchise chains and showed that survival probabilities increase when franchisors gain signs of legitimacy such as age, size, and media certification. With respect to the propensity to franchise, they argued that franchisors enhance long-term survival when their propensity to franchise matches the demands of the institutional environment. The practices of highly visible competitors are frequently observed by others and copied (Sherer & Lee, 2002). In franchising, knowledge of competitors' practices might spread through franchising consultants or the national franchising associations, which are the major clearinghouse for practitioner-focused franchising information in most countries. As others adopt the practices of highly visible competitors, the practices begin to confer legitimacy, leading still others to adopt them (Sherer & Lee, 2002). When a highly visible competitor elects to franchise, that decision is easy to observe and imitate.

In addition, RDT has also been used to look at franchising and its impact on industry but not as its central focus. However, franchising has the ability to affect power relationships within franchise systems and between franchisors in an industry. According to Hillman, Withers, and Collins (2009) 30 years have passed since Pfeffer and Salancik's seminal work on RDT. During this time RDT has been applied broadly across the research domain to explain how organisations reduce environmental interdependence and uncertainty. Hillman et al. (2009) structure their review around the five options that Pfeffer and Salancik propose firms can enact to minimise environmental dependences: (a) mergers/vertical integration, (b) joint ventures and other inter-organisational relationships such as franchising, (c) boards of directors, (d) political action, and (e) executive succession. Since its publication, RDT has become one of the most influential theories in organisational theory and strategic management. RDT characterises the corporation as an open system, dependent on contingencies in the external environment (Pfeffer & Salancik, 1978). As Pfeffer and Salancik (1978: 1) state, 'to understand the behaviour of an organization you must understand the context of that behaviour—that is, the ecology of the organization'. RDT recognises the influence of external factors on organisational behaviour and, although constrained by their context, at firm level managers can act to reduce environmental uncertainty and dependence. Central to these actions is the concept of power, which is the control over vital resources (Ulrich & Barney, 1984). Organisations attempt to reduce others' power over them; often attempting to increase their own power over others and in the case of franchising it is increasing the franchisors power over the franchisees. Pfeffer (1987) provides the basic argument of the resource dependence perspective and inter-organisational relations as (a) the fundamental units for understanding inter-corporate relations and society are organisations; (b) these organisations are not autonomous, but rather are constrained by a network of interdependencies with other organisations (such as franchisors and franchisees); (c) interdependence, when coupled with uncertainty about what the actions will be of those with which the organisations interdependent, leads to a situation in which survival and continued success are uncertain; therefore, (d) organisations take actions to manage external interdependencies, although such actions are inevitably never completely successful and produce new patterns of dependence and interdependence; and (e) these patterns of dependence produce inter-organisational as well as intra-organisational power, where such power has some effect on organisational behaviour. Thus, one major insight from using a RDT lens is the understanding that franchising has the ability to affect power relationships within franchise systems themselves and between organisations in an industry.

In addition to institutional theory and RDT population ecology has been used in the franchising literature to connect franchising and its impact and fit with the environment. Perrigot (2008) explores franchise systems and their relationship to population ecology theory. Organisations must fit to their environment in order to survive. However, in the case of franchising networks, there seems to exist a particular form of organisation that has a better fit with the environment. Perrigot (2008) found that franchise systems that had a plural format that is combining franchised units and company-owned units, offered greater flexibility and can fit more easily to the market (Bradach & Eccles, 1989). Perrigot (2008) asserts that the changes in the populations of organisations occur through selection rather than adaptation (Scott, 1995). Natural selection can be broken down into three distinct stages: variation, selection, and retention (Aldrich, 1979). The natural selection process enables us to understand three key themes: organisational foundation (Hannan & Freeman, 1989; Aldrich, 1990; Lomi, 1995; Messallam, 1998), organisational mortality (Aldrich & Reiss, 1976; Hannan & Freeman, 1989; Carroll, 1987), and organisational change (Aldrich & Reiss, 1976; Hannan & Freeman, 1977; Burton, Baron, & Hannan, 1996). However, Perrigot (2008) deals primarily with the survival of franchising networks, only the theme of organisational mortality. Because of their similar focuses on the role of the external environment, population ecology may also represent a theoretical perspective for integration with RDT. In one of the earliest attempts to integrate RDT with other theoretical lenses Ulrich and Barney (1984) do just this. The authors use these two perspectives along with transaction cost economics to develop a meta-theoretical perspective of organisations. They suggest population ecology's perspective of organisational selection and survival may be explained by a firm's ability to reduce environmental dependencies while gaining power over others. However, beyond this initial theorising, little research has considered the role that inter-organisational relationship such as franchising plays in the survival and selection process from this perspective.

Franchising and Its Impact on Society

In trying to gain a broader perspective of the impact of franchising on industry evolution there are a number of economics and law related articles that view franchising from the perspective of a utility to society. They generally explore questions regarding whether the social benefits of franchising outweigh the costs society incurs because of it. While it is recognised that many aspects of franchising may have a beneficial impact on society by improving economic efficiency, there is concern that some aspects of the franchising relationship may serve as restraints on trade. Particular franchising practices examined include resale price maintenance (the franchisor sets the price the franchisee can charge), exclusive territories (only one franchisee can do business in a geographic area), exclusive dealings (the franchisee can only do business with the franchisor), and requirements contracts (the franchisee is required to purchase certain supplies from the franchisor). Scherer and Ross (1990) provide an overview of research in this area. In addition to considering what harm franchising may do to society as a whole, these authors are concerned with how much the franchisor might abuse the relationship to the detriment of the franchisee. While the franchisee provides the capital for the franchising unit, the franchisor has decision-making power over many items quite important to the success of the unit. Topics researched in this area include how much information a franchisor should disclose to a potential franchisee when soliciting an investment (Castrogiovanni, Justis, & Julian, 1993); the ability of the franchisor to terminate the relationship after the franchisee has made a significant investment (Hadfield, 1990; Brickley, Dark, & Weisbach, 1991); and court interpretation of the franchise contract (Hadfield, 1990). This area of research is not managerially oriented. However, research from franchising and society does have relevance to management issues.

The Impact of Franchising and Competitive Advantage

In further assessing the impact of franchising on industry structure there is a definite connection between the role of firms who adopt franchising and their success or competitive advantage. Again this is an area under researched and there is a lack of studies using franchising as a central tenet. Many scholars have asked the question as to what can lead a firm to achieve competitive advantage. Perhaps franchising as an organisational form can lead an organisation to achieve competitive advantage. Thus, by entrepreneurs introducing franchising into their own firm and it leading to success or competitive advantage the entrepreneurs will have had an impact both at firm and industry level. In terms of owning resources that are unique to that firm whether developed over time or through unique technology needs to be utilised to maximise the performance of the business (Collis & Montgomery, 1995). Recognising uniqueness is not enough to gain competitive advantage; they need to be used to shape the strategy of the organisation. Many franchise systems are homogenous in their offerings and may not be identifying or utilising their resources as a means of gaining competitive advantage. Truss (2004) broadens this by including clients or suppliers as having an influence in developing people management practices and these may include external sources. Thus, franchising as a system cannot guarantee competitive advantage among rivals but it can act as a promoter of greater organisational efficiencies, brand building and development of unique resources, and core competencies as well as incentivised franchisee motivation and productivity. In order to maximise their potential competitive advantage the franchising organisation's offerings need to be judged by their customers as either sufficiently rare, valuable, inimitable, and/ or non-substitutable (Litz et al., 2000). In this way the firm's resources allow it to extract superior rents and sustain future operations. As a result, research needs to be carried out on whether franchising firms do gain a competitive advantage and thus can impact the industry in which they develop something this research shall address.

Franchising: Gaps in the Research

To summarise the review of the franchising literature, a number of gaps have been highlighted in the franchising research. First, Dant (2008) addresses the geographical bias of franchising research and claims that the reason most research of the franchising phenomenon is based in non-North American contexts (like Cochet, Dormann, & Ehrmann, 2007) is that the franchising industry in the USA is fast approaching its maturity state where a number of erstwhile controversial issues (e.g., ownership redirection thesis; cf., Oxenfeldt & Kelly, 1968; Dant & Kaufmann, 2003) have been reasonably settled. However, these issues continue to be dominant in other countries where the legal systems related to franchising are still in their developmental stages. Dant and Grunhagen (2014) also look at the rapid global expansion of the franchising enterprise. Initially this international growth was largely limited to countries that were linguistically or culturally similar to the USA. However, an emerging trend is the growth potential of global markets, developing economies like India, China, brazil, and South America appear to have the greatest potential (Dant, Grunhagen, & Windsperger, 2011) suggests that as these markets are relatively new to franchising master international franchising is among the fastest growing methods of international expansion (Alon, 2006). Kaufmann and Dant (1996) define master franchising as 'a form of umbrella licensing agreement which differs from the standard unit or location-level franchise in two ways: (a) It provides for the granting of an exclusive territory extending beyond the trade area of a single unit, and (b) It envisions from the outset the introduction of an additional layer of control between store level management and the franchisor'. Hence, if researchers want to study the evolutionary, developmental stages of franchising in completely new contexts, they need to go beyond the North American domain of enquiry something this research attempts to do.

Second, Dant and Grunhagen (2014) highlight the dominance of franchising research from the franchisors perspective (Dant, 2008; Dant, Kacker, Coughlan, & Emerson, 2007) they discuss how the enormous popularity of franchising has made prospective franchisees accept the reality of one-sided franchise contracts as 'industry standard' and hence acceptable, a state of affairs that is likely to persist so 'long as there are buyers standing in line with pen and cash in hand' (Purvin, 1994). Some notable exceptions are Baron and Schmidt (1991) who asked individuals why they joined a franchising system as a franchisee. They found that franchisees wanted to run their businesses independently but felt that the availability of backup help, a proven concept and name, and reduced risks of failure made franchising attractive. Similarly, Knight (1984) surveyed franchisees and found that the benefit of a known trade name, the higher independence and job satisfaction enjoyed, and easier business development were the primary reasons to be a franchisee. Willingness to work hard and a desire to succeed were seen as the most important characteristics of a successful franchisee. El Akremi, Mignonac, and Perrigot (2010) also addresses the issues associated with franchise relationships and they claim that these relationships are often assumed to be simple, dyadic, and highly constrained relationships between franchisors and franchisees (Clarkin & Rosa, 2005; Cochet & Ehrmann, 2007). Yet, research emphasises the complexity of franchise relationships and demonstrates collaborative and entrepreneurial teamwork between franchisees, not only between franchisors and franchisees (Clarkin & Rosa, 2005; Dormann, Ehrmann, & Cochet, 2007). Dant and Grunhagen (2014) look at a recent contemporary development which promises to bring greater parity between the franchisors and franchisees. There is a phenomenal increase in the number of multi-unit franchisees that is the number of franchisees that operate multiple units within a franchise system that function virtually as mini-hierarchies within the overall franchisor–franchisee hierarchical structure. Dant (2008) also concludes by suggesting that while a handful of franchisee-based studies exist; however, there is a virtual absence of examining the franchising phenomenon from the perspective of the customer. This despite the fact that some have scorned the franchising industry for its impact on the homogenisation of tastes (e.g. Luxenberg, 1985). Hence, in reality we have very little idea of how the customers think about the value-added aspects of franchising another gap in the franchising field.

Third, Quinn and Doherty (2000) note that much of the prior research studies in international franchising as well as other areas of franchising were based primarily on survey research and used quantitative methods. Qualitative studies, however, have complemented the portfolio of research approaches in the past few years (e.g. Altinay, 2004; Doherty & Alexander, 2004; Grunhagen et al., 2010) in an effort to gain richer insights into the rationale of key decision makers, such as franchisees, system managers, or franchise customers. Furthermore, this research will add to the qualitative research on franchising.

Finally there is a significant lack of research on franchising and its effects on industry. Elango and Freid (1997) made a call for one area in particular to be investigated, which related to franchising and industry effects and implications. Much of the franchising research has previously looked at the franchising system without considering the environment within which it operates. However, franchising is much more popular in some environments than others. Caves and Murphy (1976) argue that 'franchising appears to prevail where efficient scales of operation diverge markedly between the production of a good and the production or development of the goodwill attached to it'. Those interested in why franchising exists could benefit from analysing the characteristics of the industries where it is prevalent (Martin, 1988). They also call for use of more fine grained research methods. Stating that almost all research to date on franchising has been coarse grained, using limited information from a large sample. Fine grained methods like case studies capture details of context by studying the phenomena in depth. These methodologies are well suited to deal with complex situations and are utilised in this research to address the impact of franchising on industry evolution.

As might be understood from the review presented here, each area or discipline that studies franchising has its own perspective, and researchers in one area rarely, if ever, seem to show an interest in research in other fields. As a result, franchising research is highly fragmented. Past research has been too closely tied to theories of agency and power, while insightful; these are quite narrow in their perspectives. Therefore, there is a great need for more fine grained studies and for a broader industry perspective on franchising over time which this research hopes to achieve.

Industry Evolution

This section looks at the development of the industry evolution literature while assessing the relevance of Porter (1980) the next section more specially look at the issues relating to the field of industry evolution and its relationship to the emergence of franchising and its impact on industry evolution as well as the more recent industry change approaches.

Overview of Research on Industry Evolution

This section will look at the evolution of industry evolution research from Porter's (1980) work and will also assess the Malerba and Orsenigo (1996) seminal article on industry evolution and will identify the number of gaps in the current literature. As mentioned this research is from the strategy perspective and as such the study of industry evolution is important to strategic management scholars because it helps to explain changes in the economic, social, and cultural landscape (Durand, 2006). Porter (1980) in his work on industry evolution observed that 'industries evolve because some forces are in motion that create incentives and pressures for change', he also noted that that fragmented industries are characterised as being intensely competitive and that 'industry fragmentation has been overcome by franchising' (Porter, 1980). Furthermore, after the life cycle model (explored in more detail in the next section), Porter's (1980) industry analysis framework has been the most prominent contribution to our understanding of industry evolution in the strategy field. However, Porter's (1980) work on competitive strategy and his five forces model relating to the competitiveness of an industry have also been severely criticised, for not 'explicitly accounting for the role of government, except when the government is a supplier or buyer' (Besanko, Dranove, & Shanley, 2004). This research aims to generate a deeper understanding into the presence of franchising in Ireland's service driven market economy and its effect on industry evolution.

Looking holistically at the importance of industry evolution for the development of the field of strategy as an area of research it helps to build an understanding of the structural and architectural changes occurring in an industry over time and the processes by which firms ultimately attain superior market positions through embracing the realities of business decision making, and uncovering forces that are in motion which create the incentives for change (Porter, 1980; Winter, 2005). To date, theories originating from many disciplines including economics, sociology, and also strategic management have been exploited to explain the nature of change in industries and organisations (Garud & Van de Ven, 2002) although influential writers warn against singular theories of change advocating a multi-modal and multi-level approach (Quinn & Murray, 2007). Despite the word 'evolution' implying change, the vast majority of the work carried out has been cross-sectional (Barron, 2003) and there is only limited evidence of research of industry evolution over time (Malerba & Orsenigo, 1996; Quinn & Leavy, 2005; Quinn & Murray, 2007). Historically other scholars have built on the knowledge on industry evolution, particularly in respect to the one dynamic model; the industry life cycle (Klepper, 1996, 1997; Abernathy & Utterback, 1975) which had recently been formalised by Stephen Klepper (1996), for which, they suggest, there is limited empirical evidence in many industries. In addition, the emergence of Industrial Organisation Economics which brought with it the primacy of static analysis in the study of industry structures, market positioning, and competitive dynamics. During the 1970s and 1980s new influences entered the field as work from transaction cost economics with its focus on structural choice between markets and hierarchies, and new institutional organisation concerned with motives and the rational decision procedures of agents, or new institutionalism emerged but all have a 'static and equilibrium flavour'.

In 1996, Malerba and Orsenigo penned one of the foundational works on the evolution of industries. Their study of industry dynamics and evolution has become a cornerstone of theory within the field, and served to spur on and influence subsequent research through the foundations they established and the gaps in knowledge they identified. Fifteen years on, some but not all of the gaps identified in their paper have been addressed. Furthermore, Malerba and Orsenigo argue that while there have been many studies relating to structural dynamics of industry evolution, there is still a 'lack of empirical evidence which would allow us to construct generalisations, taxonomies, or theories about how industries evolve over time in terms of structure' (Malerba & Orsenigo, 1996). According to Malerba and Orsenigo (1996, 2002) and Malerba (2007) over the last decade more attention has been paid to industry evolution which has been informed by a range of studies, including Porter's (1980) work on competitive strategy, McGahan and Baum's (2004) and McGahan's (2004) analysis of business strategy over the industry life cycle, and Lovas and Ghoshal (2000) and Durand's (2006) work on organisational evolution and strategy (OES).

This research deals with the emergence and evolution of industries, generation and transformation of technologies and products, the development and change of capabilities, changing boundaries of firms, the development of networks, relationships between actors/agents, and the roles played by institutions. A number of scholars have looked to broaden the scope of research aside from exploring the entry, exit, size, and concentration features of industries (Malerba & Orsenigo, 1996). There have also been attempts to develop sociological models of industry evolution using organisation theory (McGahan, 2004). From this perspective the organisational ecology model adopted by Hannan and Freeman (1977) has been the most widely used for population studies. However, there still remains very little research about the structural evolution of entire industries and about the role played by institutions which this research will address.

It is important to understand the gaps in the literature and in order to assess possible research contributions. Malerba and Orsenigo (1996) observe that there are many gaps in our understanding of industry evolution, particularly in respect of empirical research in the field, as well as theoretical explanations for it. The major gaps are:

- A lack of exploration of structural dynamics or structural evolution.
- A focus on the manufacturing sector with little research on service or distributive industries.
- A lack of a dynamic model of industry evolution.
- A lack of a historical perspective.
- The need to a wider definition of industry boundaries.
- The role of institutions in industry evolution.
- The relationship between firm level activity and industry evolution.
- The need for finer grained empirical studies.

To elaborate on two of the significant gaps which are pertinent to this study, first, Malerba and Orsenigo (1996) also refer a gap in the field of industry evolution that of the role of institutions. Institutions, the humanly devised constraints that shape human interaction (North, 1990), can take many forms including governments, professions, universities, industries, religions, and families. Organisations strive for legitimacy and isomorphic pressure to conform can produce change (DiMaggio & Powell, 1983). Malerba and Orsenigo observe that 'government policies and public institutions always play a major role' in the evolution of industries, that 'one observes over time complex structural processes at work involving firms and institutions'. James Quinn and his collaborators have reported on the influence of institutions on the evolution of Irish and British grocery wholesaling (Quinn & Leavy, 2005;

Quinn & Murray, 2007; Quinn & Sparks, 2007a, 2007b). Greenwood, Hinings, and Suddaby (2002) showed that regulatory agencies, such as professional associations, play a significant role in legitimising change in the evolution of accountancy services over a 20-year period in Canada.

Second, Malerba and Orsenigo (1996) address the gap in research particularly relevant to this research that of the importance of linking industry evolution to firm level activity. Malerba and Orsenigo (1996) observe that 'any serious attempt to build theory will have to come to grips with concepts such as firm competences, boundaries and connections' and the need to 'analyze firms according to several dimensions at once: competences, innovative activities, productive specialization and organizational structure'. Some theories, particularly in the discipline of strategic management, see them as constantly evolving. For example, the emerging dynamic capabilities approach (Augier & Teece, 2008; Helfat et al., 2007; Teece, 2009; Teece, Pisano, & Shuen, 1997) endeavours to show how firms achieve sustainable competitive advantage in a changing environment exposed to strong competition (Augier & Teece, 2008). A dynamic capability is the capacity of an organisation to purposefully create, extend, or modify its resource bases (Helfat et al., 2007), helping managers to sense the changing environment and reconfigure their resources to optimise their future performance in this new environment.

Finally in the 15 years since the publication of 'The Dynamics and Evolution of Industries' (Malerba & Orsenigo, 1996) research guided by Malerba and Orsenigo has produced a body of work through which some of the gaps identified have been addressed (Dosi, Malerba, Marsili, & Orsenigo, 1997; Malerba, 2007; Malerba, Nelson, Orsenigo, & Winter, 2007; Malerba & Orsenigo, 2000). In this work they have started to address the issue of more dynamic industry evolution studies, and have looked at history friendly models, and continued to identify further challenges and progress in the field of industry evolution. There has been a noticeable shift towards a historical analysis of technological innovation and structural changes at the industry level, studies of the drivers of industrial transformations have been mainly in the economics discipline (Quinn & Leavy, 2004), with technology as their focus (Quinn & Leavy, 2004), and related to manufacturing (Quinn & Leavy, 2005), failing to address the dynamic perspective (Meyer et al., 2005; Quinn & Leavy, 2004). However, Quinn (2002) has made a significant contribution by studying the evolution of Irish wholesaling, and recently Quinn and Murray (2009) who address the transformation of industries and industry architectures through a community evolution analysis of two closely related value chains in Britain and Ireland. This research aims to build on this research. The following section examines the development of the field of industry evolution research and its relationship to the emergence and impact of franchising on industry structure.

The Impact of Franchising on Industry Evolution

This section will address the industry change and process literature that relates to the potential impact a variation like franchising can have on industry structure including approaches such as the industry life cycle model, a co-evolutionary lens and industry architecture.

In terms of understanding what possible impact on industry structure franchising may have it is helpful to approach industry evolution from a practitioner's perspective. The growth of modern economies has been characterised by the emergence, development, and on some occasions the decline of a range of industries. New firms enter an industry, some exit, some firms grow, and others decline. In addition, economic entities expand or contract their boundaries and undergo organisational change (Malerba & Orsenigo, 1996). In reality the evolution of industries has been characterised by intense change, sometimes over lengthy periods of time. From a theoretical perspective evolutionary theorists argue that to get a full understanding of how and why industries evolve we must study change over time (Barron, 2003; Quinn & Leavy, 2005). That said there are very few in-depth empirical studies of long-run change. While interest in the study of change, change processes, and industry evolution has grown only a few studies have focused fully on structural evolution as a central theme (Malerba & Orsenigo, 1996; Winter et al., 2003). The process of change continues to be the least understood aspect of how industries evolve (Dosi et al., 1997). This research supports this observation and it will address these shortfalls.

Industry Evolution—Life Cycle Model

This section looks at the relevance of the industry life cycle model in studying the impact franchising on industry evolution. The industry life cycle model has contributed significantly to the development of industry evolution in the strategy field (Abernathy & Utterback, 1975; Baum & McGahan, 2004; Klepper, 1993, 1997, 2002; Utterback, 1994). The life cycle model remains the most cited and empirically substantiated model. In addition, Klepper (1997) addressed the industry life cycle approach, while Baum and McGahan (2004) studied business strategy over industry life cycles. The industry life cycle is the supply side equivalent of the product life cycle. It poses that an industry produces a range and sequence of products and the industry life cycle is likely to be of longer duration than that of single products. The life cycle has four phases: introduction (or emergence), growth, maturity, and decline. However, much of the research on life cycles links models of innovation and technological change. Little if any research has been carried out in the service sector and the model is static and lacks a dynamic approach as not all industries go through the distinct phases. Drawing on empirical research in three industries, Malerba and Orsenigo (1996) illustrate that the patterns that the industry life cycle model would predict did not occur, whereas sectoral differences and the macro context of the industries did play a role despite being largely absent in the static paradigms and the industry life cycle.

More recently McGahan, Argyres, and Baum (2004) claimed that 'the industry life cycle model—is so widely accepted and its basic premise so taken for granted that it has become conventional wisdom in business'. However, the value of the life cycle model as a generic process model of industry evolution has been questioned with a number of limitations cited. As most of the research has address industrial demography; therefore, structural dynamics and structural evolution have been neglected. Klepper (1993:1997) claims that the life cycle model remains the only dynamic model with empirical support, while progress in the area of structural evolution remained unexplored. However, even the explanatory power of the life cycle approach is limited and concerns have been expressed with regard to the narrow product definition of industries studied that underpin the model (Malerba & Orsenigo, 1996, Klepper, 1997; Mowery and Nelson, 1999).

Organisational Change and Development Models

So taking into account, the limitations of the industry life cycle model and in order to understand the most appropriate approach to assessing the impact of franchising on industry evolution this research looks to Pettigrew's work and the Aldrich and Reuf's evolutionary model (Aldrich & Ruef, 2006). Pettigrew (1985a, 1985b, 1985c, 1987, 1990) and Pettigrew, Woodman, and Cameron (2001) have argued that change is a multi-level process that can only be fully understood in its wider context. Pettigrew (1985a, 1985b, 1985c, 1987, 1990) and Pettigrew et al. (2001) claimed that up till the 1980s there have been 'remarkably few studies of change that actually allow the change process to reveal itself in any kind of substantially temporal or contextual manner' (Pettigrew, 1987). Wilson (1992) concluded that the study of change 'needs a perspective which can blend the behavioural with the economic, the historical with the future orientated decision making and the political with the social and economic factors'. Leavy (1991) studied change in the Irish dairy industry context; Lundgren's (1995) looked at technological innovation and network evolution.

However, multi-level and multi-modal approaches of the type advocated by these scholars are still uncommon. To help address this shortfall, in their seminal work Organisational Change and Innovation Processes, Van de Ven, Angle, and Poole (2000) distinguish between four types of organisational change and development theories, based upon two dimensions of change: the unit (a single entity or multiple entities) and the mode of change (prescribed or constructive). Based upon these dimensions Van de Ven et al. (2000) identify four organisational change and development theories: the Life Cycle model (LC) (see section above), a teleological model, the dialectical model, and the evolutionary model. Aldrich and Ruef (2006), developed their framework to classify and interpret historical transformation/organisation change models into life cycle, non–life cycle (teleological and dialectical), and evolutionary models.

Aldrich and Ruef (2006) advocate the use of an evolutionary approach, which 'encompasses many levels and units of analysis, takes interdisciplinary perspective on change processes'. This approach has been chosen as the overarching framework of this study, thus adding to the gap in the research on the evolutionary approach.

In the following section some of the more exciting industry evolution developments and research trends are explored and their relevance to the study of franchising and its impact on industry evolution is noted. Next, the extension of this research into co-evolution and industry architecture is addressed to deal with some of the limitations of the previous models, as firms and industries are more frequently being understood as related and simultaneously evolving components. Then the concept of industry architecture is investigated along with its growing use in the study of industry dynamics and evolution.

The Co-Evolution Lens

The co-evolutionary lens is receiving more attention from scholars of industry evolution and this section explores why it may be of value to this study. In many domains of research from economics, management and sociology scholars attest that industries go through the life cycle phases and in the early stages of industry development many firms emerge and as industries mature this number decreases and eventually declines following the industry life cycle model (Utterback, 1994). Economists have attributed this pattern to differences in cost structures of firms, driven mainly by the discovery and/or adoption of innovations such as the adoption of franchising, leading to the success of some firms over others (Klepper 1996). Sociologists, led by organisational ecologists, have attributed this trend to legitimation of organisational fields and then subsequent firm level competition within these industries (Hannan & Freeman, 1989). However, questions remain unanswered: What happens if we only look at these industry changes through the research of single or isolated industries? Could the effect of an industry's life cycle have implications across two or more industries such is the case with this study?

Baum and Singh (1994) have explored how populations pursuing competing production technologies in the same industry will affect each other's life chance (Barnett & Carroll, 1995; Utterback, 1994). Still, others have launched a study of 'community ecology' (Ruef, 2000) in which interdependent populations within a community of populations influence each other's evolution.

Poole and Van de Ven (2004) explains that co-evolution is viewing the organisation as part of an inter-organisational community, industry or population which fits with the research on franchising in terms of franchise systems being made up of a network of franchisors and franchisees (within a franchise system) and at industry level the relationship between competing franchisors. The seminal paper by Lewin and Volberda (1999) focused on how firms co-evolve with each other and with a changing organisational environment. According to Lewin and Volberda (2011), co-evolution theory is not a new idea in organisational science; they claim that it was implicit in the early work on the emergence of bureaucracy by Weber in 'Economy and Society' (1978). Co-evolutionary effects take place at multiple levels within firms as well as between firms, as seen in the context of franchise systems in an industry. While co-evolution has been studied on a single level of analysis, McKelvey (1997) argues that co-evolution takes place at multiple levels. He makes a distinction between co-evolution within the firm (micro co-evolution) and co-evolution between firms and their niche/industry (macro co-evolution). This approach recognises that processes of variation, selection, and retention function within the organisation and interact with similar processes operating at the population level. The focus of macro co-evolutionary theory is on firms existing in a co-evolutionary competitive context, while micro co-evolutionary considers co-evolution of intra-firm resources, dynamic capabilities and competencies in an intra-firm, competitive context (McKelvey, 1997).

McKelvey (1997) has argued that evolution of organisations cannot be understood independently from the simultaneous evolution of the environment. In his paper McKelvey (1997) advocates a co-evolutionary perspective to studying organisational adaptation. He notes the importance of studying organisations over a long period of time with an historical perspective (emphasising the co-evolution of the firm and its environment). Lewin et al. (1999) have advanced a theory of the evolution of new organisation forms as an outcome of the co-evolution of the competitive environment, firm intentionality, and the institutional environment of the firm under conditions of stochastic or chaotic environmental uncertainty. More recently Lewin and Volberda (2011) argue that co-evolution has the potential to serve as a unifying framework for research in strategy and organisation studies and for reinterpreting, reframing, and redirecting the selection, adaptation discourse. Realising this potential will require dramatic increases in empirical research within co-evolutionary inquiry systems with such research requiring longitudinal methods of analysis and time series data which this research contributes to.

Building on the VSR model and the co-evolutionary dual hierarchy—genealogical and ecological (Baum & Singh, 1994)—Rodolphe Durand (2006) develops a theoretical model of the integration of evolution and strategic management. His OES model facilitates an understanding of the relationship between competitive advantage, the survival of the 'concrete firm' and industry evolution. This research poses to look beyond current research on inter-organisational relationship, networks, and alliances by considering other organisational structures such as franchising. Within the context of their approach relating to the adaptation of choices of the firm and as such investigating the motivation for a franchise system as a governance structure, the co-evolution of the firm and its environment, as well as the embeddedness of a franchise system within industry adaptation practices mediated by the institutional arrangements constraining the firm. However, one of the main criticisms of co-evolution is the lack of some co-evolutionary studies giving only a limited role to human agency. However, this research holds that co-evolution is a useful lens through which industry evolution may be investigated and also suggests that the role of human agency is an important element to consider.

The previous sections have drawn on the VSR model, organisational change and development theories, and the co-evolutionary framework. The following section will endeavour to examine the research on industry architecture and industry platforms in order to help explain the types of change that result in the evolution of industries.

Industry Platforms and Industry Eco-Systems

The emerging industry architecture research (Jacobides, 2005; Jacobides, Knudsen & Augier, 2006; Jacobides & Winter, 2005) is closely linked to research on industry platforms (Tee & Gawer, 2009) and is relevant to addressing the impact of franchising on industry evolution. Tee and Gawer (2009) observed that today's complex high-tech industries, however, has brought to the fore the idea that in many cases, industries can be better analysed as networks of interconnected firms or 'industry eco-systems' (Iansiti & Levien, 2004), to try to capture the multidimensionality and the complexity of firms' relationships such as franchise systems operating together in an industry. In this context, an important question is: What factors and processes drive value appropriation and value creation in interdependent industry ecosystems? What perhaps are the roles of industry actors? This perspective helps develop the role of the agent where industry co-evolution is limited with regards to this element.

In recent years, two theoretical perspectives, industry architectures and platforms, have attempted to explicitly address the issue of how value is created as well as captured in the context of interdependent systems of firms and institutions. Industry platforms are technological building blocks that act as a foundation upon which an array of firms, organised in a set of interdependent firms (sometimes called industry 'ecosystem'), develop a set of interrelated products, technologies, and services (Gawer, 2009a, 2009b). Research on industry platforms (Gawer & Cusumano, 2002, 2008) and ecosystems (Iansiti & Levien, 2004) builds on earlier research on technology evolution and technological dominance (Abernathy & Utterback, 1975; Tushman & Anderson, 1986; Suarez, 2004; Murmann & Frenken, 2006), as well as literature on standards and network externalities. Platform leaders tend to drive industry-wide innovation in a trajectory that allows them to exert architectural control over the overall system, as well as derive large profits and erect barriers to entry in their own market.

Perhaps, a hybrid organisational form such as franchising could be seen as a value creating industry platform with the industry eco-system comprised of the interconnected firms (franchisor and franchisees) evident in a franchise system.

Industry Architecture

Complementary to the research on platforms, a new strand of work centred on the notion of 'industry architecture' (Jacobides, Knudsen, & Augier, 2006) has emerged. It explores the rules and roles of inter firm relationships and focuses on the ways in which activities the value chain get divided among industry participants, paying particular attention to firm roles, interdependencies, and the ways in which organisations attempt to shape the industry's division of labour. The concept of industry architecture (Jacobides et al., 2006) defines the ways in which roles are distributed among interacting firms. Industries have fairly well-established rules about what activities each party undertakes, as well as roles played by industry players such as franchise systems within an industry.

According to Jacobides and Billinger (2006), more recently, research has considered how industry boundaries evolve, and how intermediate markets emerge (Jacobides, 2005). However, scant research has addressed how an industry's boundaries originate, evolve, and how they may impact individual firms. Therefore, by considering industry architectures the templates that emerge in an industry define the extent of firm reach and activity. He then argues that firms may be able to affect the architecture of their sectors, especially when it is not sharply defined, and as such create an 'architectural advantage'. Jacobides et al. (2006) suggest that this 'architectural advantage' can be manipulated by deliberate, forward-looking firms (and in this case, these behaviours much resemble firms' attempts to establish platform leadership). Certainly focusing on actors and differences in their roles can help us understand why platforms might show differences in say regional or geographic success or failure or take-up. Furthermore, Tee and Gawer (2009) discuss how environmental shocks, such as changes in regulation, can lead to significant changes in the way an industry organises itself, with important implications for control or profitability of particular types of firms (Cacciatori & Jacobides, 2005; Jacobides & Winter, 2005). Depending on the structure of the industry architecture, certain types of firms can capture more value than others.

Industry architecture research also considers the evolution of industry value chain structures. It investigates how and why the vertical integration of different industries and their changes (or lack thereof). This area of research acknowledges the agency of firms and individuals in such changes and seeks to understand the processes and circumstances of architectural change which connects to the research on franchising (Jacobides, 2008).

An important extension to the industry evolution literature is that the research on industry architectures does allow for government intervention and for deliberate separation of capabilities (Jacobides & Billinger, 2006; Jacobides, 2008). According to Quinn & Murray (2009), their article focused on the transformation of industries' architectures—how firms, institutions, technologies, and strategies co-evolve. Industry architectures are seen as the stable but evolving relationships along the value chain' (Jacobides, Knudsen, & Augier, 2006). Furthermore, the very usefulness of an 'industry' as a level of analysis is becoming doubtful: much of the change and evolution in terms of strategy, technology, and knowledge development does not happen either among firms within a stable industry, or through the growth or decline of certain sectors compared to others. Instead, the change occurs in terms of the definition, redefinition, drawing, and redesigning of the very architecture of these sectors. Technology, new systems or new firm structures such as franchising do not progress and develop within a sector; rather they shape (and are shaped by) the encompassing architecture of multiple sectors.

References

Abernathy, W. J., & Utterback, J. M. (1975). A dynamic model of product and process innovation. *Omega, 3*(6), 639–656.

Aldrich, H., & Reiss, A. (1976, Jan). Continuities in the study of ecological succession: Changes in the race composition of neighborhoods and their businesses. *American Journal of Sociology, 81*(4), 846–866.

Aldrich, H., & Ruef, M. (2006). *Organizations evolving* (2nd ed.). London: Sage.

Altinay, L. (2004). Implementing international franchising: The role of intrapreneurship. *International Journal of Service Industry Management, 15*(5), 426–443.

Augier, M., & Teece, D. J. (2008). Strategy as evolution with design: The foundations of dynamic capabilities and the role of managers in the economic system. *Organization Studies, 29*(8/9), 1185.

Alon, I., & McKee, D. (1999). Towards a macro environmental model of international franchising. *Multinational Business Review, 7*(1), 76–82.

Barnett, W. P., & Carroll, G. R. (1995). Modeling internal organizational change. *Annual Review of Sociology, 21*, 217–236.

Baron, S., & Schmidt, R. (1991). Operational aspects of retail franchises. *International Journal of Retail & Distribution Management, 19*(2), 13–19.

Barron, D. (2003). Evolutionary theory. In D. Faulkner & A. Campbell (Eds.), *The Oxford handbook of strategy* (pp. 74–97). Oxford: Oxford University Press.

Baum, J., & Singh, J. (1994). Organization-environment coevolution. In *The evolutionary dynamics of organizations*. New York: Oxford University Press.

Baum, J. A., & McGahan, A. M. (2004). *Business strategy over the industry life cycle*. Oxford: Elsevier/JAI Press.

Baum, J. A. C., & Rao, H. (2004). Evolutionary dynamics of organizational population and communities. In M. S. Poole & A. H. Van de Ven (Eds.), *Handbook of organizational change and innovation* (pp. 212–258). Oxford: Oxford University Press.

Besanko, D., Dranove, D., & Shanley, M. (2004). *Economics of strategy* (3rd ed.). Hoboken, NJ: Wiley.

Bradach, J. L., & Eccles, R. G. (1989). Price, authority, and trust: From ideal types to plural forms. *Annual Sociological Review, 15*, 97–118.

Brickley, J. A., Dark, F. H., & Weisbach, M. S. (1991). The economic effects of franchise termination laws. *Journal of Law & Economics, 34*, 101–113.

Burton, M., Baron, J., & Hannan, M. (1996). Building the iron cage: Determinants of managerial intensity in the early years. *American Sociology Review, 64*, 527–547.

Cacciatori, E., & Jacobides, M. G. (2005). The dynamic limits of specialization: Vertical integration reconsidered. *Organization Studies, 26*(12), 1851–1883.

Castrogiovanni, G. J., Justis, R. T., & Julian, S. D. (1993). Franchise failure rates: An assessment of magnitude and influencing factors. *Journal of Small Business Management, 31*, 105–114.

Caves, R. E., & Murphy, W. R. (1976). Franchising: Firms, markets, and intangible assets. *Southern Economic Journal, 42*, 572–586.

Clarkin, J., & Rosa, P. (2005). Entrepreneurial teams within franchise firms. *International Small Business Journal, 23*, 303–334.

Cochet, O., Dormann, J. and Ehrmann, T. (2007). Entrepreneurial autonomy, incentives, and relational governance in franchise chains. In *Economics and management of networks: Franchising, strategic alliances, and cooperatives* (pp. 117–143). Heidelberg: Physica-Verlag.

Collis, D. J., & Montgomery, C. A. (1995). Competing on resources: Strategy on the 1990. *Harvard Business Review, 73*(July/August), 118–128.

Combs, J. G., Michael, S. C., & Castrogiovanni, G. J. (2009). Institutional influences on the choice of organizational form: The case of franchising. *Journal of Management, 35*(5), 1268–1290.

Dant, R. P. (2008). A futuristic research agenda for the field of franchising. *Journal of Small Business Management, 46*(1), 91–98.

Dant, R. P., & Grunhagen, M. (2014). International franchising research: Some thoughts on the what, where, when and how. *Journal of Marketing Channels, 21*(3), 124–132.

Dant, R. P., Grunhagen, M., & Windsperger, J. (2011). Franchising research frontiers for the twenty-first century. *Journal of Retailing, 87*(2), 253–268.

Dant, R. P., Kacker, M., Coughlan, A., & Emerson, J. (2007). A cointegration analysis of the correlates of performance in franchised channels of distribution. In G. Cliquet et al. (Eds.), *Economics and management of networks: Franchising networks cooperatives, joint ventures and alliances*. Heidelberg: Springer.

Dant, R. P., & Kaufmann, P. (2003). Structural and strategic dynamics in franchising. *Journal of Retailing, 79*(2), 63–75.

Doherty, A. M., & Alexander, N. (2006). Power and control in international retail franchising. *European Journal of Marketing, 40*(11/12), 1292–1316.

Dormann, J., Ehrmann, T., & Cochet, O. (2007). Capitalizing on franchise autonomy: Relational forms of governance as controls in idiosyncratic franchise dyads. *Journal of Small Business Management, 46*(1), 50–72.

Dosi, G., Malerba, F., Marsili, O., & Orsenigo, L. (1997). Industrial structures and dynamics: Evidence, interpretations and puzzles. *Industrial Corporate Change, 6*(1), 3–24.

Durand, R. (2006). *Organizational evolution and strategic management*. London: Sage.

El Akremi, A., Mignonac, K., & Perrigot, R. (2010). Opportunistic behaviours in franchise chains: The role of cohesion among franchisees. *Strategic Management Journal, 31*, 930–948.

Elango, B., & Freid, V. H. (1997). Franchising research: A literature review and synthesis. *Journal of Small Business Management, 35*, 68–81.

Garud, R., & Van de Ven, A. H. (2002). Strategic change processes. In A. Pettigrew, H. Thomas, & R. Whittington (Eds.), *Handbook of strategy and management* (pp. 206–231). London: Sage.

Gauzente, Claire & Dumoulin, Regis (2012). Franchising choice in retail networks: A multi-level institutional framework. International Review of Retail, Distribution & Consumer Research; 22 4, 385–396, 12p

Gawer, A. (2009a). Platforms, markets and innovation: An introduction. In A. Gawer (Ed.), *Platforms, markets and innovation*. Cheltenham, UK and Northampton, MA: Edward Elgar.

Gawer, A. (2009b). Platform dynamics and strategies: From products to services. In A. Gawer (Ed.), *Platforms, markets and innovation*. Cheltenham, UK and Northampton, MA: Edward Elgar.

Gawer, A., & Cusumano, M. A. (2002). *Platform leadership: How Intel, Microsoft, and Cisco drive industry innovation*. Boston, MA: Harvard Business School Press.

Gawer, A., & Cusumano, M. A. (2008). How companies become platform leaders. *MIT Sloan Management Review, 49*, 28–35.

Greenwood, R., Hinings, C., & Suddaby, R. (2002). Theorizing change: The role of professional associations in the transformation of institutional fields. *Academy of Management Journal, 45*, 58–80.

Hadfield, G. (1990). Problematic relations: The law of incomplete contracts. *Stanford Law Review, 42*, 927–992.

Hannan, M. T., & Freeman, J. (1977). Population ecology of organizations. *American Journal of Sociology, 82*, 929–964.

Hannan, M. T., & Freeman, J. (1989). *Organizational ecology*. Cambridge, MA: Harvard University Press.

Helfat, C., Finkelstein, S., Mitchell, W., Peteraf, M., Singh, H., Teece, D., et al. (2007). *Dynamic capabilities: Understanding strategic change in organizations* (1st ed.). Malden, MA: Blackwell Publishing.

Hillman, A. J., Withers, M. C., & Collins, B. J. (2009). Resource dependence theory: A review. *Journal of Management, 35*(6), 1404–1427.

Iansiti, M. and R. Levien. (2004). Strategy as ecology. *Harvard Business Review,* March, 68–78.

Jacobides, M. G. (2005). Industry change through vertical disintegration: How and why markets emerged in mortgage banking. *Academy of Management Journal, 48*(3), 465–498.

Jacobides, M. G. (2008). How capability differences, transaction costs, and learning curves interact to shape vertical scope. *Organization Science, 19*(2), 306–326.

Jacobides, M. G., & Billinger, S. (2006). Designing the boundaries of the firm: From "Make, Buy, or Ally" to the dynamic benefits of vertical architecture. *Organization Science, 17*(2), 249–261.

Jacobides, M. G., Knudsen, T., & Augier, M. (2006). Benefiting from innovation: Value creation, value appropriation and the role of industry architectures. *Research Policy, 35*(8), 1200–1221.

Jacobides, M. G., & Winter, S. G. (2005). The co-evolution of capabilities and transaction costs: Explaining the institutional structure of production. *Strategic Management Journal, 26*(5), 395–413.

Kaufmann, P. J., & Dant, R. P. (1996). Multi-unit franchising: Growth and management issues. *Journal of Business Venturing, 11*, 343–358.

Klepper, S. (1993). *Entry, exit, growth and innovation over the product life-cycle.* Mimeo, Pittsburg.

Klepper, S. (1997). Industry life cycles. *Industrial and Corporate Change, 6*(1), 145–181.

Klepper, S. (2002). The capabilities of new firms and the evolution of the US automobile industry. *Industrial and Corporate Change, 11*, 645–666.

Knight, R. (1984). The independence of the franchisee entrepreneur. *Journal of Small Business Management, 21*, 53–61.

Knudsen, T., & Augier, M. (2006). *Benefiting from innovation: Value creation, value appropriation and the role of industry architectures.* Advanced Institute Management Studies working papers.

Leavy, B. (1991). A process study of strategic change and industry evolution— The case of the Irish dairy industry. *British Journal o f Management, 2*, 187–204.

Lewin, A. Y., & Volberda, H. W. (1999). Co-evolution of global sourcing: The need to understand the underlying mechanisms of firm-decisions to offshore. *International Business Review.*

Lewin, A. Y., & Volberda, H. W. (2011). Co-evolution of global sourcing: The need to understand the underlying mechanisms of firm-decisions of offshore. *International Business Review, 20*, 241–251.

Litz, R. A., & Stewart, A. C. (2000a). Charity begins at home: Family firms and patterns of community involvement. *Nonprofit and Voluntary Sector Quarterly, 29*(1), 131–148.

Litz, R. A., & Stewart, A. C. (2000b). The late show: The effects of after-hours accessibility on the performance of small retailers. *Journal of Small Business Management, 38*(1), 1–26.

Litz, R. A., & Stewart, A. C. (2000c). Research note: Trade name franchise membership as a human resource management strategy: Does buying group training deliver 'True Value' for small retailers? *Entrepreneurship: Theory and Practice, 25*(1), 125–135.

Litz, R. A., & Stewart, A. C. (2000d). Where everybody knows your name: Extraorganizational clan-building as small firm strategy for home field advantage. *Journal of Small Business Strategy, 11*(1), 1–13.

Lomi, A. (1995). The population ecology of organizational founding: Location dependence and unobserved heterogeneity. *Administrative Science Quarterly, 40*, 111–144.

Lovas, B., & Ghoshal, S. (2000). Strategy as guided evolution. *Strategic Management Journal, 21*(9), 875–896.

Lundgren, A. (1995). *Technological innovation and network evolution*. London and New York: Routledge.

Malerba, F., & Orsenigo, L. (2000). Knowledge, innovative activities and industrial evolution. *Industrial and Corporate Change, 9*(2), 289–314.

Malerba, F., & Orsenigo, L. (2002). Innovation and market structure in the dynamics of the pharmaceutical industry and biotechnology: Towards a history-friendly model. *Industrial and Corporate Change, 11*, 667–703.

Malerba, F. (2007). Innovation and the dynamics and evolution of industries: Progress and challenges. *International Journal of Industrial Organization, 25*(4), 675–699.

Malerba, F., Nelson, R. L., Orsenigo, L., & Winter, S. (2007). Demand, innovation, and the dynamics of market structure: The role of experimental users and diverse preferences. *Journal of Evolutionary Economics, 17*(4), 371–399.

Malerba, F., & Orsenigo, L. (1996). The dynamics and evolution of industries. *Industrial Corporate Change, 5*(1), 51–87.

Martin, R. E. (1988). Franchising and risk management. *American Economic Review, 78*, 954–968.

McGahan, A., & Baum, J. A. (2004). *Business strategy over the industry life cycle, advances in strategic management* (Vol. 21). Oxford: JAI Press.

McGahan, A. M. (2004). *How industries evolve: Principles for achieving and sustaining superior performance*. Boston, MA [Great Britain]: Harvard Business School Press.

McGahan, A. M., Argyres, N., & Baum, J. A. C. (2004). Context technology and strategy: Forging new perspectives on the industry life cycle. *Business Strategy Over the Industry Life Cycle, 21*, 1–21.

McKelvey, B. (1997). Quasi-natural organization science. *Organization Science, 8*(4), 352–380.

Messallam, A. A. (1998). The organization ecology of investment firms in Egypt: Organizational founding. *Organization Studies, 19*(1), 23–46.

Meyer, J. W., & Rowan, B. (1991). Institutionalized organisations: Formal structure. In W. W. Powell & P. DiMaggio (Eds.), *The new institutionalism in organizational analysis*: vii, 478. Chicago: University of Chicago Press.

Murmann, J. P., & Frenken, K. (2006). Toward a systematic framework for research on dominant designs. *Technological Innovations and Industrial Change, Research Policy, 35*, 925–952.

North, D. (1990). *Institutions, institutional change and economic performance.* Cambridge: Cambridge University Press.

Oxenfeldt, A. R., & Kelly, A. O. (1968). Will successful franchise systems ultimately become wholly-owned chains? *Journal of Retailing, 44*, 69–83.

Perrigot, R. (2008). Franchising networks survival: An approach through population ecology and survival analysis. *Recherche et Applications en Marketing, 23*, 21–36.

Pettigrew, A. M. (1985a). *The awakening giant: Continuity and change in imperial chemical industries.* Oxford: Blackwell.

Pettigrew, A. M. (1985b). Contextualist research: A natural way to link theory and practice. In E. E. Lawler (Ed.), *Doing research that is useful in theory and practice.* San Francisco, CA: Jossey Bass.

Pettigrew, A. M. (1985c). Examining change in the long term context of culture and polities. In J. M. Pennings (Ed.), *Organizational strategy and change.* San Francisco, CA: Jossey-Bass.

Pettigrew, A. M. (1987). Researching strategic change. In A. M. Pettigrew (Ed.), *The management of strategic change.* Oxford: Basil Blackwell.

Pettigrew, A. M. (1990). Longitudinal field research on change: Theory and practice. *Organization Science, 1*(3), 267–292.

Pettigrew, A. M., Woodman, R. W., & Cameron, K. S. (2001). Studying organizational change and development: Challenges for future research. *Academy of Management Journal, 44*, 697–713.

Pfeffer, J. (1987). A resource dependence perspective on interorganizational relations. In M. S. Mizruchi & M. Schwartz (Eds.), *Intercorporate relations: The structural analysis of business* (pp. 25–55). Cambridge, UK: Cambridge University Press.

Pfeffer, J., & Salancik, G. R. (1978). *The external control of organizations: A resource dependence perspective*. New York: Harper & Row.

Poole, M. S. (2004). Cental issues in the study of change and innovation. In M. S. Poole & A. H. Van de Ven (Eds.), *Handbook of organizational change and innovation* (pp. 3–31). Oxford: Oxford University Press.

Poole, M. S., & Van de Ven, A. H. (2004). *Handbook of organizational change and innovation*. Oxford: Oxford University Press.

Porter, M. E. (1980). *Competitive strategy*. New York Free Press.

Powell, W., & DiMaggio, J. (1991). *The new institutionalism in organizational analysis*. University of Chicago Press.

Purvin, R. L. (1994). *The franchise fraud*. New York: John Wiley and Sons.

Quinn, B., & Doherty, A. M. (2000). Power and control in international retail franchising. *International Marketing Review, 17*(4/5), 354–372.

Quinn, J. (2002). *Industry evolution: A comparative study of Irish wholesaling*. Unpublished doctoral dissertation, Dublin City University, Dublin.

Quinn, J., & Leavy, B. (2004). Government activism and industry change: The structural evolution of Irish wholesailing. *The Irish Journal of Management, 25*(1), 110–125.

Quinn, J., & Leavy, B. (2005). The drivers of industry evolution: A study of Irish wholesaling. *Journal of Marketing Channels, 13*(1), 37–62.

Quinn, J., & Murray, J. A. (2007). *Evolutionary change, industry architecture and the emergence of new forms*. Unpublished Power Point, Trinity College Dublin.

Quinn, J., & Murray, J. A. (2009). The community context of evolving industry Architecture. *Journal of Marketing Channels, 16*(4), 327–357.

Quinn, J., & Sparks, L. (2007a). Research frontiers in wholesale distribution. *International Review of Retail, Distribution and Consumer Research, 17*(4), 301–311.

Quinn, J., & Sparks, L. (2007b). The evolution of grocery wholesaling and grocery wholesalers in Ireland and Britain since the 1930s. *International Review of Retail, Distribution and Consumer Research, 17*, 391–411.

Ruef, M. (2000). The emergence of organizational forms: A community ecology approach. *The American Journal of Sociology, 106*(3), 658–714.

Scherer, F., & Ross, D. (1990). *Industrial market structure and economic performance* (3rd ed.). Boston, MA: Houghton-Mifflin.

Scott, W. R. (1995). *Institutions and environments*. Thousand Oaks, CA: Sage.

Shane, S., & Foo, M.-D. (1999). New firm survival: Institutional explanations for new franchisor mortality. *Management Science, 45*, 142–159.

Sherer, P. D., & Lee, K. (2002). Institutional change in large law firms: A resource dependency and institutional perspective. *Academy of Management Journal, 45*, 102–119.

Tee, R., & Gawer, A. (2009). Industry architecture as a determinant of successful platform strategies: A case study of the i-mode mobile Internet service. *European Management Review, 6*(4), 217–232.

Teece, D. J. (2010). Business models, business strategy and innovation. *Long Range Planning, 43*(2–3), 172–194.

Teece, D. J., Pisano, G., & Shuen, A. (1997). Dynamic capabilities and strategic fit. *Strategic Management Journal, 18*(5), 510–533.

Truss, C. (2004). Who's in the driving seat? Managing human resources in a franchise firm. *Human Resource Management Journal, 14*(4), 57–75.

Tushman, M. L., & Anderson, P. (1986). Technological discontinuities and organizational environments. *Administrative Science Quarterly, 31*, 439–465.

Ulrich, D., & Barney, J. B. (1984). Perspectives in organizations: Resource dependence, efficiency, and population. *Academy of Management Review, 9*(3), 471–481.

Utterback, J. M. (1994). *Mastering the dynamics of innovation*. Boston, MA: Harvard Business School.

Van de Ven, A. H., Angle, H. L., & Poole, M. S. (2000). *Research on the management of innovation: The Minnesota studies*. New York: Oxford University.

Wilson, D. C. (1992). *A strategy of change: Concepts and controversies in the management of change*. London; New York: Routledge.

Winter, S. G. (2005). Developing evolutionary theory for economics and management. In M. A. Hitt & K. G. Smith (Eds.), *Great minds in management: The process of theory development* (pp. 509–546). Oxford: Oxford University Press.

Winter, S. G., Kaniovski, Y. M., & Dosi, G. (2003). A baseline model of industry evolution. *Journal of Evolutionary Economics, 13*(4), 355.

5

Case Study of the Irish Fast Food/QSR Industry

Introduction

This chapter presents an industry history of the Irish fast food/quick service restaurant (QSR) industry from the beginning of the 1900s to the present day. Both firm- and industry-level changes over the decades are examined in a chronological account; see Table 5.1 below for a timeline on the industry. The historical account is based on primary and secondary data collected from the Irish fast food/QSR industry. This case study is presented as a story, tracing the industry from its emergence right through to the introduction of franchising to the present day. The case-based empirical evidence is presented to show the reasons for the emergence of franchising and its impact on industry evolution.

Fast Food/QSR Industry

Today, the fast food industry, also referred to as the QSR Industry, is described as 'being a limited menu establishment which lends itself to production line techniques of producing food that is served packaged for

© The Author(s) 2017   **91**
R. Beere, *The Role of Franchising on Industry Evolution*,
DOI 10.1007/978-3-319-49064-9_5

Table 5.1 Timeline of the Irish fast food/QSR industry

1920s	1950s	1960s	1970s	1980s	1990s	2000s	2010s
20 fish & chip shops	Chippers expand nationwide	120 chippers	Franchising occurs	2 firms dominate[a]	2 firms dominate[a]	4 firms dominate	3 firms dominate
		Wimpy (1968)	250 chippers	Burger King (1981)	Abrakebabra 60[b]	McDonald's 66[b]	AIL 190[b]
			100 Indian/Chinese	Abrakebabra (1982)	McDonald's 35[b]	Abrakebabra 55[b]	McDonald's 75[b]
			Burgerland (1975)	O'Briens Sandwich (1988)	Domino's (1991)	Supermac's 45[b]	Supermac's 90[b]
			McDonald's (1977)	Four Star Pizza (1986)		O'Briens Sandwich 60[b]	Domino's 42[b]
			Supermac's 1978			Burger King 34[b]	Four Star Pizza 37[b]
			KFC (1979)			Four Star Pizza 26[b]	Burger King 30[b]
						Domino's 17[b]	260 chippers (180 ITICA)
							Other 541

[a]2 firms dominate
[b]Number of outlets

immediate consumption, on or off the restaurant premises. Fast food/ QSR customers normally order at a counter and pay before eating'. Overall, the fast food/QSR industry is regarded as a competitive industry. The firms operating within the industry have basic product offerings (such as burgers, fish and chips, pizzas, curries, and sandwiches) considered as basic/normal goods. Thus, the focus of this study is related to all fast food/QSR restaurants in Ireland.

Fast Food/QSR Industry Today

Today, the fast food industry, also referred to as the Quick Service Restaurant Industry (QSR), is described as 'being a limited menu establishment which lends itself to production line techniques of producing food that is served packaged for immediate consumption, on or off the restaurant premises. Fast food/QSR customers normally order at a counter and pay before eating'. Overall, the fast food/QSR industry is regarded as a competitive industry. The firms operating within the industry have basic product offerings (examples are; burgers, fish and chips, pizzas, curries and sandwiches) considered as basic/normal goods. These goods are usually inexpensive and therefore during times of recession, are not adversely affected.

The boundaries that defined the Irish fast food/QSR industry throughout the twentieth century have undergone considerable transformation. Since its inception in the 1860s, the industry as a whole has grown considerably in revenue terms. At the beginning of the twentieth century, the industry comprised primarily of independently owned fish and chip shops. During the 1950s, a new wave of ethnic cuisine came to Ireland with the opening of Chinese and Indian restaurants and takeaways nationwide. From the late 1970s and early 1980s, international competitors began to enter the market bringing new product and service offerings. During this time, franchising was introduced by the international fast food chain McDonald's, which resulted in a rapid adoption of franchising by many industry players during the 1980s. In the late 1990s, the industry underwent further changes. There was an even greater increase of international competitors such as Burger King, Domino's, and Four Star Pizza. Since entry, these firms have grown in size and dominance (see Table 5.1). From the late 1990s, the growth in the number of firms has stabilised but the level of industry concentration has increased. Independent operators are now in the minority and a new industry structure has emerged, centred on national and international branded franchise systems. Following the introduction of franchising, the industry has witnessed significant efficiency gains, the importance of branding has come to the fore, and new industry leaders have emerged.

The industry has always been affected by changes in economic cycles, social change, and regulatory changes. Competition within the industry has increased substantially since the 1920s, when just 20 fish and chip shops operated in Dublin. Today, the independent operators still exist, but they lack the competitive advantages of the branded franchising chains. In addition to the increased international competition, the industry still has a large number of small, independently owned fast food/QSR outlets across Ireland. These include approximately 300 fish and chip shops, and 541 Chinese/Asian restaurants and takeaways (see Table 5.2 below). The sector faces increasing concentration in its customer base, particularly among the branded franchised fast food chains. In recent years, a new industry structure has emerged, with a concentration of three large nationwide franchise systems; the multi-brand Abrakebabra Investments Limited (AIL), McDonald's and Supermac's. Prior to 2008, there were four dominant firms including O'Briens Sandwich Bars. In 2008, AIL acquired O'Briens which led to further industry concentration. Today, the three

Table 5.2 Irish franchise systems fast food/QSR number of outlets annual turnover 2012

Fast food/QSR brand	Number of outlets	Average size (sq ft)	Annual turnover 2012 (million)	Turnover per outlet
AIL[a] multi-brand	190	2000	€254.5	€1,339,473
McDonald's	75	4000	€200	€2,666,666
Supermac's	90	2000	€58.8	€653,333
Burger King	30	3600	€38.2	€1,273,333
Four Star Pizza	37	1200	€15	€405,405
Domino's Pizza	42	1700	€12	€285,714

[a]Multi-brand including: Abrakebabra 60, O'Briens 72, Bagel Factory 42, Gourmet Burger Kitchen 8, King Chick 6, and Yo-sushi 2

Source: Annual returns and outlet number information was obtained by contact with each company's head office

Table 5.3 Selected competitors' restaurant numbers in Ireland 2012

Name	Eat-in	Number of outlet	Country of origin
McDonald's	Seating	78	USA
Supermac's	Seating	90	Ireland
Abrakebabra AIL	Seating	60	Ireland
O'Briens AIL	No seating/some	72 (230 Intl)	Ireland
Gourmet Burger AIL	Seating	8	UK (master)
Bagel Factory AIL	No seating/some	42	UK (master)
King Chick AIL	Seating	6	UK (master)
Yo Sushi AIL	Seating	3	UK (master)
Domino's	No seating	48	UK
Four Star Pizza	No seating	33	USA
Eddie Rockets	Seating	30	Ireland
Burger King	Seating	27	USA
KFC	Seating	17	USA
Chippers	26	No seating (180 ITICA)	Ireland
Other restaurants	Seating	541	Ireland

Including: 187 Chinese, 125 Indian, 50 Asian, and 179 Italian

leading firms account for 45 per cent of the market (see Table 5.3 above). All three industry leaders have been in existence since the late 1970s and early 1980s. AIL and Supermac's are Irish-owned, and McDonald's is a US multi-national. Indeed, all three firms have successfully expanded, utilising a franchise model of growth and they maintain a solid national presence across Ireland. The growth of the franchise chains has increased the level of buyer concentration and power, thus making the industry a highly competitive one. Recently independent chippers have instigated co-operative action in order to help them compete with the franchise chains.

The Early Development of Fast Food/QSR Industry

Eating Outside the Home

The origin of the industry can be attributed to the rise in food consumption outside of the home. In Ireland, this began in the early nineteenth century. It was then predominantly a male-dominated affair and consisted of visits to the local inn or pub. The majority of the population would have frequented cafes and coffee houses together with pubs and hotels, such as Bewley's of Grafton Street (opened in 1927), the Mansion House Supper room (1881), Switzers (1892) and the Royal Hibernian Hotel (1892) all located in Dublin City. In fact, the origin of the fast food/QSR phenomenon has its roots in the UK, with the opening of the first fish and chip shop. In 1994, Walton wrote a book, Fish and Chips and the British Working Class, 1870–1940. In his study, he states that 'fish and chip shops' were, in many ways, pioneers of fast food/QSR industry. Fish and chips became an important meal in the working class diet, thus the fish and chip shops became an essential component of urban centres. In the UK, by the year 1905, there existed a fish and chip shop for every 400 citizens of London, Leeds and Bradford. By 1913, there were 25,000 outlets. The trade spread to Scotland, where Italian immigrants began to make the fish and chip trade their own, with many doubling up as ice-cream parlours. By 1914, Scotland had approximately 4500 'chippers'.

The Origins of Fast Food/QSR—The Influence of the Italians

Indeed, it was 20 years after the emergence of the fish and chip industry in London that the first fish and chips were sold in Ireland. In Dublin in 1885, an Italian immigrant, Giuseppe Cervi, began selling chips outside a pub, with a handcart on Great Brunswick Street (now Pearse Street, Dublin). According to Walton (1989), by 1909, there were 20 fish and chip shops in Dublin, run by Italian immigrants, serving a population of 290,000, predominantly working class customers. Many of these early traders built their business around selling fish and chips and some also sold Italian ice-cream.

Almost all of Ireland's Italian chipper families came from Frosinone in Val Di Comino, 140 km southeast of Rome. Initially, they drifted into Dublin and Cork in the late nineteenth century, selling religious statues and their celebrated ice-cream. These families began to operate fish and chip shops, enabling them to integrate into Irish society. Most named their establishments with their family name: Borzas, Caffollas, Macaris, the Fuscos, Marsellas and Apriles. According to Walton (1989), the popularity of the fish and chip shop fundamentally aided the social needs of the urban working classes at the time, by reducing the domestic workload of women, easing tensions in the home, and supplementing a poor diet. In terms of social influence, the Italian Chippers were predominately Catholic and encouraged the Catholic religious tradition of eating fish instead of meat on Fridays. By the middle of the twentieth century, many of these businesses had developed a full service structure, providing a wide range of fast food items and a high degree of personal service. These fish and chips shops became important establishments within their communities. In 1912, the famous Irish Burdocks and Beshoff's fish and chip shops began trading both of which are still successfully operating today. Meanwhile, in the USA in 1904, the first hamburger was sold from a burger stall at a Louisiana fair by Fletch Davies, who began serving grilled steak between two pieces of toast. However, it would take more than 50 years before the hamburger arrived in the UK or Ireland.

Changing Industry Structure

In the post-war period, significant changes took place in the industry. Competition intensified as the number of outlets increased. Throughout the 1950s, there was an increase in the growth of fish and chip shops outside the Dublin area. By the 1960s, every town in Ireland had a chipper, bringing the national total to approximately 120. The picture painted was of a small industry with small firms many of which were over 10 or 20 years old. These firms were run by families with many extended family members operating one or two outlets. During this time, chippers began to expand their menu offering to include sausages, battered sausages, hamburgers and the Irish spice burger. During the 1960s, many fish and chip shops began stocking frozen chips which made the operational process more efficient and reduced overall costs. In Dublin, the first sit-down restaurants began to open up: the Beaufield Mews and the Trocadero both opened in 1956 and are still trading today.

New Entrants: 1950–1970

The fast food industry changed considerably from the late 1950s. Customer profiles broadened, competitive new entrants appeared, and new food offerings began to emerge. During this period, Asian immigrants came to Ireland and brought with them new and exciting cuisine, resulting in the opening of the first Indian and Chinese restaurants. In 1956, The Golden Orient became the first Indian Restaurant to open on Leeson Street, Dublin. The proprietor, Mike Butt, was an East African Indian who adapted many dishes to suit the taste palate of the Irish which was slightly bland. Chinese immigrants also came to Ireland in the late 1950s, and Ireland's first Chinese restaurant, 'the Universal', opened in 1957, on Leeson Street. 'Luna' and 'Sunflower' Chinese restaurants, followed in quick succession. The number of Chinese restaurants in Ireland is much greater than the number of Indian restaurants, due to the larger number of migrants moving to Ireland. Another development, in the late 1950s, was the beginning of 'pub grub'. By the late 1960s, Pubs began to serve a variety of food, including 'chicken in a basket', steak, shepherd's pie, fish and chips, sausages and chips, and the traditional Sunday roast.

Managing New Challenges: Fast Food/QSR Revolution

The 1960s brought with them improved economic and social prosperity, with Irish cities commencing their developmental sprawl. During this time, the genesis of the Celtic Tiger began to emerge. There was wider access to education, good housing, motor cars, television, good food, and health services for most women and men. As the economy improved and air travel became cheaper, more people began travelling abroad for their holidays. The introduction of the 'package holiday' opened consumers' eyes to new ways of living, socialising, and eating. Expenditure on 'convenience food' rose by 31 per cent between 1955 and 1960, and in 1966, accounted for 20 per cent of total food consumption. 'Convenience food' (defined as: a food, typically a complete meal that has been pre-prepared commercially and so requires little preparation by the consumer) became popular, helping reduce the domestic workload of the growing proportion of married women, taking up paid employment outside the home. Television advertising campaigns for convenience foods increased considerably and branding in general became increasingly important.

A greater emphasis on convenience and preference for labour-saving items created a demand for eating outside the home. By the end of the 1960s, the fast food industry was under pressure from several quarters. New entrants were increasing the competitive nature of the industry. The traditional fish and chip shop incumbents began to feel the pressure and the era of the American hamburger was fast approaching.

Wimpy Bar—Opens in Ireland

The first Wimpy opened in Ireland in the 1960s. However, the Wimpy brand was created in the UK in the 1930s. The name was inspired by the character of J. Wellington Wimpy from the Popeye cartoons created by E.C. Segar. In the UK, by the early 1950s, businessman Eddie Gold was running 12 restaurants serving hamburgers and fries to the public. In 1954, the Wimpy fast food concept came to the attention of the company directors of J. Lyons and Co., a large-scale British food manufacturing and hotel conglomerate. Lyons Inc. licensed the brand for use in the UK, and in 1954, the first 'Wimpy Bar' was established at the Lyons Corner House in Coventry Street, London. Originally, the bar had a special fast food section within the more traditional Corner House restaurants, but the success soon led to the establishment of separate Wimpy restaurants serving only hamburger-based meals. By 1970, the business had expanded to over a 1000 restaurants in 23 countries. In the 1960s, Wimpy opened in Galway. Irish born Jimmy Sheils from Derry, witnessed first-hand how successful managing a Wimpy bar franchise could be when he was living in England. In particular, he noticed that fast food restaurants were very popular during the 1960s—so much so that he bought a franchise and opened a Wimpy restaurant in Galway. Sheils claimed 'I was going to open the restaurant on the Strand Road in Derry but a friend convinced me to come to Galway, so I did and it proved to be very successful'.

Industry Change: The Impact of Franchising 1970–1980

In the 20-year period between 1950 and 1970, new entrants were mostly independent fish and chip shops, and Chinese or Indian outlets. By the 1970s, there were approximately 250 chippers and 100 Indian and Chinese restaurants in Ireland. In 1971, the original American hamburger and fries were introduced to Ireland by Captain America's restaurant on Grafton Street, Dublin. In 1975, Burgerland was the first fast food/QSR burger bar since Wimpy's to open in Ireland, and by 1979, had two outlets in Dublin's city centre. For many industry incumbents, it was becoming apparent that in order to survive, they would have to learn to operate in a more intensively competitive environment.

International Competition

At the end of the 1970s, the US-based fast food leader, McDonald's, began to express their interest in the establishment of fast food outlets in Ireland and other European Economic Community (EEC) markets. This global new entrant would spur the Irish industry incumbents to change. Upon the arrival of McDonald's to Ireland, the fast food industry underwent a period of profound transformation. The small independent traditional fish and chip shop was blindsided by the professional image and finely honed operating model of McDonald's. McDonald's brought to the industry a new focus on brand building and the novel organisational structure of franchising. Between 1977 and 1982, McDonald's, Wimpy, Supermac's, and Abrakebabra entered the industry. These firms were focused on building their brands, and for the first time, the industry witnessed professional marketing practices and improvements in operational efficiencies. However, none of the new entrants came to dominate the industry at this point, and product offerings remained narrowly focused. Although there were several significant players, they only competed when products or geographical locations overlapped and full head-to-head competition became the norm.

The Emergence of New Industry Leaders

By the late 1980s, two firms, McDonald's and Abrakebabra, were the two leading fast food operators, with outlet and turnover figures larger than other industry competitors. Both firms offered similar product ranges including burgers, French fries and soft drinks, with Abrakebabra offering their unique kebabs. The financial success and brand recognition of both firms enabled them to carry out a rapid nationwide expansion strategy using the franchising model, further enforcing their brand power and industry dominance.

McDonald's Opens in Ireland

McDonald's arrived in Ireland in 1977 and opened its first fast food outlet on Grafton Street, Dublin. The famous McDonald's burger and French fries had finally arrived in Ireland and with it, the first franchising business endeavour on Irish soil. The fast food phenomenon was so new to Irish customers that it took them some time to adapt to this new style of eating, that is queuing for food, paying at the till before sitting down to consume their meal, without using knives and forks. McDonald's Inc. sold the Irish Master franchise to Irishman Mike Meagan, who had worked for McDonald's in Canada. Meagan approached McDonald's about operating a McDonald's franchise in Ireland and was granted the licence. His first franchise outlet was so successful that he opened another six McDonald's outlets in Dublin between 1977 and 1982. However, in 1989, McDonald's bought back the rights to the Irish region, as they had huge plans for expansion beyond Meagan's own ambitions.

McDonald's global has always been focused on rapid growth. The company is not just a very large multi-national corporation (MNC), it is a phenomenon in its own right. McDonald's was founded in 1937 by the McDonald brothers. They began franchising in 1955, when Ray Kroc, a milk-shake mixer salesman, negotiated a franchise deal which gave him exclusive rights to franchise McDonald's in the USA. The concept was innovative, the menu was short, simple and cheap, and the hamburgers, fries and milkshakes were of the highest quality. By 1960, Kroc had opened 200 restaurants throughout the USA, and within five years, the company went public becoming the McDonald's Corporation. From its entry into the Irish market, McDonald's has followed a dual approach to its growth strategy, opening both company-owned and franchised restaurants. The company-owned outlets allowed McDonald's to try out new concepts, and spot potential franchisee and management talent. McDonald's Ireland recognised that its success and profitability was inextricably linked to the success of its franchisees. Franchisees benefited greatly by having a well-developed and universally recognised brand and product range. This was backed by national and international marketing campaigns. Additionally, McDonald's operating processes were the core of their success. Their well-honed cooking processes were broken down into small, repetitive tasks. This enabled staff to be highly efficient and adept at all tasks, and provided franchisees with a ready-made operational model.

The cost of a McDonald's franchise varied, it depended on the capital available to potential franchisees. They could choose between two financial routes: the Conventional Franchise or the Business Facilities Lease. With the Conventional Franchise, franchisees would buy an existing restaurant at 25 per cent of the purchase price, or open a new restaurant for 40 per cent of the total purchase price. The Business Facilities lease would be for potential franchisees who did not have sufficient capital. This model used the cash flow of the restaurant to purchase the franchise within the first three years of trading. For both options, there was a monthly rent and service fee, as well as a contribution to an annual marketing budget. All this would be based on a percentage of sales. McDonald's also required franchisees to undergo unpaid training for nine months. The programme would cover all relevant areas including team building, customer relations, people skills, business management, health and safety, hygiene and general first aid. Training would be split between restaurant experience and residential courses at their training centre. McDonald's claimed that a certain type of person with certain characteristics would make a successful franchisee. Usually they would be successful in business or in a previous career, having experience of people management and development, sales building, and marketing. Joe Byrne, a McDonald's franchisee in Waterford, began working at McDonald's while he was still at school. He spent 17 years with the organisation and worked his way up to becoming a restaurant manager at 29 years of age. Byrne was attracted by the support offered by McDonald's with proven operational methods. This helped to reduce the risk of failure in opening a new restaurant. Another franchisee, Gerry Riordan had worked in the banking industry for a number of years prior to opening his McDonald's franchise restaurant in Blackrock, Dublin. According to Riordan, the management skills and the successful business systems that he gained from the McDonald's training programme would have taken him years to acquire on his own. Finally, Paul Crocker, had run a number of successful petrol station businesses before taking on a McDonald's franchise in 1996, and within five years, he had opened five outlets. Crocker claimed 'the secret to McDonald's success was their combination of finely tuned operational performance and the ability to entice new customers into the restaurant'.

Wimpy Bars in the 1970s—Emergence of the Burger King Brand

In 1977, the Wimpy business was acquired by the English firm United Biscuits. In the UK by the late 1980s, Wimpy was beginning to lose ground to McDonald's, who had opened their first UK restaurant in 1974. New management at Wimpy began to streamline the business by converting some of the traditional table service into counter service restaurants. In 1989, the business was sold to Grand Metropolitan (now Diageo). Grand Metropolitan had acquired Burger King the previous year and they began to convert to the 'counter service' restaurants in Burger King Restaurants. In 1990, the remaining 220 'table service' restaurants were purchased by a management buy-out backed by 3i. A second management buy-out occurred in 2002. By the mid-1990s, there were 12 Burger King outlets in Ireland, and some were combined with petrol stations.

Supermac's Opens in Galway 1978

Supermac's was founded by Pat McDonagh in Galway in 1978 directly after McDonald's entered the Irish market. McDonagh was a former school teacher and initially wanted to open a pool hall but failed to get planning permission. He settled on a shortlist of other business alternatives for his location, a furniture shop or a takeaway. He chose the latter and Supermac's was born. The name was based on McDonagh's nickname which he had acquired playing school Gaelic Athletic Association (GAA).

Supermac's used its 'Irishness' to set it apart from its competitors, in particular from the international global giants McDonald's and Burger King. According to McDonagh, it gave the brand a unique identity. The company focused on opening sit-down, family-style restaurants, using the franchise business model of expansion. Initially, Supermac's concentrated its growth in the West of Ireland. Important lessons were learned about selecting suitable franchisees and the right locations. Many franchisees began working for Supermac's as employees and worked their way up to become managers. In 1984, John Kennedy a franchisee in Athlone, joined Supermac's directly from school. Initially he worked part time, and then became a full-time manager. In 1997, he became a franchisee, 'I liked the opportunity to become your 'own boss', to work for yourself, and to have more control over the standards of your own business'. He attributes his success to having a good support team as Kennedy prefers to focus on the day-to-day running of the restaurant while others focus on the administration. Another franchisee, Danny McHugh opened three Supermac's in Mayo. He worked for Supermac's for 12 years before training to become a manager. In 2005, he opened his first franchise in Roscommon. He believed Supermac's offered the ability to conduct both localised store marketing and brand-wide marketing as well as the ability to get involved in the local business community. Another franchisee, Jim Casey, opened his first Supermac's outlet in 2005, a Supermac's Express (smaller Supermac's run out of a large motorway petrol station) on the Dublin to Athlone motorway. He already owned the premises and operated a garage there; thus, the Express Supermac's launch was for him a natural progression.

The Industry's Trade Association

By the early 1980s, franchising as a business model was gaining a degree of publicity, particularly after the success of many US-franchised businesses during the 1970s. In Ireland in 1983, the Irish Franchise Association was established as a point of reference for firms considering franchising, as well as individuals wishing to become franchisees. At this time, franchising was mainly concentrated in the fast food/QSR industry. The Irish Franchise Association aimed to encourage franchising as a successful way to achieve businesses growth and expansion. The Association's mission statement has always been 'to develop and promote best practice franchising in Ireland and create an environment within which franchise businesses can grow'. The declared objective of the Irish Franchise Association;

> To protect and further the interests of properly constructed franchising companies and by these means to establish and maintain a clear definition of ethical franchising standards to assist members of the public, press, potential investors and government bodies in differentiating between sound business opportunities and any suspect investment. In consequence of these aims, a code of ethics and strict criteria for membership are produced.

Up until the 1980s, in the fast food/QSR sector, there was a distinct lack of industry regulation this being laissez-faire with little or no interference from government. A restaurant licence was unnecessary in order to open a fast food/QSR, only a restaurant certificate was required if the restaurant had seating. However, Ireland having joined the European Union (EU) in the 1990s produced new directives under the Maastricht Treaty relating to industry policies which were set to change.

Abrakebabra Founded in 1982 and Adopted Franchising in 1985

In 1982, Graeme Beere, with his brother Wyn, established a new fast food restaurant, targeted at Dublin's late night pub-going population. A product mix of kebabs, burgers and chips, late night opening, and the option to 'eat-in' were all innovative to the Irish market. Graeme called his new restaurant 'Abrakebabra'. He realised that location was the key for this new venture to work. The restaurant needed to be situated close to pubs, and in an area where his target market lived and socialised. The first outlet was opened in the Dublin suburb of Rathmines. Abrakebabra proved hugely popular with customers, and by 1984, had opened four successful shops. However, the brothers experienced problems managing four busy restaurants. Having witnessed the unrivalled success of McDonald's using franchising, the brothers saw the potential it offered to expand the business rapidly, and they decided to pursue this model. It provided solutions to two key challenges to the further growth of their business—cash flow and management capacity.

The period between 1985 and 1987 was one of very rapid growth for Abrakebabra. The company used a dual strategy to drive the growth process. By 1997, Abrakebabra had 60 restaurants in total, 12 company-owned restaurants, and 48 franchised restaurants across Ireland. The logic of this dual strategy was that by franchising, the company could expand quickly, as franchisees provided capital and management. The success of the franchised outlets provided the resources to fund company-owned restaurants. The larger the chain became, the greater the brand recognition, and the easier it became to attract franchisees. Abrakebabra would approach an established local fast food restaurant suggesting a franchise conversion. However, teething problems began to emerge with the franchises early on, namely, an inability to control franchisees financial performance and restaurant standards. Consequently, Abrakebabra decided to be more rigorous in choosing franchisees. They set about formulating a selection process. The process would involve franchisees completing a formal application form. If selected, they would be interviewed to evaluate their ambitions, experience, and personal characteristics. Abrakebabra wanted people with experience in management and entrepreneurship. They wanted people with ambition and passion to run a restaurant full time, serving customers to the best of their ability. Previous education was not as important as previous experience in business, especially in the food industry. When a franchisee was selected and deemed suitable, their official training would begin under the instruction of an established franchisee. This form of training would take from two to three months.

Abrakebabra, required a franchisee entry fee and an on-going levy of 6 per cent on each franchisee's gross revenues (excluding the 1 per cent advertising levy which was charged to every franchisee and pooled into a fund specifically for brand advertising campaigns). Franchisees paid the franchisor for expertise in operational issues, access to economies of scale, supply chain management, bulk buying, marketing and branding. All of these benefits made the franchisee more cost efficient, 'bulk buying offered Abrakebabra operators an extra 10 per cent profit margin over and above the industry norm of 60 per cent'. There were a number of reasons why franchisees would decide to choose an Abrakebabra franchise. A Dublin-based franchisee believed Abrakebabra had the most attractive franchise package when compared to McDonald's and Supermac's. A Waterford franchisee was attracted by the strong brand name and innovative product range. Originally, a fish and chip shop owner, he claimed 'I was already in the business, and I knew that one of the chains would eventually open up in my area, so I chose Abrakebabra as they had a national presence'. Another, Cork-based franchisee, who converted his restaurant to an Abrakebabra acknowledged, 'we owned our own restaurant and McDonald's came to town we saw our trade drop by 30 per cent so Abrakebabra was something to do battle with McDonald's'. When citing the reasons for success, franchisees consistently commented on the importance of Abrakebabra's branding and marketing as well as bulk buying benefits. One franchisee in Sligo claimed, 'as franchisees, we were part of a bigger picture in terms of marketing and branding and from a financial point of view we were purchasing supplies at least 12 to 13 per cent cheaper than as an independent operator'. A Cork-based franchisee said, 'Advertising and bulk buying would be the two main benefits. Abrakebara's back-up services were very good and they helped to solve operational problems'.

New Focus: Image, Branding, Efficiency

Increased International Competition

In the years following late 1980s, industry change was particularly swift and extensive. At the lower end of the market, the inexpensive fast food/QSR sector once dominated by independent chippers and Chinese and Indian takeaways began to change. The industry began to experience increased competition from international franchised fast food restaurant chains such as McDonald's, Burger King, and Domino's, as well as from the Irish-owned Abrakebabra and Supermac's. Increased competition, combined with a recession in the late 1980s, brought further challenges to the industry. New store openings by the franchise systems increased dramatically and price competition intensified. The two key elements for success in the industry became branding and operational efficiency. The 1990s also brought changing customer preferences—customers were becoming increasingly health conscious—and this increase in buyer power made success in the industry increasingly difficult. In response, competitors extended their food offerings to incorporate more health conscious options and also began to invest heavily in marketing strategies, which caused alarm across the industry's independent operators. Independent chippers were severely hit and their numbers declined particularly in the Dublin region. Many fish and chip owners converted and became franchisees of the franchised chains. The 1990s unleashed unprecedented price competition in the industry, the introduction of 'meal deals' and McDonald's famous 'happy meal' were unique to the Irish market and after its success, McDonald's rolled-out the concept to all its global restaurants.

Intensifying Competition and Industry Failures

During this period of growth and competitive intensity, there was one international fast food chain which struggled to enter the industry. In the midst of the success of most of the international fast food/QSR market entries, Kentucky Fried Chicken (KFC) experienced a market entry failure.

Kentucky Fried Chicken (KFC): KFC, a hugely successful American fried chicken chain, first entered the Irish market in the late 1970s opening four outlets. However, KFC has operated intermittently ever since and in the early 1990s, closed most of its outlets in the Republic. This was attributed to management issues. KFC was a tiny part of the worldwide Pepsi organisation and during this period, its Irish division reported directly to the USA instead of the UK or Europe. 'They were trying to run the stores by US remote control', according to UK-based Kevin Higgins of Tricon's.

In 1997, Pepsi spun off its restaurant business, which also included Pizza Hut and Taco Bell, to Tricon. As a result, the responsibility for the Republic of Ireland was transferred to the UK headquarters. Although KFC had a chequered history in the Republic, the company had thrived in Northern Ireland opening 31 outlets. These are operated by two separate franchise firms, the Belfast-based Herbel Restaurants and Ladbury restaurants (also a Pizza Hut franchisee in Ireland). The KFC management in the UK were convinced that KFC would be successful in Ireland so they decided to re-enter the Irish market. They opened a small outlet in Liffey Valley shopping centre in 1998, and a drive-through was established at Blanchardstown shopping centre.

Industry Boundaries Expand

Traditional fast food, typically represented by products such as fish, chips and burgers began to expand and the QSR began to broaden their scope. Both night-time and day-time trading became part of the industry and in the 1990s, the day-time sandwich and snack trade became direct competitors. Industry level changes in the 1990s were not dramatic, and firms further developed their product offerings and consolidated their positions. Despite entries and exits, the basic methods of trading remained the same. Throughout this period, different segments of the industry varied in their overall performance, however, McDonald's and Abrakebabra remained industry leaders.

O'Briens Sandwich Bars Founded in 1988, Adopted Franchising in 1994

Brody Sweeny founded O'Briens Sandwich Bars in 1988 and had previous first-hand experience of franchising in the Irish printing industry. Brody's father, Frank Sweeney, a solicitor, was granted the licence to operate Prontaprint (a UK printing franchise) in 1980. Brody took over the business and bought his father's share. He then spent eight years setting up Prontaprint franchise outlets all over Ireland. The company expanded rapidly, at a loss. Brody finally sold Prontaprint back to the UK Company in 1988. In the same year, he opened O'Briens, bringing some valuable insights from his printing experience.

From the beginning, Brody Sweeny wanted to create a modern Irish image for his sandwich bars. He chose the name O'Briens, as it is the most common surname in Ireland. Sweeney wanted the design to be young and friendly, with no plastic sandwich packaging. He used high quality ingredients, thick slices of fresh bread filled with the customer's own choice of healthy, non-processed food. He wanted it to incorporate all the positive traditional Irish values, yet reflect modern Ireland and the changing lifestyles with a proposition that would have universal appeal. His research indicated that the biggest sector of the fast food/QSR market in the UK was the sandwich sector. 'In other words, more sandwiches were sold in the UK than hamburgers, pizza, chicken, Chinese, and fish and chips all put together and it was the only one of those sectors without a chain' (Brody Sweeny). The business concept was developed with a view to international expansion, as such Sweeney sought the help and advice of Howarth, an International franchise consultancy, who helped him put together a franchise package and franchisee agreement.

Despite initial success, O'Briens continued to lose money for the first six years and by 1994, the company was in financial trouble. Sweeney developed O'Briens as a franchise business, writing manuals and focusing on expansion. In 1994, when happy with his franchise package, he opened the first O'Briens franchise. By 1999, there were 61 franchised O'Briens Irish Sandwich Bars operating: 25 in Ireland, 25 in England and Scotland, two in America, two in Singapore, two in Australia, and two in Germany. The company's motto was 'an O'Briens' franchise partner is in business for themselves but never by themselves'. The operations team supported the franchisee through every stage of the franchising process. The franchisee was supported with property acquisition, store design, on-going staff recruitment and training, group purchasing, business development, employment law, health and hygiene. As well as training in sandwich preparation, speciality coffee making and the office and outside catering arrangements. Communications with franchisees were maintained through regional meetings, weekly phone calls, newsletters, and an annual international conference. All O'Briens marketing campaigns were supported by a proactive public relations team who helped launch each new outlet. Thus, gaining valuable recognition with positive media coverage focused on raising the profile of the O'Briens brand. A mix of leaflet drops, high quality point of sale material, promotional campaigns, local radio ads, national media activity and public relations helped promote sales and profits. Having a strong brand was essential for O'Briens strategic planning and ensured differentiation from competitors. They believed that the strength of their brand could be seen in every aspect of the business, be it the franchise partners and the staff they attracted, or the supplier partners who joined their distribution network. The idea of optimal standardisation across the network of stores was key and O'Briens claimed a customer could predict with certainty what they would find when they walked into any O'Briens outlets worldwide.

As a franchisee, Andi Cooke set up two Dublin O'Briens Sandwich Bars. Before becoming a franchisee, she was Operations Manager for O'Briens for six years. She wanted to start up a business within the catering sector. She saw O'Briens as being a market leader with excellent support services for franchisees'. Laura Hill, another O'Briens franchisee, in Mayo. 'I worked as an accountant prior to opening my outlet. I had no previous experience as an entrepreneur and therefore decided a franchise opportunity would suit me'. Laura felt that O'Briens had a proven track record. The back-up provided was particularly beneficial to her in the early days, offering advice and support in relation to set-up, store location, layout, systems and suppliers, as well as continuously developing new products and marketing ideas which she would never have had the time to do on her own. It appears that while O'Briens were excellent at strategising on branding and expansion they were weak at financial and operational planning.

Franchising Dominates

Economic and Social Changes

By the end of the 1990s, the Irish economy was heating up for what was to be a period of unprecedented economic growth and prosperity known as the Celtic Tiger years. Irish consumerism became an unstoppable machine and international retailing giants began to enter the Irish market. Irish indigenous firms also began to prosper and thrive, bringing full employment and a culture of 'cash rich, time poor', where convenience was the number one criteria for consumption. In terms of food shopping and supermarkets, the smaller operators were now competing with larger convenience-store chains such as Spar, Centra and Londis, foreign discount supermarkets Lidl and Aldi, and large native national supermarket chains Dunnes Stores and Superquinn and British chains, such as Tesco Ireland (formerly Quinnsworth).

In the fast food/QSR industry, increased competition, an ensuing recession and increased health conscious consumers—caused many incumbents to focus more on branding, advertising, product innovation/extension and price in order to differentiate themselves from their competitors. Fast food also suffered from its own obsession with cost and margins at the expense of marketing effectiveness. Many operators paid staff minimum wages and failed to attract a high quality workforce, and in many cases, their company operational infrastructure was weak. Although the 1990s was a period which presented numerous challenges to the fast food industry, on a whole, the industry continued to expand. McDonald's, Abrakebabra and O'Briens continued to dominate as the independents declined. Competition in the industry intensified, resulting in the demise of many independent fish and chip shops.

Coping with Change: Nationwide Expansion and Branding

Industry Expansion

During the 1990s, some key issues affected all fast food/QSR operators. These included staff shortages, unemployment being at an all-time low, making minimum wage jobs difficult to fill. Additionally, customers had increased disposable income and began opting for more expensive restaurants over inexpensive fast food/QSR outlets. Furthermore, for the first time, comprehensive Irish Health and Safety (H&S) regulations were firmly established in 1993 under the guidance of the Irish Health and

Safety Authority (and the European Union Maastricht Treaty directives). In general, people's working lives had become increasingly fast-paced, with more people eating outside of the home. The industry experienced further expansion; this was reflected in the increase in pubs and petrol stations which began selling hot food. From the late 1990s, pubs had begun to experience a decline in sales of alcohol, therefore food became a critical component of sales. In some cases, food accounted for 50–65 per cent of turnover. Another extension of the fast food/QSR sector occurred when petrol stations began to sell hot food, such as breakfast rolls, sandwiches, tea, and coffee. In the early 1990s, Statoil garages began to sell 'the breakfast roll' and their food and drink sales became as important as their fuel sales. According to Frank Gleeson of Topez garages, 'in the food channel, we began to compete against Quick Serve Restaurants (QSR), convenience shops, and symbol stores, we become a roadside utility to satisfy people's convenience needs'.

The demand for fast food/QSRs and restaurants, continued to grow. The industry key firms were McDonald's, Abrakebabra, O'Briens and Supermac's. McDonald's began to expand and had opened 35 outlets by the late 1990s (see Table 5.4). However, the real industry leader was Abrakebabra who opened over 60 outlets by the late 1990s. During this period, there was additional growth among independent burger bars, pizzerias and sandwich/snack bars across Ireland and a variety of internationally franchised pizza chains also entered the Irish market. In an ever-competitive industry, many industry incumbents began to expand

Table 5.4 Selected competitors: restaurant numbers in Ireland 1997

Name	Eat-in	Number of outlet	Annual turnover (million)
MacDonald's	Seating	35	€46
Abrakebabra	Seating	60	€50
Supermac's	Seating	16	€10
O'Briens	Seating	50	€30
Four Star Pizza	No seating	10	€4
Burger King	Seating	12	€35
Domino's Pizza	No seating	9	€2.5

Source: Annual returns and outlet number information was obtained by contact with each company's head office.

their product offering to include ethnically diverse fast food items, as well as catering to the more health conscious customer. Branding and price continued to be a priority, particularly as customer buying power increased. Within this context, franchising offered benefits in terms of brand power and cost reduction. Franchised chains, such as Abrakebabra and McDonald's, achieved important margin increases for their franchisees by bulk buying at discounted prices and capital injections from new franchisees's fees fuelled firm expansions. All of these factors combined helped the leading franchise systems stay ahead of the competition. In the late 1990s, efforts to develop stronger brand identities were intensified in response to the growing competition from the industry's leading firms.

According to many of the industry incumbents such as McDonald's, Abrakebabra and O'Briens, when the market was at its most competitive, organisational changes were necessary to tackle industry challenges. To differentiate themselves, fast food/QSR firms began to focus on becoming more customer-centric, enhancing their quality of service, improving cost effectiveness, and building the capabilities needed to improve overall business performance. Statistics on the number of firms in the industry from 1970 until the late 1990s are not available, but information from industry sources suggest that the number of firms had not changed substantially since the late 1970s particularly with reference to the 250 chippers and 100 Chinese and Indian takeaways. However, in terms of the franchised chains, growth was dramatic.

Industry Regulation

McDonald's Influences Industry Regulation

Government regulation regarding fast food/QSR industry was broad and rather vague up until the late 1980s when the Health and Safety Authority (HSA) began to monitor the industry. However, McDonald's global model of operations, which maintained the highest H&S standards, had been developed in the USA during the 1950s and 1960s. Annette Kelly (McDonald's Trainer) claims that

Only in the mid-1990s did we have visits from the Health and Safety Authority.

McDonald's, from its entry into the Irish market in 1977, was instrumental in setting H&S industry standards. McDonald's worked in conjunction with the HSA on its policies, guidelines, and standards.

> We would work quite closely with the food safety authority, and they love what we do and they have taken a lot of our systems and used them as an industry benchmark. (Chris Pollock)

Industry regulation and increased Health and Safety awareness became important for firms in the 1990s when HSA (Health and Safety Authority) officers began to inspect all restaurants and fast food outlets, carrying out cleanliness and food safety audits. In the late 1990s, new directives were introduced at a European level regarding Health and Safety policies and industry monitoring became increasingly more stringent. New auditing procedures were introduced whereby every restaurant and food serving outlet would be inspected regularly each year. If standards were not met or maintained, then a restaurant or food service operation would be shut down and a re-application for a restaurant licence would be needed. Customers could also report to the HSA directly if they suspected that basic standards were not being met by a restaurant.

Industry Competition—New Tactics

Industry dynamics changed considerably in the early 2000s and the two previous industry leaders (Abrekebabra and McDonald's) were now joined by Supermac's and O'Briens (see Table 5.5). Both firms gained a foothold after a decade of company expansion and brand building, enabled by their adoption of franchising. For the first time, the pizza chains began to have an impact on the industry structure and gained an increased market share.

For the industry incumbents, the early 2000s were characterised by intense price wars, further product expansion and costly marketing cam-

Table 5.5 Main franchise restaurant outlets operating in Ireland 2005

Name	Eat-in	Number of outlet	Annual turnover (million)
Abrakebabra	Seating	55	€40.5
Supermac's	Seating	45	€29.4
McDonald's	Seating	66	€176
Burger King	Seating	10	€17
Four Star Pizza	No seating	26	€10
Domino's Pizza	No seating	17	€10

Source: Annual returns and outlet number information was obtained by contact with each company's head office

paigns. The leading firms competed intensely for customers and were always focused on obtaining new sites for their outlets, often at the expense of the independents. As the market became more crowded, there were casualties.

Such intense competition led to further industry consolidation and by 2008, Abrakebabra Investments Limited (AIL formed in 2008) had begun to diversify its brand offering to increase market share. The company embarked on a Master franchise acquisition strategy. AIL acquired O'Briens Irish Sandwich Bars, after the company went into liquidation in 2009. Having looked at the success of the US multi-brand Yum (KFC, Pizza Hut and Taco Bell) AIL decided to build a diversified brand portfolio. In addition to O'Briens, AIL acquired the Master franchise to Bagel Factory (UK), Gourmet Burger Kitchen (UK), Yo Sushi (UK), and King Chick (UK), making it the first fast food/QSR multi-brand franchise system in Ireland.

Social and Economic Change—2000 Onwards

By the late 2000s, the Irish franchise market was considered to be in its infancy compared to the USA and considered to have potentially great future growth. In recent years, one of the key changes in retail was the increase in new shopping centres across Ireland, a factor that affected the locations of fast food/QSR outlets. The brand recognition that is an inherent part of franchising is a very attractive proposition for a shopping centre owner or developer. Ireland's shopping centres now account for an increasing volume of retail sales, representing a move away from the traditional focus on the Main Street. In most Irish shopping centres, many of the large fast food/QSR franchise chains now have a presence.

Consumer lifestyle changes and increased availability of new product and service offerings have been an underlying driver of consumption between the years 2000 and 2008. High employment, dual income families, and a young workforce meant people were choosing to eat out. A recent report assessing the eating habits of Irish families revealed that a large portion of meals in Ireland are not eaten or prepared at home. According to Professor Patrick Wall, of the UCD School of Public Health and Popular Science;

In Ireland, 33 per cent of food is eaten or prepared outside the home.

As a testament to this increased consumption of fast food/QSR, Tallaght, a sprawling suburb in County Dublin with high unemployment rates among its inhabitants (a population of 71,467 according to the 2010 census), consumes more pizza than anywhere else in the world. The Tallaght branch of Domino's Pizza is the busiest of its 8000 stores worldwide, selling a record 1 million pizzas per annum (13 pizzas per year per capita).

Another change affecting the range of convenience foods demanded in Ireland has been the influx of immigrants from Central and Eastern Europe. Ireland opened its labour market to 10 new member states of the European Union in 2004, and triggered an influx of Polish and Latvian immigrants, reaching a high of 10,000 workers per month. To reflect these changes, even small supermarkets routinely stock large ethnic food sections containing Indian, Chinese, Thai, Polish, Tex-Mex American (Mexican), and specialty foods from Poland and the Czech/Slovak/Slovene regions. As a result of this, the fast food/QSR industry incumbents have begun to offer more varied product range to cater for a more diverse customer base.

The Response of the Traditional Chippers

As a result of increasing industry pressure, traditional Irish chippers have decided to come together and form a branded association and create a unified identity. The association named the Irish Traditional Italian Chipper Association (ITICA) was formed in 2010,

to celebrate the unique identity of the traditional Italian chippers in Ireland
and to mark the contribution we have made to the Irish community.

ITICA is a unique association, with only Italian-owned chippers allowed to become members. There are strict rules governing the association. The chippers must be family-run, the chips have to be made from freshly cut potatoes and the batter must be made on the premises. Johnny Soave CEO of ITICA says,

> 99 per cent of Italian chippers are still run by people whose forefathers came to Ireland.

Soave says there are probably 300 takeaway chippers in Ireland and not all of them, would meet ITICA's criteria for membership. ITICA already has more than 180 members out of 260 Irish Italian chippers in 2010. The number of chippers has remained relatively stable since the 1970s, which is impressive considering the growing competitive intensity of the industry. Therefore, chippers have had to innovate and to address the increasingly diverse consumer tastes. Most have expanded their menus offering a range of curries, gravies, salsas, cheeses, kebabs, pizzas, Tex-Mex food, chicken tandoori, and chicken curry in addition to other formerly unknown menu selections.

Economic Collapse

Following the 2008 Irish economic collapse, national consumption patterns altered once again as the population's disposable income decreased. Consumers began to opt for cheaper fast food/QSRs takeaways as opposed to expensive sit-down restaurant meals. Fast food outlets once again began to experience a steady increase in sales from 2008 onwards. Domino's UK and Ireland have seen a change in customer habits,

> many consumers are 'trading down', to cheaper QSR options, which means that they are eating out less often and staying at home. (according to Domino's' Chairman Stephen Hemsley)

Industry Growth

By the end of 2012, the economic collapse was still permeating Ireland; the fast food/QSR industry experienced continued growth with increased levels of consumption. By 2012, AIL, McDonald's, and Supermac's were still the main industry leaders, followed by a number of other key industry competitors.

Industry Leaders

AIL (Abrakebabra) 2012

In the late 1990s, Abrakebabra made the decision to sell all of its company-owned outlets, and focused solely on operating as a franchisor. The management team acknowledged the obvious benefits of franchising as a system of growth and they redefined the advantages of such a structure. Through franchising, Abrakebabra had achieved rapid expansion and market penetration with relatively low capital investment, as well as increasing market coverage, market share and brand equity with limited financial exposure. Due to the early adoption of a franchise strategy, Abrakebabra had a solid and largely unrivalled position. By 2006, Abrakebabra faced another difficult decision. The company had 60 own-branded outlets but decided that the market was at saturation point for its kebab shops. Abrakebabra realised that its brand was limited to late night eating and a narrow demographic. The company made a key strategic decision to acquire other master franchise brands. Abrakebabra looked to the UK to find popular brands in the QSR industry. They bought the master franchise rights for: the Bagel Factory, Gourmet Burger Kitchen, King Chick, and Yo-sushi. Within a two-year period, Abrakebabra had opened 42 Bagel Factory's, eight Gourmet Burger Kitchens, six King Chick's, and two Yo-sushi's.

O'Briens 2012

In 2008, O'Briens went into liquidation. Under an arrangement sanctioned by the High Court, AIL's subsidiary, Impless, immediately acquired and began to operate O'Briens Sandwich Bars. A statement issued by AIL founder, Graeme Beere: 'with over 25 years' experience in the franchise sector and we intend to work with O'Briens franchisees, new and old, to ensure that in these testing retail times they feel renewed confidence in the brand, a brand that we believe in strongly'. In 2008, there were 85 O'Briens stores in Ireland and more than 200 franchised outlets across the globe. O'Briens had always focused on innovation in its product offerings and also had focused on recruiting good quality franchisees. AIL's intention was to maintain O'Briens' position as a leader in the day-time sandwich market.

McDonald's 2012

By 2012, McDonald's Ireland had 75 restaurants with over 3000 employees, serving more than 150,000 customers daily. Of the restaurants operating across Ireland, approximately 75 per cent would be operated by franchisees. McDonald's has always regarded people and continuous training as central to the company's success,

> We provide training at every level to a high standard, with an investment above the national average. (According to Michelle Ryan [McDonald's Trainer])

According to Chris Pollock, the head of McDonald's franchising in Ireland, the biggest advantage McDonald's derives from franchising is to take the global brand and make it local, so that the franchisee is the local voice of a big global corporation.

> I see very few negatives in franchising if it's done properly, its advantages far out-way risks. (Chris Pollock, the head of franchising McDonald's Ireland)

As a testament to its success, McDonald's has consistently been voted one of the '50 Best Companies in Ireland to Work For' between the years 2005 to 2012. In Ireland, McDonald's is the only franchise system operating an independent HR department, managing both its company-owned stores and its franchisee-operated outlets. While the HR function managed the traditional aspects of policies and procedures, it also manages the relationship between McDonald's and its franchisees. This is accomplished through a consultative approach, getting involved when required, setting best practices, and influencing rather than regimenting change. McDonald's has always focused on its branding and customer service, to ensure that customers always receive a positive and consistent experience, throughout all outlets. To achieve their business goals, McDonald's has identified 'People', their employees, as a key source of competitive advantage. In the QSR industry, McDonald's has continuously set the standard for operational excellence by identifying and measuring key indicators of product quality and fast and accurate service.

Turnover for McDonald's Ireland's 78 restaurants in 2012 was €200 million. Sales were expected to continue to grow in 2011/2012. However, 'the actual spend per customer is declining', says John Atherton (McDonald's Ireland MD). '*What we're seeing in our restaurants is that people are trading down*'. In a recent interview with the Irish Times, Atherton would not divulge a figure for 'system-wide profits' but said tax paid in 2009 was €3.3 million. Based on a 12.5 per cent rate, this would indicate an annual profit of €26.4 million.

Supermac's 2012

In 2012, Supermac's turnover was €58.8 million. The company's turnover was derived from the operation of its fast food outlets and service stations in Ireland together with its nine subsidiaries engaged in fast food, patent technology, forestry development and franchising technology related to fast foods. McDonagh and his wife Úna have made the move to multi-brand franchising, as well as Supermac's and they hold the country franchise for the Papa John's Pizza Chain and a sub-franchise for the Quiznos sandwich chain. McDonagh also owns Claddagh Irish Pubs, a 15-strong US pub/restaurant chain. He wants to expand the chain to 80 outlets within five years, possibly through franchising. By 2012, Supermac's brand had over 2500 employees and 103 branches, serving an average of over 320,000 customers per week. McDonagh is very much a 'hands-on' CEO and is highly involved in the day-to-day operations of the company. The company's success is built on a unique menu, ideally suited to local tastes, using high quality food and ingredients locally sourced where possible. This quality philosophy has been recognised by the Gilbey's Award for Food Excellence and the Excellence Ireland Hygiene Mark. Similarly to McDonald's, Supermac's places emphasis on quality of staff and service.

McGurk Consulting, who recently completed a brand audit of Supermac's, said the brand was associated in everyone's mind with 'real Irish country food'. Supermac's opened a number of new outlets in 2012. A typical new store fit-out costs €250,000 and McDonagh intends to invest a total of €8 million for refits of existing restaurants in 2012. Changes in customer behaviour, coupled with what McDonagh described as an 'overcrowding' of legislation in relation to the traditional Supermac's business have also prompted the company to look at other models, such as the smaller, cheaper Fresh Express outlets which have done well in service stations. This has led McDonagh to invest in a number of service stations. According to McDonagh, 'Applegreen went with Burger King and Topaz went with McDonald's and we have decided maybe we can do serviced stations ourselves'.

Changing Environment—Changing Priorities: Franchised Competitors

In 2012, as well as the industry leaders, key industry players were Burger King, and the pizza chains Domino's and Four Star Pizza. In 2012, amidst the success of many industry leaders, KFC decided to attempt another market re-entry.

Burger King 2012

In 1981, the first Irish Burger King outlet opened on Grafton Street, Dublin. Today, there are 34 outlets located throughout Ireland with 17 located in Dublin. Burger King was founded in 1954 by James McLamore and David Edgerton in Miami, Florida. They had a guiding principle of offering reasonably priced quality food, served quickly, in attractive, clean surroundings. OKR Group was the sole franchisee for Burger King in the Republic of Ireland and employed over 900 people. According the Daniel Fitzpatrick, Burger King's Chief Operations Officer (COO)

> we think of each of our restaurants as a standalone business, we really make life simple for the restaurants. The last thing we want them focused on is things like IT. We want them focused on serving customers and serving great food. We get very granular information on every single item we sell; it's all about getting full visibility into what's happening at the restaurant.

Fitzpatrick says the company's current make-up is about 90 per cent franchisee and 10 per cent company-owned restaurants. In 2009, Burger King changed hands again, and was acquired by private investment firm 3G Capital for $3.3 billion and Fitzpatrick was appointed chief brand and operations officer. Based back in Miami, he reports directly to the US Head Quarters and CEO, Bernardo Hees. Fitzpatrick said:

> We wanted to make sure that our marketing of the brand and our opera-tions of the brand were very consistent, over 30 per cent of our customers are kid's parties, we have a balanced customer portfolio.

However, in 2012, Burger King Ireland saw profits fall nearly 13 per cent with pre-tax profits of €4.82 million, down from €5.53 million in the previous financial year with 30 outlets in Ireland.

Burger King has 17 Dublin outlets as well as restaurants in all the major Irish cities. Burger King, like Supermac's and McDonald's has begun to combine fast food with petrol stations and now has an outlet in Urlingford, County Kilkenny, which is the location of the rest stop for buses between Dublin and Cork; and an outlet in Celbridge, County Kildare. These outlets are located in Petrogas (Applegreen) petrol sta-tions, as Petrogas hold the Master Applegreen franchise in Ireland.

Domino's Pizza 2012

Domino's Pizza Group Limited (DPG) is a wholly owned subsidiary of Domino's Pizza UK & IRL plc which is quoted on the London Stock

Exchange. DPG is the UK and Ireland's leading pizza delivery company and holds the master franchise to own and operate Domino's Pizza stores in these markets. The first UK store opened in 1985 and the first Irish store opened in 1991. Domino's Pizza was founded in 1960 by Tom Monaghan, whose original goal was to open three pizza delivery stores hence the three dots on the company's logo. His modest plan grew into something far bigger and more successful than he could have imagined. By franchising his pizza delivery model to like-minded entrepreneurs, Domino's Pizza has become the world leader in pizza delivery and one of the most successful franchise businesses in the world. The company is still growing today with more than 8000 stores in more than 50 international markets.

Domino's Pizza Group (DPG) is a QSR, they are not a fast food restaurant, they are not a takeaway (on average, only 30 per cent of their pizzas orders are collected) and they are not a restaurant (their stores do nt have eat-in facilities). DPG invests a lot of time and money in branding and their marketing activity is financed through a National Advertising Fund (NAF) which is made up of franchisee contributions. They carefully select targeted marketing campaigns that reach their core audience of 18–35 year olds. DPG provide support to franchisees in areas such as information systems, operations training, and marketing. New franchisees take part in a four-week intensive Franchise Development Programme. This training course is designed to equip them with the knowledge and skills that they need to run a successful Domino's Pizza delivery business. The full cost of a new store is approximately £280,000. In 2012, DPG saw profits rise to £23.4 million. The company also announced it had witnessed a broadening customer base with many families ordering pizzas at home. In Ireland, the average branch makes an annual profit of £100,000.

Four Star Pizza 2012

Four Star Pizza was founded in 1981 in Washington, Pennsylvania, a suburb of Pittsburgh, USA by Alan B. Cottrill. In 1986, Four Star Pizza USA opened a model store in Dublin with the intention of selling the Master franchise to an Irish company. The benefits of owning a Four Star Pizza franchise included pizza delivery chain-brand leader and realistic costs, affordable initial investment, and start-up package. Four Star Pizza also offered full franchisee support on customer service, product information, advertising, record-keeping, training, promotion, communication, and day-to-day business operations.

However, in 2012, the company behind the Four Star Pizza sought protection from the High Court from its creditors. Four Star Pizza's parent company, Zowington, was deemed insolvent, unable to pay their debts. The takeaway company owed National Irish Bank €4.9 million and other creditors including suppliers, a printing firm and the Revenue Commissioners. Four Star Pizza currently has 37 outlets in Ireland. However, onerous lease costs have put a strain on franchisees and sales have declined by about 30 per cent in the past three years due to increased competition and heavy price discounting. About 35 people are directly employed by the holding company, with another 400 working in the franchised outlets. In 2012, the latest accounts for Four Star show the holding company made a loss of €83,000.

Kentucky Fried Chicken (KFC) 2012

In 2012, after two unsuccessful attempts to enter the Irish market, KFC made a third attempt, this time backed by a multi-million pound investment programme. KFC plans to build at least 30 new outlets in the Republic over the next four years, two-thirds to be located in Dublin,

> having seen these operations; seen the sales and the return on investment, looked at staffing and all the other issues we are now comfortable that we can make a success of KFC in the Republic

says Kevin Higgins, the business development director at Tricon's UK operation. KFC is likely to face a significant battle for both franchisees and locations, as Ireland's other main fast food/QSR operators are also currently expanding. The company estimates that demographics show the Republic could support 70 outlets. The investment programme will be significant, as a typical outlet set up cost of £500,000 and land costs could add a further £200,000 to each unit. Thirty outlets would require a £21 million investment while building 70 KFCs would cost up to £49 million, not including the cost of a major advertising and marketing campaign. However, KFC has committed to the rollout and is confident in its success.

The Latest Developments in the Fast Food/QSR Industry

The fast food/QSR industry, over recent years, has become dominated by a few large firms. There is a shared view among operators in the market that Ireland's population of 4.6 million (2011 Census), there is a market saturation point of between 70 and 100 outlets per brand. In terms of potential new industry entrants, the single biggest problem has been available retail space, which is slightly easier to obtain during the current recession. Assessing why franchising works so well in fast food/QSR, the resounding two key elements are good margins and branding. It is important to note that consumers choose to differentiate between a Burger King burger and a McDonald's burger which are fundamentally similar products. This perceived differentiation is a testament to the huge influence branding has on this industry. In addition to branding, the product quality and value is very important and the total franchise package appears to work because there are high margins associated with fast food/QSR products sold which contribute to high profits. The fast food/QSR industry came under increased pressure in 2011/2012 with operators competing on value menus and reduced price promotional offers, in addition to the introduction of wider product ranges. Meanwhile, reduced disposable incomes continued to have a negative impact on consumer spending. During 2012, consumers further restricted spending as concerns over Ireland's economy escalated. It appears that Irish tastes and preferences have begun to move away from fast food, which is considered to be less healthy than other food types. However, a look at the global picture shows growth in regions such as Latin American and Asian in fast food/QSR. In these regions, consumers perceive the fast food/QSR offering as relatively healthy.

Ireland's economic downturn is continuing into 2011/2012, with no sign of abating. If anything, as 2011/2012 progressed, the situation worsened as the full extent of the banking crisis became evident and the government floundered under increasing pressure from a disgruntled population, opposition parties, and the EU. Consumer food service operators were not immune to the crisis, as consumers continued to reduce discretionary spending as a result of lower disposable incomes. Businesses continued to suffer high operating costs which further squeezed profit margins, with approximately 80 per cent of restaurants running at a loss. For many operators, 2011 and 2012 have been about adjusting to a new operating environment and accepting that fundamental changes had taken place within the market that will have implications for many years to come. Franchised chains, especially international operators, appear at first glance to be performing well in Ireland. However, on closer inspection there is some evidence that international companies are subsidising their Irish operations. With many operations currently running at a loss, subsidising is necessary to maintain outlet numbers and retain brand presence. The effect on independent operators is a continued decline in numbers as they find themselves unable to compete with the franchised chains due to their high operating costs and reduced revenues and profitability. However, franchising continues to play an important role in the fast food/QSR industry in Ireland as witnessed by the success and brand awareness of popular brands. The success of franchising can be attributed to the strength of a national (or international) brand with the benefits of well-established local knowledge and reputation to respond to smaller local markets, allowing substantial market penetration and increased brand recognition. Today, there has been considerable industry consolidation and the four industry leaders reduced to three in 2008. In 2012, McDonald's, Abrakebabra Investment Limited (AIL), and Supermac's are still industry leaders, followed closely by Burger King, Four Star Pizza, and Domino's. By the end of 2012, McDonald's has been overtaken by Supermac's in terms of the number of outlets it has operating. Abrakebabra became an even greater industry leader with its acquisition of O'Briens, and AIL as a multi-brand has over 191 outlets (Abrakebabra 60, O'Briens 72, Bagel Factory 42 etc.). Faced with intensifying competition from the branded franchised chains, the newly founded Irish Traditional Italian Chipper Association (ITICA) intends to help create a collective identity for the original industry founders, the independent traditional chippers, as they try to collectively ward off competition from the larger franchised chains.

Conclusion

This chapter presented an industry history of the fast food/QSR industry in Ireland. It traced the industry from its emergence pre-1900s, to the first fish and chip shops right through to the wave of international fast food/QSR entrants, and the increases in the competitive landscape. The impact of franchising is addressed and the structural changes that take place once it is introduced are presented. The case follows the story of the industry through the recessionary and boom times and finishes with the overview of the industry today. The next chapter presents the industry history of the Irish real estate industry.

Reference

Walton, J. K. (1989). Fish and chips and the British working class, 1870–1930. *Journal of Social History, 23*(2) (Winter): 243–266. Published by: Peter N. Stearns.

6

Case Study of the Irish Real Estate Industry

Introduction

This chapter presents an industry history of the Irish real estate industry from the beginning of the 1900s to the present day presenting following both firm and industry-level changes over the decades in a chronological account. The historical account is based on primary and secondary data collected from the Irish real estate industry. This case study is presented as a story, tracing the industry from its emergence right through to the introduction of franchising to the present day.

Real Estate Industry

Limiting the case to real estate industry raised the issue of defining it. The Irish real estate sector comprises two segments: residential and commercial property. The majority of Irish real estate agents deal with residential property sales, with only a few expert firms focusing on commercial property. The focus of this study is on real estate agents predominantly trading in the residential property market. In other words, the scope of

© The Author(s) 2017
R. Beere, *The Role of Franchising on Industry Evolution*,
DOI 10.1007/978-3-319-49064-9_6

this case study is mostly limited to domestic (Irish) residential real estate services and leaves out other services, such as commercial property services, mortgage and insurance services, property investments, and online property listing firms.

Irish Real Estate Industry Today

The Irish real estate sector comprises two segments: residential and commercial property. The majority of Irish real estate agents deal with residential property sales, with only a few expert firms focusing on commercial property. In Ireland the commercial property specialists are DTZ Sherry FitzGerald, Douglas Newman Good (DNG), Caldwell Banker, Lisney, Hooke & MacDonald, Knight Frank, and MEPC.

The focus of this study is on real estate agents predominantly trading in the residential property market. There are seven leading residential real estate agents in Ireland, namely Sherry FitzGerald, DNG, RE/MAX, HOK, Gunne, Lisney, and Property Partners (a co-operative organisation based in Galway comprised of independent property real estate agents). However, in recent years, Sherry FitzGerald and DNG have emerged as the two industry leaders, with both firms claiming to hold 60 per cent of the total market share (see Table 6.1). The two firms have a nationwide presence in Ireland, and have grown using franchising as a business model Sherry FitzGerald first introduced franchising to the industry in 1999 pending the imminent threat of entry from the international

Table 6.1 Industry leaders number of outlets 2012

Real estate brand	Number of outlets average size	Annual turnover 2012
Sherry FitzGerald	84 franchises & 14 company-owned	−€15.5 million loss
DNG	90 franchises	
RE/MAX	40 outlets	
Property partners	20 franchises	
HOK (Savills)	5 outlets	
Gunne	5 outlets	
Lisney	6 outlets	

Source: Annual returns and outlet number information was obtained by contact with each company's head office

franchise chain RE/MAX who entered the Irish market in the same year (2004) DNG adopted franchising. Today Sherry FitzGerald claims to hold the number one position in the industry with DNG in second position, based on sales and outlet presence. The industry consists of a large number of small independent real estate agents who have built up a reputation for themselves within their local areas. In recent years, many have become involved in co-operative or network affiliations, such as Property Partners, Real Estate Alliance (REA) Ireland, and Property Team. These co-operative networks have helped independent real estate agents to develop collective marketing campaigns, and share market knowledge, which is vital for success in such a competitive industry.

Since the 1920s, the industry has undergone significant changes, and the number of real estate firms and agents has increased, decade by decade (see Table 6.2) for the industry timeline. However, in recent years, the level of industry competition has intensified dramatically. The industry and firm level growth has always been dictated by economic cycles. In recent years the sector has been adversely affected by the recent economic downturn.

Early Industry Development: Pre and Post 1920s

The Origins of the Real Estate Industry

Company histories show the emergence of the real estate sector in Ireland dating as far back to the beginning of the nineteenth century. Real estate agents (known then as auctioneering firms) have been operating in Ireland since 1815, when the first recorded real estate agent was established to conduct business. The main corpus of legislation relating to real estate can be traced back to Georgian times with the first appraiser's licenses being granted by King George III in 1806. By the 1800s an auctioneer was the individual to undertake the sale of Lands and Estates and auctions were held in coffee houses, Marts, or Auction Rooms. Some of the first established real estate agents in Ireland were based in Dublin; in 1815 Battersby and Co., in 1829 James H. North & Co., in 1847 Ganly and Sons, and in 1887 James Adam and Sons were established.

Table 6.2 Timeline of the Irish real estate industry

1920s	1940s	1970s	1980s	1990s	2000s	2010s
4 leading firms[a]	3 new leaders	IAVI renamed	5 firms dominate	6 firms dominate	3 firms dominate	2 firms dominate
IAA formed	Lisney (1922)	IPAV formed	Lisney, HOK	Lisney, HOK,	Sherry FitzGerald 104[b]	Sherry FitzGerald 98[b]
67 agents	HOK (1928)	Education key	Sherry FitzGerald (1982)	Sherry FitzGerald,	RE/MAX 80[b]	DNG 90[b]
	JacksonStops (1924)		and Gunne (1981)	Gunne, RE/MAX (1999),	PropertyPartners (2000) 60[b]	PropertyPartners 40[b]
	580 agents		DNG (1983)	& DNG	DNG 10[b]	RE/MAX 20[b]
			Mergers occur	Franchising occurs	469 total firms	Lisney 6[b]
					157 Dublin firms	Gunne 5[b]

[a]The four leading firms: Battersby and Co. (1815), James H. North & Co. (1829), Ganly and Sons (1847), and James Adam and Sons (1887)

[b]Number of outlets

Between 1815 and 1900s these agents would have been involved in the sale of a variety of properties including large estates, breweries, distilleries, theatre/cinemas, aerodromes, factories, and government buildings. Many smaller regional real estate agents would also have been involved in selling antiques, cattle, and all manner of livestock, in addition to dead stock such as machinery and furniture. Real estate agents would also have been involved in house lettings, property management, and valuations of many items for probate, family division, loans, mortgages, and so on. Historically, these regional real estate practices were passed down from generation, to generation. No formal qualifications were needed to operate as a real estate agent and the main emphasis was on mentoring and apprenticeships usually in small family-run businesses. In most provincial districts, it was very common that real estate agents were also active farmers, managing day-to-day farming duties. What emerges is a picture of a small industry with many small firms, some over 50 years old.

The First Trade Association—IAA

The twentieth century transformation of Irish real estate determined the industry's structure for the next century. It is around this time that the first signs of industry-level cooperation became evident with real estate agents joining the first industry trade association. The Auctioneers Association of Ireland (IAA) was established in 1922, with the purpose, of bringing a professional identity and unity as well as offering support to real estate agents in Ireland. A striking aspect of the real estate industry in Ireland has been its continuity, with family-run businesses being passed down from one generation to the next. The IAA yearbook provides annual membership listings. Many of the original firms are still operating today, for example Craigie and Ganly in Dublin, Coonan in Kildare, Marsh in Cork, Palmer in Waterford, Armstrong in Kells, McMahon in Ennis, Quirke in Clonmel, and Smith in Navan .

The IAA was focused on establishing educational standards and membership requirements for the association encouraged members to gain qualifications. In many respects, this affected entry requirements into the industry. From the outset the IAA were instrumental in driving forward the industry and influencing incumbent's business conduct. The IAA drew up a scale of fees, as guidelines, applicable to private sales, auction sales, valuations, inventories, and other services—acknowledged by Government departments, courts of law, and the public. In 1925 the IAA was instrumental in improving legislation relating to real estate agents' licenses, and lobbied against unqualified and unprofessional persons being allowed to act as real estate agents. The IAA disapproved of some solicitors who began placing advertisements, offering properties for sale and to let. By the late 1920s, every person, exercising or carrying out trade as a real estate agent was required to hold a license paying the annual duty of excise of £10. Persons acting as house agents were required to take out an annual license and pay a duty of £2. Where two or more agents acted in partnership, each was required to have a separate license. At this time, entry into the major real estate firms was prestigious and young entrants regularly paid an apprenticeship fee (in the 1920s approximately £100, later rising to £300) to secure a position with a leading practice. The apprenticeship period typically lasted for three years, at the end of which membership of the IAA was sought.

A New Era of Growth: 1920–1940

The industry in the late 1920s was dominated by four firms all based in Dublin, Battersby and Co., James H. North & Co., Ganly and Sons, and James Adam and Sons many of which had been trading for over 100 years and were family businesses. Outside of Dublin small independent firms were operating, usually covering a particular region. At the time the IAA recorded 67 registered real estate agents throughout Ireland.

The 1920s triggered a flurry of legislation relating to lands, rents, and property; including the State Lands Act 1924; the State Land Bill 1925; Land (Finance) Rules 1925; the Land Registry Rules 1926; and the Land Act 1926. Section 29 of the Land Act 1927 was of particular importance to real estate agents. It made them personally liable for all arrears due to the Land Commission on any lands let by them. These legislative developments had an enormous impact on economic activity, social change, and the housing market. Larger, more established real estate agency practices operated where population density and housing demand was greater, in the major cities and towns such as Dublin, Cork, Galway, and

Limerick,. In more rural areas, one agent would usually cover a number of local towns, where population density was low.

From the 1930s onwards, the Government set about providing public housing, building 5000 dwellings in Dublin alone, between 1923 and 1930. The Government estimated that a further 18,000 new dwellings were required to meet the capital's housing problem. Reconstruction costs, covering redevelopment of buildings, at the end of the Civil War, were estimated at around £20 million. This period marked a change in home and land ownership, and a new class of homeowner was born. Agricultural lands were suddenly turned into suburban building sites. The population of Dublin and other larger towns were now showing signs of rapid increase, with manufacturers, as well as private citizens beginning to discover the drawbacks of operating in crowded central areas. By the late 1930s, land prices had risen so much that an acre worth £10 in 1926, was offered for sale at £300–500 in 1936.

Real estate agents were quick to adapt to the changing demands of society and during the 1930s began to focus on advertising and customer service. At first, professional photographs of properties for sale would be displayed in the windows of the real estate offices. Additionally, they also began to print property listings in national newspapers. To improve customer service and sale negotiation, many real estate agents began to drive prospective purchasers to inspect a property, accompanied by one of the firm's area supervisors.

Another testament to the increase in housing demand was the growth of Building Societies, who were at the forefront of lending to the new home owners. The most significant increase in the assets of building societies occurred in the 1940s when assets grew from £1.4 to 9.5million.

Industry Power Struggle

Real Estate Agents' 'New Blood'

New entrants to the real estate industry had minimal levels of regulation to adhere to, and limited start-up costs. However, they had to contend with the well-established real estate agents who had built up a brand name and reputation in their area of operation.

From the 1940s onwards, the IAA focused on education. In 1943 a six-month professional course was introduced by the City of Dublin Vocational Education Committee for aspiring real estate agents, which was taught at Bolton Street Institute of Technology. The course was based on the syllabus of the auctioneers & real estate agents Institute of the UK.

According to IAA records, real estate agent numbers doubled from 1940 to 1950 giving a total of over 500 real estate agents operating in Ireland. After the war, the sector benefited from the release of pent up demand in house sale activity. During this time the real estate industry prospered, and in addition to new firms, partnerships and mergers were taking place. By the end of the 1940s the four firms who had previously dominated the industry were swept aside and three new Dublin-based firms quickly became industry leaders: Lisney's, HOK and Jackson Stops McCabe. All three were leading with sales and employee numbers of 20 or more. The three new firms emerged as more flexible and efficient compared with the industry incumbents, and contributed to the climate for change in the sector.

Lisney

Lisney was founded, in 1922 as Franks & Franks. The company specialised in real estate management, and operated from offices at number 23 St Stephen's Green. In 1932, Harry Lisney took over the firm, and subsequently changed the name to, Harry Lisney & Company. At that time the business was a small valuation practice. By the 1940s the business had become one of the most highly respected estate agencies in Ireland. In 1964 there were a total of 30 employees and the company later moved to the larger premises at No. 24 St. Stephens Green.

Hamilton Osborne King

In the late 1920s Osborne King & Megan, was a commercial property consultancy firm, based in Belfast, associated with a UK private partnership of chartered surveyors. It was among the oldest firms of its kind in Ireland. Hamilton Osborne King was founded in 1942, under the name of Hamilton & Hamilton and located at No. 17 Dawson Street. In 1947, James Osborne King took over his father's firm and formed Osborne King and Megan with Jervis Megan. The company offered a full range of property services to both public and private sectors. Known mostly for its public sector work and contracts in defence, county councils, government offices, and educational facilities. Over the years, the firm has changed names frequently, for example Osborne King & Megan, J Trevor & Sons, Hamilton Osborne King & Osborne King.

Jackson Stops & McCabe

In 1908, at the age of 24, Herbert Jackson Stops opened an office in Towcester Town Hall, a village in the UK. Initially Jackson Stops practiced as an auctioneer, holding weekly livestock auctions. In 1924, he decided to open an office in London's Mayfair, not satisfied with expanding in the UK, Jackson Stops had a desire to develop an international business. Two of his London team, John McCabe and Owen Sebag Montefoire established an associate firm in Dublin called Jackson Stops & McCabe. They operated at No. 35 Kildare Street, Dublin 2. The two businesses never had a written agreement and continued to have a close co-operative relationship.

Prosperous Times: Industry Growth 1950–1970

Between 1954 and 1961 fundamental changes took place, influenced mainly by a shift in national economic policy from protectionism to export-led growth, promoting increased industry competition, and efficiency. During the 1950s the Irish pace of life quickened discernibly. A post-war building drive led to cities expanding their boundaries into the rural countryside. Dublin led the way, with its peripheral expansion continuing from Howth to Killiney. The Government helped foster economic growth, leading to increased prosperity and increased demand for residential housing and commercial property. Public and private housing areas developed separately, driving an invisible social wedge between the classes. Residential flats and office buildings were now beginning to be viewed as lucrative property investments, and white collar employment, such as office jobs, rose to 40 per cent in 1960s. Therefore Ireland entered the 1960s, looking forward to more prosperous times.

Property Boom

The 1960s marked a period of economic expansion after years of static growth, leading to Ireland's first ever 'property boom'. In terms of industry structure things remained stable with Lisney, HOK, and Jackson Stops McCabe continuing to lead the industry. A steady stream of new entrants into the industry was sustained but none making any significant impact. Demand for housing continued as rural workers moved to the cities in search of new opportunities and urban populations grew more rapidly. As a result, between 1961 and 1971 employment in agriculture fell by 28 per cent. A more affluent society provided opportunities for new retail developments as international influences began to percolate through to Irish consumers. By the end of the decade, two property companies were quoted on the Ireland Stock Market (ISEQ), namely Associated Properties and Dublin Artisan Dwellings.

Strategies promoting economic expansion and urban development rejuvenated the building and property sectors. Regional development stimulated considerable commercial building activity, while tax incentives encouraged private sector housing and commercial development. All of this spurred growth in the real estate industry. The 1963 Planning & Development Act was a major landmark, laying the foundations for the modern commercial property industry in Ireland. As a result, a new office property era dawned in Dublin and demand for industrial space rose significantly. Purpose built office blocks, commercial investment properties, and the wider availability of development finance, presented unprecedented challenges, together with corresponding opportunities. In 1966 the Stillorgan Shopping Centre was built. It was the first planned suburban shopping development in the Republic and cost £1.5 million to build. The project was managed by the commercial property firm Marine Environment Protection Committee (MEPC). During the period 1966–1990, 51 planned shopping developments opened for trade in Dublin alone. Three new suburban towns were also created in West Dublin—Tallaght, Blanchardstown, and Clondalkin. These were intended to rehouse and improve the lives of inner city dwellers. However, in many cases, they merely transplanted social problems into suburban ghettos.

As a result of all of these developments new commercial property agents began to emerge and some incumbents set up commercial property subsidiaries or departments within their organisations to capitalise on such growth. Numbers of residential property real estate also began setting up offices and some located in the newly developed West Dublin to aid the selling of properties in this locale. Independent real estate agents numbers continued to rise and during the 1960s reached the 1000 mark according to the IAA records.

Building Societies

Building societies also grew to become a major force in the 1960s and 1970s. Building societies operated as financial institutions, owned by their members. They offered banking and related financial services, specialising in mortgage lending. In 1989 the introduction of the Building Societies Act, which granted the building societies the power to engage in banking transactions, dramatically changed their status by allowing them to extend credit for non-housing purposes and provide payment facilities and a wide range of financial services.

The term 'building society' first arose in the eighteenth century in Great Britain, from co-operative savings groups. Five Building Societies, in particular became prominent in the Irish mortgage lending sector, these were Irish Nationwide Building Society, First Active, Irish Permanent, EBS Building Society, ICS Building Society, and Irish Life Building Society.

Irish Nationwide Building Society, established in 1873, was one of Ireland's oldest financial institutions and was originally called the Irish Industrial Building Society. In 1975, it had just five staff and changed its name to Irish Nationwide Building Society. First Active was founded in Dublin in 1861 as the Workingman's Benefit Building Society, by a small group of skilled tradesmen. The Society's members, many of whom were railway workers, subscribed for shares, and their regular deposits were used to make house purchase loans. In 1875, when the Society had more than 200 members, it was incorporated under the Building Societies Act 1874. In 2003 First Active plc, Ireland's oldest building society, was acquired by Ulster bank and continued to operate as a separate brand. Irish Permanent, founded as the Irish Temperance Permanent Benefit Building Society established in 1884, changed its name to Irish Permanent Building Society in 1940. EBS Building Society was founded in 1935 by teachers to provide affordable housing finance for teachers and other civil servants. ICS Building Society first opened for subscriptions on 2 June 1864 gaining a reputation for financial strength, customer service and innovation. In 1984 ICS became part of Bank of Ireland Group. ICS Building Society launched the first Mortgage Store in 1989, with the opening of their Grafton Street premises. The objective of the store was to provide a fresh alternative to the traditional mortgage experience offered by banks and building societies. In 1939 Irish Life Assurance Incorporated was established, as part of the amalgamation of nine British and Irish life assurance companies. The Minister for Finance held 18 per cent of the shares of the company, and in 1979 it rebranded as the Irish Life Building Society.

With Building Societies offering mortgages and finance for property purchases and property investment, this fuelled the demand for properties for sale. These developments significantly influenced the competitiveness of the Irish real estate industry.

Industry Expansion—Branding and Operational Efficiency

From the early 1960s, the range of real estate agents services increased, the differences between real estate agents blurred, and profit margins within the industry compressed, thus reducing the barriers to entry and increasing competition. During the 1960s, economic growth paved the way for real estate agents to grow and prosper, particularly in the Dublin region. New office blocks, suburban Shopping Centres, and satellite towns, were being developed. With the increase in housing demand and supply, real estate agents services were in demand more than ever before. To differentiate themselves in an increasingly competitive landscape, they needed to focus on building a reputation and brand, marketing their services, listing properties, and improving customer service. Many of the agents who were established before the 1950s began to witness enormous growth and needed to respond quickly to capture this demand. Change was predominately centred in the Dublin area. In the regional areas one agent covering a few small towns, remained largely unchanged.

Industry Consolidation: 1970–1980

In 1970, the IAA increased membership requirements, allowing entry only to those with a recognised qualification. As a result of the Irish Auctioneers and Valuers Institute (IAVI)'s restrictions, a new trade association called the IPAV (the Institute of Professional Auctioneers, Valuers, and Livestock Salesmen) was formed in 1971. This was specifically set up for non-IAA members, and was, subsequently renamed, the Institute of Professional Auctioneers and Valuers (IPAV). Its membership comprised of smaller real estate agents in rural locations. As a consequence of the IPAV's formation in 1971, the IAA was renamed the IAVI—Irish Auctioneers and Valuers Institute with 698 members and 47 students.

The Dublin-based Lisney, HOK and Jackson Stops McCabe were still leading the industry in terms of sales and market share with the rest of the industry represented by small geographically spread independent estate agents. Changes in the industry since the 1940s had not been dramatic, with firms developing their service offerings and consolidating their positions. Despite entries and exits the basic methods of trading remained the same.

Regulation—Growing Concern

In 1973 The National Prices Commission conducted a study, investigating the charges accruing to the real estate profession. The report was opposed by both the IPAV and the IAVI. The report compiled a full list of licensed real estate agents; it revealed that there were a total of 1649 real estate licenses granted with 139 licenses in Dublin 1 & 2 districts. This figure having grown steadily since the 1950s directly reflected the upturn in the economy, in addition to the lucrative level of fees charged at the time. Not all licensed real estate agents dealt in property; some were dealers in livestock or food. To obtain a real estate license, an annual excise duty of £10 was required, as well as an insurance bond. The report identified the three main ways to sell a property in Ireland: by auction, by private treaty, or by tender. The report noted that the presence of a high number of auction sales was unique in Ireland. At the time 50 per cent of Dublin residential properties were sold by auction.

However, stamp duty, a major government duty, was about to be introduced. This would prove to be disadvantageous for real estate agents. A period of heated debate followed with a spotlight being shone on the industry, specifically real estate agents, their prices and overall professionalism. It was a time when numbers grew in the industry's trade associations and it appeared that real estate agents valued the work the associations had achieved in managing the industry's public relations.

Recession: New Focus—Image, Branding and Efficiency

The 1980s was a period when the property market plummeted. The period brought many entries, exits, and acquisitions. A number of established players grew through acquisitions and new ventures, creating the need for more professional management. Recession ensued from 1981 to 1985, and brought with it emigration. As a result there was a flood of second-hand housing on the market and a diminishing demand for new housing. The Economist magazine in 1988, called Ireland the 'Poorest of the Rich'. The average house price at this time was IR£50,000 in a contracting property market.

For the first time since the 1940s the real estate industry was to undergo dramatic change. The recession had an adverse effect on the real estate industry. Many real estate agents closed down and ceased to trade. A number of key mergers and acquisitions occurred in order to pool resources, spread costs, and create brand awareness as a method of survival. A merger resulting in the formation of HOK took place. At the time HOK, Lisney, and Jackson Stops McCabe, were still the leaders in the industry. However, during the early 1980s three new entrants to the industry were about to change industry dynamics and become the new generation of leaders. Gunne (1981), Sherry FitzGerald (1982) and Douglas Newman Good (DNG) (1983) were established, and emerged as a new breed of real estate agents, highly ambitious, focused on growth with a new survival tactic, capturing economies of scale with nationwide expansion. By the end of the 1980s competition in the real estate industry was high. There was a distinct increased emphasis on firm branding and marketing by the new entrants that dramatically altered the industry's playing field. Marketing and promotional expenditure in the industry, across all three leading firms, totalled £15 million in 1988; this constituted an enormous amount for advertising at that time, not previously witnessed.

Emergence of a Few Dominating Firms: 1980–1990

Increasing Competition

In the 1980s efforts to differentiate from the competition resulted in firm level investment in developing stronger brands and market identities and a new breed of entrants appeared to set the pace in terms of this development.

Gunne Founded 1981

Gunne was originally established in Monaghan in 1950 by P.B. Gunne. He operated a successful cattle market business, and expanded into Carrickmacross in 1956. Widening his horizons into real estate, Gunne opened a branch in Dundalk in 1964. It was not until 1981 that Gunne opened in Dublin. By 1987, the firm had established itself as a competitive force, as a nationally operating real estate agency. Within 15 years the company ranked in the top four estate agencies in the country.

Sherry FitzGerald Founded 1982

In 1982 two companies amalgamated, FitzGerald & Partners (founded in 1972) and Sherry & Sons (founded in 1949). During this difficult economic decade, the company recruited a team of young property professionals, with a gender-balanced business philosophy. Sherry FitzGerald's business opened a second branch in 1989, in Terenure, Dublin. The firm targeted the middle market in residential sales, becoming successful in the early 1990s as the housing market prospered. They opened eight new branches across Dublin (Drumcondra, Dun Laoghaire, Dundrum, Sutton, Bray, Lucan, Killester, and Templeogue). Moreover, in 1992, Sherry FitzGerald launched their Dublin house price index, and became the first entity outside of the Department of the Environment to provide any coherent house price information to the general public. In 1998 Sherry FitzGerald, opened its first branch outside Dublin, in Galway, and in the same year launched one of the first property websites, SherryFitz. ie. Sherry FitzGerald, formed a joint venture with the global property advisory firm DTZ Holdings, and became DTZ Sherry FitzGerald. At its peak in the late 1990s DTZ Sherry FitzGerald had over 150 employees.

Douglas Newman Good (DNG) Founded 1983

Douglas Newman Good (DNG) was founded in 1983, and initially focused on the Dublin market. The company grew quickly and became the largest sellers of residential property in the Greater Dublin area, with 20 per cent of the market share.

Hamilton Osborne King (HOK)

In 1987 two of the largest real estate firms—Hamilton & Hamilton and Osborne King and Megran merged to form Hamilton Osborne King.

The newly merged agency, HOK, grew and expanded rapidly with a focus on selling large country estates and auctioning the contents of these houses, including furniture and paintings.

The End of the 1980s Recession—1990 Onwards

In 1989, the Building Societies Act authorised building societies to extend their product range; thus, allowing them to compete more effectively with the banking industry. As a result, lending for home ownership and property investment became more widely available. The 1990s brought with it the emergence of franchising as a growth model for a number of industry incumbents. Overall the industry witnessed a few large firms who began to dominate and competition among independent real estate agents increased. International real estate agents began to enter the market as a property boom began. The population of Ireland had increased to a total of 3.6 million, with unemployment at an all-time low. Population density changed, with more people moving back into Dublin's City Centre. The new Dublin road network had a significant impact on residential housing and increased the demand for housing in the west of Dublin city. By the end of the 1980s and the beginning of the 1990s five Dublin-based firms strengthened their positions as leaders in the industry: Lisney, HOK, Gunne, Sherry FitzGerald and DNG.

The 1990s saw over four-fifths of Irish households living in owner-occupied accommodation, one of the highest rates in the world. The Economist in late 1997 published an article: 'The Celtic Tiger: Europe's shining light'. By the end of 1997, the average home price had jumped to over €93,000 (from €50,000 in 1988). A total of 30,575 new houses were completed during 1995, almost double the 1988 level, with many suburban houses selling from £1 to 3 million. Hooke & MacDonald, already successful in commercial property (established in 1967 and headed by Ken MacDonald), was the first estate agency to specialise in apartment sales, thus carving out a lucrative company niche. Additionally, during the 1990s the Irish populace became aware of investment opportunities, buying and selling property abroad. Thus property investment, both domestic and foreign, began on a large scale. Moreover, the government introduced property investment legislation with Section 23 and Section 29, which encouraged such investment. Another initiative was driven by the Irish Government which stimulated industry and employment and encouraged international financial firms to locate to the newly developed Irish Financial Services Centre (IFSC) in Dublin's city centre. In 1996 it was acclaimed as the fastest growing Off-Shore Fund Centre in Europe, with some 400 companies located there.

During this time Information Technology became important to the real estate industry. The leading, Dublin-based real estate agents began adopting IT systems and developing their own company websites. The first Irish property sold having been featured on the internet was by HOK in 1996. This technology utilisation would change the face of real estate forever, in terms of increasing operating efficiencies and consumer access to property information. Many older regional firms were to be left behind in terms of technology adoption and it was a race to see who would lead in terms of internet adoption and exposure. Three of the industry's leading firms believed that the internet was the way forward. To such an extent that they bought into what would be the first successful Irish property listings website, www.myhome.ie (which at its peak had over 8500 real estate agents listing properties). The main stakeholders were Sherry FitzGerald (23.5 per cent stake), Gunne (19 per cent) and DNG (19 per cent) and the AIB Group (18 per cent stake) with CEO Jim Miley owning 10 of the website. Myhome.ie would ultimately be sold in 2006 to the Irish Times for €50 million.

Industry Competition Increases

By 1995 the number of Irish real estate firms was reaching over 300 nationwide. The industry was changing once again, with increased market growth and increased residential sales this encouraged new entrants into the industry and in particular international competitors were attracted to the Irish market. The number of real estate agents expanded considerably, but mostly at the smaller end of the scale. Unambiguous statistics on changes since the early 1980s are not available, but information from industry sources suggests that the number of firms changed substantially since the 1980s. While turnovers would undoubtedly have increased, size distribution would be unlikely to have changed since then.

From 1995 onwards the housing boom resulted in an unprecedented increase in apartment developments. In 1996, according to The Irish Times, the four biggest Dublin residential sales agencies were Sherry FitzGerald, DNG, HOK and Gunne, handling 71 per cent of the 1221 auctions for that year. The top five firms in the late 1990s, according to Business & Finance were, in alphabetical order: Gunne, Hamiltion Osbourne King, Jones Lang Wooton, Lisney and Sherry FitzGerald. Each of these firms also operated substantial commercial property operations. However, Jones Lang Wooton claimed to be the only specialist firm, involved exclusively in commercial property. In 1996 The Property Valuer magazine stated:

> In agency terms the market has undoubtedly become more competitive, though the names of the key firms have changed little. Some medium-sized firms may be finding it more difficult to prosper in an environment where specialisation is the norm for both small niche firms as well as the larger firms.

A study carried out by David McKenna, in the late 1990s, on the Property Service Industry (PSI) shows that, both in volume and value terms, real estate agents were disproportionately concentrated in Dublin. Small practices outside of Dublin, would find it virtually impossible to compete for property services within the Dublin region. During the property boom, real estate agents were challenged to stay informed of changing legislation and practices, as new trends were emerging. They needed to focus on creating market specialisation in order to prosper in such an increasingly competitive environment.

Industry Change: The Introduction & Emergence of Franchising

By the end of the 1990s five firms were leading the industry: Sherry FitzGerald, DNG, Gunne, Lisney and HOK. During this time one of the most important events in the Irish real estate industry was the introduction of franchising as an organisational structure by Sherry FitzGerald in 1999. Sherry FitzGerald began to use franchising as a means to expand nationwide and to build a brand that would be recognisable outside of Dublin. At the same time, in 1999 the industry was exposed for the first time to international competition in the form of the American international real estate RE/MAX, which used franchising exclusively as a growth model. RE/MAX was also unique as it allowing unqualified agents set up RE/MAX real estate franchises, a practice frowned upon in Ireland, but internationally it was quite commonplace. At the time many industry sceptics, including the two trade associations, questioned whether franchising was appropriate for the Irish real estate industry, but no-one could deny the success US based franchise systems like RE/MAX had experienced on a global scale.

1999 Sherry FitzGerald Begins to Franchise

In 1999 Sherry FitzGerald became Ireland's first ever, property franchisor. The company's first franchisee was real estate agent McMahon Estate Agents, already operating in Ennis and Shannon. In the same year, Sherry FitzGerald was listed on the Dublin Stock Exchange, which helped raise the required capital to pursue a national expansion strategy. Shortly after flotation, the Group acquired the Ross McParland New Homes business, Ireland's most successful new homes specialist, later rebranded Sherry FitzGerald New Homes. Sherry FitzGerald also opened offices in Cork, Limerick, Castleknock, and Swords.

Sherry FitzGerald embarked upon the franchising process because they saw the potential in nationwide growth. The company had already opened offices in Galway, Limerick, and Cork. In a branded market place, Sherry FitzGerald understood that branding was a way to add value to their franchising model. The company had 15 years of brand building experience and they recognised that they could transfer their operating systems and leverage their brand nationwide. However, it became clear how important having a local real estate agent, with local knowledge, was in operating their regional branches. Customers wanted everything a big brand could give them, but they also wanted to deal with local personalities they could trust. Thus franchising as a growth strategy offered this advantage. Sherry FitzGerald were very aware that international property franchise systems were looking to enter the booming Irish property market,

'we knew they (RE/MAX) were coming but we knew an Irish brand was going to win out over an international brand', according to Triona Gorman.

Sherry FitzGerald believed that they had first mover advantage as customers recognised and trusted their brand and they planned to capitalise on this lead. Philip Sherry (MD of Sherry FitzGerald) travelled throughout Ireland visiting every town looking for potential franchisees. He and his team compiled a dossier on all the possible agents, the biggest agents in each town were not necessarily their targets, and instead they wanted,

'Like-minded professionals with a willingness to change for the future and for the better' said, Philip Sherry (MD of Sherry FitzGerald).

Post market research, they could design a franchise package, and sought the expertise of an international franchise consultancy firm known as Howarth. This expert firm which helped them to draw up their franchise agreement; and also helped them understand how best to manage potential franchisees. This was an entirely new operational strategy for the company, requiring different skills and knowledge. By April 1999 the company had 11 franchisees with 13 offices. By 2007 they had reached the 100th franchisee outlet, which they believed was the saturation point in terms of the Irish market. Sherry FitzGerald claims that they could have expanded organically, but they would not have had the capital to fully penetrate the market to the level of 100 outlets in eight years;

Ultimately it just wouldn't have been cost effective to have over a hundred offices all around the country, trying to manage each office separately.

Sherry FitzGerald has a strict and formalised approach to monitoring their franchisees in relation to standards of service and operations. They organised mystery shopper programmes and customer service satisfaction surveys. Sherry FitzGerald has also had a number of business development managers who would visit each franchisee regularly,

'To make sure the office is looking well, that they are trading properly', says Triona Gorman.

The company had an awards system for ranking the best performing franchisees. Some of the problems encountered in the earlier years were mostly franchisees not adhering to their branding guidelines. One of the biggest challenges they faced was making sure all franchisees used the brand name consistency across their systems, on all promotional items, to ensure brand uniformity.

Once a franchisee had signed their franchise agreement, Sherry FitzGerald's offered training by its full-time training and development department. The training covered all aspects relating to their property business, such as sales, marketing, strategic planning, HR, and information technology systems. They were the only real estate franchisor with a HR training centre. In addition, Sherry FitzGerald also recognised, earlier than most, that consumers were using the internet to access property information. Sherry FitzGerald offered their clients two of the most successful property websites in Ireland, sherryFitz.ie and myhome.ie. Sherry FitzGerald, as a franchisor, also offered property advisory services throughout Ireland, in residential, commercial and overseas markets, mortgages, and investments. Additionally, they had a full-time research department which provided up to date market trends and forecasts. Franchisees benefited from this huge pool of property expertise. Furthermore, there was an international dimension to Sherry FitzGerald, which franchisees had access to, via their commercial partner DTZ, and their property investment and fund management partner, Signature Capital. Sherry FitzGerald's London residential business, Marsh & Parsons, also provided an opportunity to promote franchisee's properties to an audience outside Ireland.

One Sherry FitzGerald franchisee, Sean Daly, founded his original real estate and financial services business in 1977. The directors felt that joining the Sherry FitzGerald franchise would offer them access to a recognised brand and a property network of over 100 Sherry FitzGerald offices, in which to market their local properties. Another franchisee began trading as Rainey Estate Agents, in Letterkenny, in 1958. The founder, Dermot Rainey Snr originally operated his real estate business in conjunction with long established furniture and hardware business. In 1980 the firm decided to concentrate exclusively on the real estate business. In 1999 the firm recognised the importance of having a link with a national brand name became a franchisee of Sherry FitzGerald. Tony Kavanagh a franchisee based in Galway says,

> Our intention was to continue to lead the market in Galway city, to provide a quality service and deliver real value for money to our customers. Sherry FitzGerald helped us focus on the customer and their needs.

1999 RE/MAX Enters the Irish Market

RE/MAX entered the Irish market in 1999. According to RE/MAX, branding and exceptional levels of client care have differentiated them from their competitors. In terms of branding, the RE/MAX hot air balloon logo, one of the world's 13th most recognised brand. RE/MAX Ireland was founded in 1998 by Dennis Curtin and Tamara Libbey. Dennis Curtin was the first RE/MAX franchisee in the USA, opening his Kansas City franchise in 1975. Tamara Libbey specialised in the area of business planning, sales promotion and training and began working from the beginning. Ireland was considered a RE/MAX region, and Mark Campbell was the Irish Regional Director based in Dublin with a support team and Franchise Sales Consultants nationwide. In 1999 RE/MAX opened its first franchise office in Wicklow and by 2000 had ten outlets located in Dublin, Kildare, Port Laoise, Limerick, Athlone, and Roscommon. In 2002, RE/MAX had achieved rapid growth and had opened over 60 offices across Ireland. In 2009 RE/MAX Ireland had over 80 agents, and had a target of expanding to 120 franchisees. However, the company was forced to close or amalgamate a number of its offices, as a result of the downturn in the property market due to the 2008 recession.

Initially the group began recruiting franchisees by targeting small to medium-sized Irish practices. In some cases agents approached RE/MAX directly. RE/MAX preferred that their franchisees were already operating as real estate agents, and also preferred members of recognised trade associations, either the IVAI or the IPAV, they did make exceptions to this rule. RE/MAX claimed their franchisees and Associates were the best trained, most motivated, and most client-focused in the industry. Every RE/MAX franchise office was independently owned and operated. RE/MAX representatives received mentoring, coaching, training, and technological and marketing support from RE/MAX. The company's services were always supported by 'hi-tech' sales and information systems (putting properties on a world-wide network, and including automatic language translation). The company has always invested heavily in IT and training. RE/MAX always insisted that franchisees adhered to brand uniformity and used standardised processes and procedures such as letter and contract templates. The cost of buying a RE/MAX franchise was €10,000 for a rural firm, and €15,000 for an urban firm. RE/MAX operated on the basis that each franchise office would cost €10,000 and that 10 real estate agents could rent a desk, splitting the overhead costs between them. RE/MAX franchisees would work on 9 per cent of commission income. According to Mark Campbell he believed that,

> we were the ones with a real franchise system in Ireland.

RE/MAX always tried to help franchisees build a business. Some individuals who became RE/MAX franchisees, were not qualified real estate agents,

> we had everybody from bank managers to school teachers.

John Fogarty, a franchisee with offices in Waterford, Tramore, and Carlow previously traded as part of the Property Partners group believed that new franchisees would come from independent small firms operating in both cities and towns. He cited branding as the reason for becoming a RE/MAX franchisee.

> 'RE/MAX's cost model allowed them to operate on a lower cost base than an independent office', said John Fogarty.

Fogarty said he had already had several approaches about joining from independent agents as well as some presently in a group practice.

Property Partners Founded in 2000

As a result of increased competition in the industry, Property Partners was established in 2000 as a co-operative of National Property Consultants. They claimed to provide an unrivalled service, by utilising the strength of their network of offices throughout Ireland. Each office, within the co-op, would run as an independent real estate agency, yet would benefit from a pool of property information, marketing collateral, and nationwide reach. The affiliated agents promote the Property Partners brand and represent professionalism and quality of service. This is backed by a strict code of practice, bespoke property marketing tools and service excellence. With 150 property professionals nationwide, Property Partners have their head office located in Galway. The co-op has always been recognised as a leading player in the Irish property market. Continuously offering professional development programmes to monitor and enhance their service levels, and the skills of all their negotiators.

Emergence of the Celtic Tiger

The late 1990s saw the beginnings of the Irish economic boom referred to as the 'Celtic Tiger', which was fuelled by an unprecedented property boom. Established agents prospered and grew quickly, and new entrants were vying to enter into the profitable market. Competition increased among the industry leaders: Sherry FitzGerald, DNG, HOK, RE/MAX, Lisney, and Gunne. The industry had been transformed. These industry leaders had propelled it to higher levels of efficiency and professionalism, and many of the older players had been relegated to a significantly reduced market share. Up until the emergence of franchising in 1999, most real estate agents had traded in their local area, building up a local client base. After the introduction of franchising, the Dublin-based operators began to focus on national growth. Franchising was the favoured growth model for both Sherry FitzGerald and RE/MAX. It offered branding, operational efficiencies, and was a successful growth accelerator in what was a highly competitive industry. Franchising could accomplish company growth, at a fast pace, and with maximum brand impact. In 2000, according to Business and Finance, the top real estate agents and spenders, in press advertising were Sherry FitzGerald IR£8,419,990, DNG IR£1,782,980, and HOK IR£5,003,460 (Source IAPI Advertising Spend).

However, there were a number of key differences in the real estate adoption of the franchise model. First, the majority of their franchisees were mostly conversions of existing real estate businesses, rather than new startups. RE/MAX; however, had initially recruited both qualified and unqualified real estate agents. Second, the franchisor's brand name could be used alongside the established franchisee's trading name. Finally franchisees were able to offer 'Speed to Market' and 'Superior Service Delivery' by replicating franchisor methods in every transaction, such as, standard signage, accounting systems, client relationship management, and data management.

One issue arising at this time was the increasing tension between the trade associations and the franchise systems. The IAVI initially disapproved of RE/MAX's entry into Ireland, objecting to unqualified agents becoming real estate franchisees under the RE/MAX brand. The IAVI began lobbying for government intervention, in the form of increased industry regulation. This would take another ten years to occur.

Managing New Challenges

By the mid-2000s it was clear that in order to compete and secure a leading position in the real estate industry, firms would have to focus more on creating efficiencies and also concentrate on building their brands. The industry leaders were lean and competitive, finding opportunities in the nationwide expansions, brand building and the complacency of incumbents. The older incumbents faced serious problems, including a diminished position in the industry, poor brand and reputational image, and obsolete technology usage. Specialists emerged to serve both residential and commercial customer categories, with further specialisation in the residential sector between sales and rental, and apartment and house categories.

2004 DNG Begins to Franchise

The Douglas Newman Good (DNG) Group adopted franchising much later than their competitors. Founded in 1983, the company had consistently been the largest residential property agency in the Greater Dublin area. In 2004 the company embarked on a franchise-lead growth strategy, and within a short period of time had become the second largest franchise network in Ireland, second only to Sherry FitzGerald. DNG rebranded and became DNG Nationwide and initiated a national franchise expansion strategy. By 2007, the company had 88 branded offices nationwide, supported by teams of marketing, technology, and property specialists. DNG franchise system focused on providing a first class service, by ensuring stringent standards, professionalism & expertise— qualities that DNG claimed all their nationwide franchisees possessed. The company had ambitions to grow rapidly, but had difficulty achieving organic growth. According to CEO Keith Lowe,

> We realised we had to franchise to help us grow quickly because if we didn't, we believed we would get left behind and our competitors would pass us out.

In 2004 DNG believed that franchising was the appropriate method of national growth. They were eager to compete with Sherry FitzGerald, the largest franchise operator in the real estate industry. In 2004 DNG's aim was to overtake Sherry FitzGerald as the number one leader in Ireland. At the time Sherry FitzGerald had 90 offices nationally. Property Partners at that time occupied the number two spot, with nearly 70 branches. In 2005 DNG CEO Keith Lowe, had sales of over €2 billion that year. Even before adopting franchising, DNG's business had been increasing by 15 per cent through its Dublin offices, indicating a very buoyant market. During this period the company also spent heavily on advertising, marketing and branding. DNG always supported their franchisees' businesses by working closely with them on branding, administration systems, local marketing advice, and human resource training. One of the key competitive advantages they could offer their franchisees was access to a strategic alliance with GMC Nationwide, the second largest mortgage retail broker in Ireland. This helped their franchisees develop mortgage income for their businesses. Franchisees, also had access to DNG sales and management training programmes as well as DNG's Property Research Department. In terms of branding, the company focused heavily on developing a website, media, and print tools to drive the brand forward. DNG approached a franchising expert Michael Glynn, who had helped Sherry FitzGerald establish their franchising network. Glynn was happy to oversee technology investment and mortgage marketing. DNG senior partner Tony Forte oversaw the franchisee recruitment and management side of the operation. However, when converting agents to the DNG brand, the most successful number one and number two agents were already operating for the competition. This was a disadvantage to DNG's late adoption of franchising.

During a franchisees' initial set-up stage, DNG provided shop design and planning support, through their creative agency. The DNG operational support manual outlined everything a franchisee needed to know, from start up through to staff training, sales and negotiation, customer care management, team leadership, and information technology. DNG had a training consultant with ten years of property training experience, and franchisees were invited to attend business and property training courses on a regular basis. DNG also made considerable investments in its IT systems. All aspects of the sales process were automated using a system called 'Property Selector' (similar to a Client Relationship Management [CRM] system), to manage data from client's details, client meetings, property valuations, advertising budgets, and fees that might have been discussed with the client. The brochure production system was also automated and used information from the system generating webpages. The strength of this system lies in the fact that it enabled the operator to extract all kinds of information instantly. Data from each branch was uploaded nightly to the firm's head office.

In 2004 DNG already had 20 company-owned branches in the Greater Dublin area, and by 2007 had 65 franchise offices throughout the country. By 2007, DNG had earned over €2 billion in turnover. DNG always supported the trade associations IAVI and IPAV, and its franchisees were members of both. DNG knew their rival, Sherry FitzGerald, were the larger franchise operator. However, DNG have always had the largest Dublin presence, with Sherry FitzGerald having the larger nationwide presence. In fact DNG claimed that, Sherry FitzGerald had been diluting their own market, as within each of their regions had three or four franchisees operating beside each other. In 2005 Thomas Reid joined DNG as a franchisee:

> I was delighted to join one of the leading property franchises in the country.

Reid's Waterford-based estate agency was already firmly established as one of the leading providers of property sales advice and services in Waterford. Reid suggested being part of a larger organisation would only serve to improve his business. The opportunity to join with other equally well placed and respected estate agents across the country would further enhance his offering to clients while still utilising his firm's local knowledge and expertise. Another franchisee based in Cork stated that the benefits of joining DNG were branding and expertise,

> the DNG nationwide franchise network and its customers benefit from significant national and local 'board' presence and selling expertise unsurpassed in Ireland.

The Emergence of Two Industry Leaders

From 2003 onwards, enormous changes were happening in the Irish real estate industry. Ireland was still in the throes of an economic boom, and competition was increasing with seven major real estate agents: Sherry FitzGerald, Douglas Newman Good (DNG), HOK, Gunne, Lisney, Property Partners (Co-op) and RE/MAX dominating the industry. Sherry FitzGerald and RE/MAX had been the two market leaders but in 2004 another firm would compete and vie for joint industry leadership with

Table 6.3 Real estate agents' number of outlets 2004

Real estate brand	Number of outlets
Sherry FitzGerald	90 franchises and 14 company owned
RE/MAX	80 franchises
DNG	10 franchised and 16 company owned
Property partners and property team	60 franchises

Source: Annual returns and outlet number information was obtained by contact with each company's head office

Sherry FitzGerald. DNG adopted a franchise model, to compete with Sherry FitzGerald and RE/MAX, as well as the smaller quasi-groupings such as Property Partners and REA and Property Team, all nationwide co-op networks. By 2004 Sherry FitzGerald had 90 franchised outlets, RE/MAX had 80 franchisees, Property Partners and REA and Property Team in total had approximately 60 offices (see Table 6.3). By 2004 DNG had 16 Dublin offices and 25 franchised outlets.

Franchising a Possible Threat to the Trade Associations?

Initially it would appear that the industry's trade associations viewed franchising as being almost a competitive threat to their existence. However, on closer inspection, this was a more complex issue. The IAVI's CEO claimed,

> We were facing the challenge, of franchising, and some were saying the institute should have been offering services that franchisors were offering.

However, by 2005 the IAVI supported both Sherry FitzGerald and DNG who complied with industry regulations. Moreover, both franchise systems helped to set and maintain high standards of professional practice and conduct, and most of their franchisees were either IAVI or IPAV members. However, the IAVI objected to the RE/MAX model of franchising, as unqualified and unregulated agents were allowed to operate. In some cases, a RE/MAX agent might have two jobs, only working part time as a real estate agent. But the trade association's main issue related to

US franchise's operating procedures, which conflicted with Irish national licensing laws. In certain cases some agents had been obliged, under their franchise contract, to act contrary to Irish agency/contract law.

Government Intervention

The New Regulatory Environment

In line with increasing industry regulation and greater attention to ethical issues, the two industry trade associations introduced an industry-wide voluntary code of conduct. In 2005 the Auctioneering/Estate Agency Review Group was set up to assess and report on the real estate industry. Under the review, the two main Property Services Providers (PSPs) classifications were agency and professional services (including valuations and property management). The property services industry was defined as consisting of the member firms of the IAVI, IPAV and the Society of Chartered Surveyors (SCS). In 2004, the number of real estate licenses was 2103. A total of 469 real estate and surveying firms in Ireland, with 157 practices located in Dublin and 312 located outside of Dublin. In 2004 the SCS had 205 members, the IAVI had 788 members, and the IPAV had a membership of 200 working in the industry. The number of firms under this umbrella principally described themselves as real estate agents, auctioneers, valuers, surveyors, and property consultants. The conditions for obtaining a real estate license were certification of qualification, stating that the candidate was of sound character, a lodgement of €10,000 deposit to the High Court, a tax clearance cert from the tax office, and the license to be taken up within 28 days of receipt of deposit from the High Court. In 2004 a total of 2500 people were employed in Irish property services. The majority of firms had only one outlet, fewer than ten staff and an output of less than €100,000 per annum. With 87 per cent earning less than €250,000 and only a handful earning, in excess of £1 million. In terms of foreign entrants into the industry, the majority of companies were found to be Irish-owned with less than 2 per cent originating outside of Ireland. In ownership terms, the industry was a mix of partnerships, limited companies, and sole traders.

According to the review, housing in Ireland totalled 1,406,000 dwellings in 2004. The Irish population maintained a preference for home ownership, and this coupled with other factors, increased demand for property. In 2004 the Irish property market witnessed the delivery of record house completions, totalling 76,954 houses. As a result of the review the National Property Services Regulatory Authority was established in 2005 as a regulatory authority, to underpin a new regulatory framework governing the auctioneer/real estate sector. The Authority aimed to achieve uniformity and transparency in licensing, regulation and the provision of information for the public. Thus Auctioneers, Real Estate agents, Letting agents, and Property Management agents would all be regulated by the new Authority.

The Property Bubble Bursts

The Irish property bubble began in 2000 and peaked in 2006. According to the Economist, by 2006, the average price had soared to €311,000 (from €50,000 in 1988 and €93,000 in 1997). However, by September 2009 average prices were down to €232,500 and were continuing to fall. The economy slowed and large numbers of migrant workers, previously employed in construction and hospitality sectors, began returning home. This lowered demand for rental properties, leaving lower returns and high inventories. Rent prices fell by up to 30 per cent. Many property developers went bust, leaving newly built developments vacant or half built. Lending to builders and developers had comprised roughly 28 per cent of all banks' lending which left the banking system unstable as Banks were calling in loans and developers were going into receivership.

Industry Competition: New Structure

Ireland's economic bubble burst during 2008. By the second quarter of 2012, house prices had fallen by 35 per cent, compared with the second quarter of 2007, and the number of housing loans approved, fell by 73 per cent. The fall in domestic and commercial property prices contributed to the Irish banking crisis. As of first quarter of 2012, prices continue to fall. In 2012, of the 1200 real estate agents, approximately 470 were in franchise or quasi-franchise groupings. Although only 30 per cent of these firms had over 75 per cent of the total market share.

Sherry FitzGerald 2012

In 2012, Sherry FitzGerald had 84 franchised offices and 14 company-owned offices, coupled with 14 offices in London. Sherry FitzGerald claimed to account for over 20 per cent of the total industry market share. However, due to the economic recession, the company initiated a significant cost-cutting programme during 2008. Total staff numbers fell from 476 in 2007 to 202 in December 2012. Sherry FitzGerald made a pre-tax loss of €15.5 million in 2008, a year it described as 'exceptionally difficult and challenging'. Turnover for 2008 was €39.97 million, down from €64.95 million the previous year, 'when pre-tax losses were €3.79 million'.

DNG 2012

In 2012 DNG's aim was still to overtake Sherry FitzGerald, as the number one industry leader in Ireland. In 2012 DNG had 60 offices, and Property Partners occupied the number three spot, with nearly 40 branches.

> Like any industry, the real estate business is consolidating', said Lowe. 'As the big brands become stronger, it will become more difficult for the smaller operator to survive.

The company was spending heavily on advertising, marketing, and branding. Lowe claimed that in the UK, the public perception of estate agents is unfavourable.

> In Ireland, there is a much more professional and ethical code to agencies, however this has changed in recent years with people allowed to open up business, with no qualifications, simply appearing in court, to get a license.

All DNG agents were qualified and were members of either the IAVI or IPAV. Lowe claimed than in the current downturn, having a solid reputation, a respected brand and high levels of service would help DNG to survive.

Property Partners 2012

The Property Partners Real Estate Group was established as an independently owned real estate group, with more than 40 offices nationwide. Founded in 2000, Property Partners was established as a co-operative of National Property Consultants. Property Partners claimed that by listening to their customers and responding to their needs, they have been able to develop their services to meet their buyers and seller's specific requirements. They claimed to provide an unrivalled service with access to the widest audience by utilising the strength of their network of offices throughout Ireland. Each office operates independently, yet benefits from a pool of property information and marketing collateral that reaches the property markets, both nationwide and abroad. Property Partners' claimed that their agents offer a brand of professionalism and quality service with a combined staff of 150 professionals nationwide. Property Partners in terms of scale is a leading player in the Irish property market. Similar to other real estate agencies Property Partners claimed to continually monitor and enhance customer service levels and strive to improve the skills of all their real estate agents through a comprehensive professional development programme.

RE/MAX 2012

In 2012, Waterford-based auctioneer, John Fogarty, acquired the RE/MAX Irish franchise from its American owners. His plan was to double the number of RE/MAX offices in the country to 40 over the next few years. Fogarty, had offices in Waterford, Tramore, and Carlow and previously traded as part of the Property Partners group. He believed that the new franchisees would come from the smaller firms needing a big brand to help them survive the current recession.

Latest Developments in Real Estate Industry

A few key firms dominate the industry and these firms continue to operate successfully, namely Sherry FitzGerald, Douglas Newman Good
(DNG), Property Partners, Gunne, Lisney, and RE/MAX. However,
Sherry FitzGerald and DNG have forged ahead and secured their industry leadership with the largest market share of over 60 per cent between
them (see Table 6.4). Therefore, branding and operational efficiencies, the
cornerstones of the franchising model, have provided the bigger franchise
systems with a competitive advantage over smaller independent firms.

There has been a noticeable claw-back of RE/MAX franchised operations from 80 to 20 franchises. This can be attributed to both changes in
industry legislation (not permitting unqualified people to act as property
agents) and to the economic downturn. Another development has been
the success of the co-operative, Property Partners since its formation in
2000. In 2012 the co-operative holds third place in the industry with
over 40 offices nationwide.

There are indications that the government would begin to regulate the
industry more heavily in the very near future and the IAVI and IPAV
claim to welcome this move. The IAVI see the government as having
greater powers to enforce standards that the IAVI is striving to set and
maintain. The question is whether the franchising firms stand for or
against the trade associations. It appears that individual franchisees independently decide which of the two trade associations they wish to join.
The standards, which both trade associations appear to be upholding, are
in line with the franchise systems standards. This ensures that agents are
under observation and appear to have stringent operating standards, and

Table 6.4 Industry leaders number of outlets 2012

Real estate brand	Outlet number
Sherry FitzGerald	98
DNG	90
Property partners and property team	40
RE/MAX	20
Lisney	6
Gunne	5

professional codes of conduct, together with on-going internal training and development. In recent years it appears that both trade associations have become less involved in the sectors affairs.

The Trade Association Merger—SCSI

In 2011, after six years of discussions, the IAVI and the SCS merged to form the new Society of Chartered Surveyors Ireland (SCSI). The SCSI will represent up to 4000 property and construction professionals. Its goals are:

1. to enhance the brand of chartered surveyors in Ireland;
2. to ensure high and uniform educational standards;
3. to produce a higher and clearer profile of the profession;
4. to enhance and augment services and the pooling of resources.

The merging of the two trade associations was especially significant in light of the economic crisis since 2008. The move was anticipated to produce a substantial saving of administration costs, as well as the ability to offer joint education programmes. As a result of this amalgamation, the IPAV will be the only other representative body for real estate agents and auctioneers in Ireland. Current opinion is that the industry has already consolidated and further consolidation may be accelerated by the economic downturn. It is evident that there are currently two leading firms in the industry, DNG and Sherry FitzGerald, both of which are franchise systems who the co-operative Property Partners in third position. The majority of industry incumbents are small independent real estate agents operating in their local region, similar to their industry founders over 100 years ago.

Conclusion

This chapter presented an industry history of the real estate industry in Ireland see Table 6.5 for industry timeline. It chronicled the industry from its emergence pre-1900s, to the first auctioneers right through to the

Table 6.5 Timeline of the real estate industry

Year	Number of licenced agents	Leading firms
1921	67	Leading firms Dublin are based: James North & Co., Ganley & Sons, Battersby & Co, and James Adam & Sons
1930	330	Agent and firm numbers increase
1940	340	New firms appear on the horizon. partnership and mergers begin leading firms
1949	580	Lisneys, HOK, and Jackson Stops and McCabe—partnerships and mergers
1965	1054 licenses	1960s real estate agents trying to differentiate themselves from the competition—branding and efficiencies become important
1970	698 (47 students)	IAVI renamed and IPAV formed
1980	1600 licenses	1980s staff cuts and key mergers & amalgamations to survive competition and economic downturn
		Four key firms dominate: Gunne, Sherry FitzGerald and HOK, Lisney coming to fore in Dublin market and mergers to survive competition
1996	1406 licenses	Five key firms dominate: Gunne, HOK, Jones Lang Wooton (commercial), Lisney, and Sherry FitzGerald—the five firms holding 71 per cent auctions
1997	1520	Three key firms dominate: Sherry FitzGerald, Douglas Newman Goode (DNG), Hamilton Osbourne King (HOK), with Gunne, Lisney, Property Partners (Co-op) also important firms
2005	2000	469 firms with 157 firms based in Dublin—two key firms dominate—Sherry FitzGerald and DNG
2010	2750	DNG and Sherry FitzGerald dominating the market with Gunne, Lisney, and HOK in the top five
2012	5800	DNG and Sherry FitzGerald dominating the market and Property Partners co-op in third position with Gunne, Lisney, and HOK in the top six

wave of international new entrants and the increases in the competitive landscape. The impact of franchising is addressed and the structural changes that took place after franchising was introduced are presented. The case follows the story of the industry through the recessionary and boom times and finishes with the overview of the industry today. The next chapter presents the analysis of the two individual cases as well as the comparative case analysis.

7

Franchising—From Industry Fragmentation to Consolidation

This chapter looks at franchising and its impact on industry evolution. Indeed, the previous chapters have explored both the literature and the empirical evidence in terms of the emergence of franchising and the impact it has on industry structures. One of the main contributions of this research is that it provides a focused engagement with franchising over time. Overtime the industry is radically altered and threshold capabilities change. This chapter explores some of the following questions: What happens next once the industry has moved to a more consolidated position, what do you need to succeed in such an industry?

Furthermore, an opportunity to develop a clearer understanding of the relationship between franchising and its industry setting was identified—something not adequately covered in the existing literature. This research therefore allowed for an understanding of why franchising emerges in an industry along with its structural impact over time. It also introduced the opportunity to use industry evolution material to explain this—and therefore engaged with a need in the evolutionary literature to understand the emergence of new organisational forms/institutions such as franchising. The review of the franchising literature highlighted the

© The Author(s) 2017
R. Beere, *The Role of Franchising on Industry Evolution*,
DOI 10.1007/978-3-319-49064-9_7

fragmented nature of previous research and the role of franchising as a driver of industry-level change which has not been previously explored. This research also makes an empirical contribution by providing evidence on how the Irish fast food/quick service restaurant (QSR) and real estate industries evolved over time, particularly in terms of structure as research in service sectors still suffers from the 'lack of empirical evidence' (Malerba & Orsenigo, 1996). By exploring franchising and its impact on the structural evolution of industry, this research enhances the franchising and industry evolution literature.

Linking Empirical Findings to the Literature

This section will link the empirical findings to the franchising and industry evolution literature and will address the role franchising has on industry evolution by addressing two questions: First, why does franchising emerge? Second, how does franchising impact industry evolution?

Why Does Franchising Emerge?

This section explores the emergence of franchising and links this question to the literature on franchising and industry evolution and then assesses the relevance of the literature to the findings of this research.

Franchising

Importance of a Multi-level and Multi-Modal Approach

Franchising research to date has mainly focused on the reason or decision to franchise at firm level mostly using agency theory (AT) and resource scarcity explanations. Little research has been conducted relating to the emergence of franchising at the macro-environmental level (government impact, economic and social change, or technology effects) or the industry context (industry competition, branding, or industry standards),

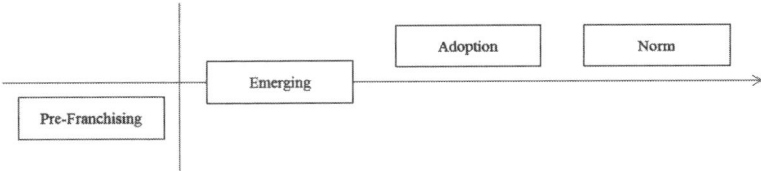

Fig. 7.1 Pre-emergence and emergence of franchising

so there remains a substantial gap in the research which this research looks to address. Furthermore, to date franchising research has failed to assess the emergence and pre-emergence of franchising from a multi-level approach, and instead research has focused on the adoption rather than pre-adoption conditions of franchising and with a main focus on firm level issues as opposed to industry-level analysis (see Fig. 7.1).

Therefore, this research looks at the factors evident prior to the emergence of franchising from a multi-level approach incorporating macro-environmental and industry level and firm level in the two case studies under investigation. The data show that in the fast food/QSR and real estate industries macro-environmental level changes, including environmental, governmental, economic, and social conditions, were important factors in the emergence of franchising as was the influence of industry competitive pressures and potential new entrants. In addition, at firm level the influence of agency and entrepreneurs was instrumental in the adoption of the franchising model for their individual organisations. Despite the rapid adoption of the franchising concept, there is still a lack of understanding and consensus on the theoretical determinant and creation of this organisational form and business strategy (Inma, 2005). Due to several distinct structural properties of franchising, it offers ample opportunities to research topics of more general theoretical and managerial interest. This research investigates the exploratory power of different theoretical perspectives. In doing so it has looked at the franchising literature and has assessed its relationship to research on industry evolution using a multi-modal approach. In addition, the complementary use of the five organisational level theories (transaction cost economics [TCE], AT, resource dependency theory [RDT], neo-institutional theory [NIT], and population ecology) in explaining the emergence of franchising on

Table 7.1 VSR and the five organisational level theories

Perspectives	Variation	Selection	Retention
Firm level			
Transaction cost economics	Variation into via intended rational action	Selection involves actions to minimise transaction costs	Retention via transaction specific investments
Resource dependency	Variation introduced as managers try to avoid dependence	Selection via asymmetric power relations	Retention a temporary result of coalitions and bargaining
Agency theory	Variation via new organisations internal incentives offered to employees	Selection via asymmetric power relations	Retention a via contacts and bargaining
Industry level			
Neo-institutional	Variations introduced from external origins, for example imitation	Selection via conformity	Retention through transmission of shared understandings
Population ecology	Variation depending on co-ordination of relationships	Selection results from fit between organisation and environment	Retention through transmission of shared understandings and efficiency

industry evolution has been useful which will be addressed later in this chapter (see Table 7.1).

Importance of Macro-Environmental and Industry Context

As mentioned much of the literature pertaining to the emergence of franchising relates to firm level decision and choices. However, there is some research that looks at the environmental context but this is limited and focuses mainly on institutional theory. Notably Shane and Foo

(1999) and Barthélemy (2011) look at franchising and link it to institutional theory which can help to connect some environmental factors to the emergence of franchising. The application of institutional theory has proven to be especially helpful to this stream of entrepreneurial research. However, even so the majority of franchising literature fails to properly address the macro-environmental conditions evident in the emergence of franchising (including government impact, economic and social change, and technology effect) which this research looks to address. The literature suggests as highlighted by Elango and Freid (1997) that franchising is suited for environments characterised by intense competition, rapidly changing customer tastes, and a trend towards localised market segments. Indeed, one area of the franchising research that has been given attention is the importance of the competitive environment (at the industry level) with regards to the adoption of franchising. Most industries and firms are having to face increasingly turbulent and ambiguous and hypercompetitive environmental conditions (Volberda, 1998; Brown & Eisenhardt, 1998). In these conditions, the need to search for and 'explore' new organisational forms appears necessary for organisational survival (March & Simon, 1958; Lewin, Weigelt, & Emery, 2004). The findings of this research show that in addition to increasing competition at industry level, the macro-environment of both industries became more demanding and as such firms needed to react to these changes. There became a need for organisations to adapt to change as well as increased efficiency and operational improvements, image and branding demands coupled with the need for transparency of business practices, which all emerged as an important determinant of industry success. Thus, as a consequence of this the pattern of strategies of the fast food/QSR and real estate industries also changed over time. Henceforth, industry incumbents began to pay less attention to the protection of industry boundaries through erection of barriers, and focused instead on the improvement of the reputation, branding, and operating efficiencies within their industry. The fast food/QSR industry and the real estate industries exhibited similar evolutionary patterns and their strategies were generally driven by similar contextual developments. At the same time, they responded differently to these developments. This research supports the current franchising research on the importance of the competitive environment and the increasing pressures that such a competitive environment creates at firm level which in turn promotes the emergence of franchising. However, the data also show that the emergence of franchising was as a result of the macro-environmental context including the influence of government, economic and social change, and technology effects (not previously explored in the franchising literature) as well as industry-level effects such as competition and the influence of agency and entrepreneurs. Therefore, the choice to franchise, in this view, is embedded within the firm's history and strategic portfolio and co-evolves with the firm's strategy, the institutional environment (macro-environment), the organisational and competitive environment, and with management's (entrepreneurs) strategic intent for the creation of the franchise system.

Indeed, to look in more detail at the industry effects in relation to the emergence of franchising Martin (1988) asked some key questions: Why does franchising exist and why does franchising exist in certain industries? Martin (1988) addressed the first question when he examined franchising from an industry perspective and found that capital needs, market competition, monitoring costs, and the need to reach minimum efficient scale were reasons to franchise. The second question Martin (1988) asked was why is franchising successful in some industries and not others? He found that from multiple quantitative studies there seems some consensus on the following: First, retail sales, fast food, and customer service franchisees were found to have low closure rates, while beauty, health, automotive, and hotels had the highest failure rates (Justis, Castrogiovanni, & Chan, 1992). Second, the longer established the franchise system the lower the failure rates (Lafountaine & Shaw, 1998). But these findings do not uncover the core issue at hand and further research is needed to truly address these fundamental questions. Elango and Freid (1997) made a call for one area in particular to be investigated, which related to franchising and industry effects and implications which this research has endeavoured to address. The findings of this research show that according to the data franchising emerged was as a result of varied contextual developments. At the same time, the anticipation of contextual changes at industry level was also important in driving the adoption of franchising. The data show that in both industries many actions of the fast food/QSR and real estate industry incumbents were aimed at keeping the existing context and industry status quo and preventing environmental changes. However, in the fast food/QSR industry it was McDonald's entry in 1977 that first brought franchising to Ireland and changed the industry forever and in the real estate industry it was the threat of entry of the USA RE/MAX that prompted SherryFitzgerald to adopt franchising. Some studies suggest that the increasing competition towards the end of the twentieth century forced firms to examine alternative ways to do conduct business including new organisational forms such as franchising. The cross-case analysis showed that throughout different stages of each industry's evolution the introduction of franchising occurred under similar industry-level contextual circumstances. These findings provide empirical support to previous studies in the field. Thus, as Martin (1988) suggests firm level co-operation at industry level such as the introduction and emergence of franchising often became a response to changing environmental forces and to economic and political pressures which this research supports.

The Role of Agency—and the Role of Entrepreneurs

The franchising literature has focused a good deal on research relating to entrepreneurship or indeed has been from an entrepreneurial perspective. However, the role that entrepreneurs play with regard to the emergence of franchising has not been extensively explored and has mainly been from a quantitative perspective. As such there is limited research using qualitative and more in-depth and inductive methods as adopted by this research. Furthermore, the franchising literature has mainly focused on the franchisor perspective and not accounted for the importance of the franchisee. Dant (2008) highlights that much of what we know about franchising is based on investigations of the franchisors to the virtual exclusion of research focused on the franchisee perspective. Furthermore, franchising research has rarely been looked at from a strategy lens which this research adopts. Oxenfeldt and Kelly (1968), Caves and Murphy (1976), and Norton (1988) have suggested from their research that entrepreneurs use franchising to gain access to significant resources that are in short supply in the early stages of the development of their franchise chains from a quantitative perspective. Chirico, Ireland, and Sirmon

(2011) also recognise that many, if not most, franchisors and franchisees are family-run enterprises, and they use this insight to draw implications about franchising from research on family firms. However, most of the research fails to explore the role of agency or entrepreneurs in the emergence of franchising as a central focus. The findings of this research and the evidence from the data suggest that agency and the role of the entrepreneurs were of enormous significance in the emergence of franchising in both industries. Entrepreneurship was widely evident in both cases especially as an instigator of the adoption of franchising whereby key individual entrepreneurs championed the adoption of franchising within their own firm. This type of industry leadership served as an exemplar for others to follow. In both the fast food/QSR and real estate industries the role of entrepreneurship and individual entrepreneurs (both franchisors and franchisees) were critical in making the decision to adopt franchising as a growth model in a resource and capital constrained environment. Entrepreneurship was manifested in the leading role of entrepreneurs such as; Mike Meagan (McDonalds), Wyn Beere, Graeme Beere (AIL), and Pat McDonagh (Suprmacs) in the fast food/QSR industry and with Philip Sherry and Mark Fitzgerald (SherryFitzgerald) and Keith Lowe (DNG) in the real estate industry.

In order to further the stream of entrepreneurial research the concept of innovation was also looked at whereby entrepreneurs that is franchisors and individual franchisees engage in innovation and experimentation to generate more efficient processes and better products (Bradach, 1997). In spite of considerable anecdotal evidence; however, no formal examination of the claim that franchising is a vehicle for innovation has occurred. One potentially fruitful avenue for future inquiry might be to investigate whether the benefits of franchisee innovation for the franchisor are moderated by the quality of franchisor–franchisee relations. Whereas many innovations developed by franchisees are not communicated to franchisors (Darr, Argote, & Epple, 1995), franchisors with good franchisee relations might be better able to identify and implement local adaptations that will benefit the entire chain (Bradach, 1997). This research found that from the data that franchise systems were instrumental in bringing innovation and new systems into the industry; for example, McDonalds was innovative in their efficiency and operating models which had an effect on the fast food/QSR industry, and SherryFitzgerald was innovative in terms of their uptake on technology and CRM systems which influenced other industry incumbents in the real estate industry.

A point to note is that from the data is that there were multiple similarities with regard to the patterns evident in both cases prior to the emergence of franchising. However, there was one principal difference across the adoption of franchising in both industries: The emergence of franchising and its rate of adoption in the fast food/QSR industry franchising occurred much earlier in 1977 and its diffusion was much faster. In contrast, in the real estate industry franchising was adopted 20 years later in 1999 and its diffusion although quick was not as fast or as intense as the fast food/QSR industry. Although the timing of emergence may have been different many of the influencing factors such as macro-environmental, industry, and agency were similar in both industry cases.

Industry Evolution

This section will look at the relevant industry evolution literature with its contribution in explaining the emergence of franchising and comparing it with this research's findings. First the section will look at Porter's (1980) work on fragmented industries and its relationship to the findings of this research. The contribution of the Variation, Selection, and Retention (VSR) approach will be explored followed by the importance of the role of agency in industry evolution.

Fragmented Industries

Taking into account the analysis of the comparative case studies the question can be asked; does the industry evolution literature offer an explanation as to why franchising emerges? It appears that there are a number of shortcomings with regards to the industry evolution literature. Some of the key findings from this research have not been previously explored in the research field. There are a number of gaps in the literature that have been highlighted; the service sector is rarely investigated and to date franchising has never been studied from an industry evolution perspective. In terms of the industry evolution literature after the life cycle model, Michael Porter's (1980) industry analysis framework has been the most prominent contribution to the development of industry evolution in the strategy field. However, Porter (1980) is one of the few strategy theorists to mention franchising in the context of industry and he talks about fragmented industries prior to the emergence of franchising. The data from this research are able to support this assertion as both industries were fragmented prior to the emergence of franchising. In addition, Porter (1980) suggested that technology, demographics, trade barriers, political conditions, and regulations influence industries. Drawing from Porter's work this research sought to assess what was happening in the macro-environmental and industry context that precipitates the opportunity for change and therefore pre-emergence conditions for franchising as well as the structural consequences of the impact of franchising. Many of Porter's (1980) suggestions were valid but there were other contextual factors he did not mention and which this research has unveiled. The findings of this research confirm Porter's (1980) assertions, as the data show in the fast food/QSR and real estate industries that the emergence of franchising often took place as a response to some external variation. For example changes in government impact, economic change, social change, technology effects and increasing international competition, as well as a range of other factors accelerated the need for firms to adopt franchising to help them remain competitive in a changing macro-environmental context. In addition, there were other industry contextual factors that prompted the introduction of franchising such as; increased industry competition, the threat of or the entry of international new entrants as well as branding/industry standards, changes in industry recipe, and continued industry self-regulation. Moreover, the industry evolution literature does not give a great deal of information regarding the pre-emergence conditions; however, it does look at some external factors or environmental conditions but nothing in great depth.

Variation, Selection, and Retention in Explaining the Emergence of Franchising

From the literature review in Chap. 2, the VSR model when applied to evolutionary theory (Aldrich, 1999) could be used to explain how particular forms of organisations come to exist in specific kinds of environments and is a useful model in terms of studying industry evolution and indeed the emergence of a new variant such as franchising. According to Aldrich and Ruef (2006) evolutionary theory is an overarching meta-theory applied across multiple levels of analysis; it is open to multiple approaches for explaining particular kinds of change and it is a meta-theory that requires downstream links to other theories such as the five organisational level theories used in this research (TCE, AT, RDT, NIT, and Population ecology; all five theories are dealt with in greater detail later in this chapter [see Table 7.1]). The evolutionary approach serves as a meta-theory within which the value of these approaches can be recognised and appreciated. Table 7.1 looks at how these chosen perspectives deal with the issues of VSR. VSR is applicable in this research as franchising is a variation that is selected and retained.

In both cases franchising became the preserved and most replicated business model and ultimately became the dominant form of organisational model for industry leaders. Thus, the external variation and the opportunities to create change caused franchising to be adopted and to restructure industry dynamics. Franchising resulted from the external variation and new external pressures. In terms of the impact on industry, franchising created new variations, adapted to variations, and dealt with selective pressures. The findings of this research address the question of why variations occur and how this relates to franchising and its emergence. The empirical findings of this research generally support the conceptual propositions embedded in the theoretical framework. Furthermore, change and variation are encompassed in evolutionary economics as firms are seen as vehicles of innovation and drivers of change at the industry level (Nelson & Winter, 1973, 1974, 1982). As shown by the data in both industries firm level changes in business strategies, organisational structure and search activities such as the adoption of franchising affected firm profitability and market share; these changes generated fluctuating degrees of expansion and contraction of individual firms, leading to dynamic changes at the industry level (Nelson & Winter, 1974). Variation, the threat of variation, and selection as evolutionary processes drove the emergence of franchising as a new variation. Thus, the external variation and the opportunities to create variation caused franchising to emerge. Therefore, the introduction of franchising resulted from the external variation and new external pressures.

The findings show that in both the fast food/QSR and real estate industries the emergence of franchising took place as a response to some external variation caused by changes in government policies, increasing competition, at both national, European and international levels. For example, increasing competition imposed not only risk, but also an opportunity for firms to expand into new segments. The period from the 1970s to 1990s imposed industry and European Union (EU)-level structural changes and created external variations. Organisational restructuring and optimisation through the adoption of franchising allowed some firms to adjust to variations caused by their external environment. Moreover, it helped the franchise systems to deal with changing selective pressures by meeting new efficiency and branding requirements and customer expectations. The case data suggest that despite industry-level variations, the emergence of franchising in both industries exhibit similar characteristics. Since the 1980s both industries faced the necessity to legitimise themselves in the eyes of consumers, governments, and industry stakeholders. There is also evidence of new selective pressures emerging in both industries, which are embedded in increasing customer and government expectations of higher standards and transparency.

Role of Agency

The industry evolution literature can in many ways appear disconnected and often fails to adequately explain the macro-environmental, industry context and role of agency with regards to the emergence of franchising, whereby franchising is viewed as a change or variation that is introduced. Furthermore, one of the major gaps in the literature is the lack of attention to agency or indeed the influence of entrepreneurship in the evolutionary process and it has only recently been mentioned by Jacobides (2006) in his work on industry architecture and also in the dynamic capabilities (Augier & Teece, 2008) literature. Aldrich and Ruef (2006) mention its relevance to industry evolution and Jacobides (2006) looks at the roles of industry actors/agents. Jacobides, Knudsen, and Augier (2006) suggest that 'architectural advantage' depends on two factors: complementarity and mobility of assets and that these industry architectures can be manipulated by deliberate, forward-looking firms (and in both cases, these behaviours resemble many firms' attempts to establish platform leadership by adopting franchising). Jacobides (2006) claims that by focusing on actors/agents and the differences in their roles can help us understand why platforms might show variances in say regional or geographic success or failure or take-up. This area of research acknowledges the agency of firms and individuals in such change and seeks to understand the processes and circumstances of architectural change. However, apart from Jacobides (2006), the influence of entrepreneurship is not widely acknowledged in the industry evolution literature and this research aims to link the importance of the role of entrepreneurship in the emergence of franchising something not previously explored. The findings of this research show that in both the fast food/QSR and real estate industries the role of entrepreneurs in the introduction of franchising was of great importance. In the fast food/QSR industry McDonald's Inc. sold the Irish Master franchise to Irishman Mike Meagan; Meagan approached McDonald's with regard to operating a McDonald's franchise in Ireland and was granted the licence. His first franchise outlet was so successful that he opened another six McDonald's outlets in Dublin between 1977 and 1982. However, in 1989 McDonald's bought back the rights to the Irish region, as they had huge plans for expansion beyond Meagan's own ambitions. The entrepreneurs and owners of Abrakebabra and Supermacs quickly followed suit and also adopted franchising. In the real estate industry it was the entrepreneurial vision of Phillip Sherry and Mark Fitzgerald who introduced franchising to the Irish real estate industry followed by the entrepreneurial foresight of Keith Lowe of DNG.

As noted the conceptual framework identifies certain factors which helped to drive the emergence of franchising and the data correspond to the industry evolution literature in terms of assessing the macro-environmental context and its influence on the emergence of franchising, the influence of government impact, economic change, social change, and technology effects are supported by the literature. However, from the findings, macro-environmental context factors play a more powerful influencing role than the industry context factors in terms of the emergence of franchising. The industry context factors have a role to play in the emergence of franchising; the industry evolution literature supports that certain influences such as the increased industry competition, and international new entrants can bring about industry recipe changes such as the introduction of an organisational model like franchising. One significant shortcoming of the industry evolution stream of research is that it fails to properly identify and explore the crucial role of entrepreneurs or agency in terms of enabling the adoption of franchising. One of the key findings of this research is that the role of agency and entrepreneurs is of major importance to the emergence of franchising which extends the current body research in the field.

What Impact Does Franchising Have on the Structural Evolution of an Industry?

Franchising

This section will look at the franchising literature in terms of addressing the impact of franchising on industry structure and will discuss the relevance of this research and its findings to this field of research. To date there is a significant lack of research on franchising and its effects on industry. In the field of franchising Elango and Freid (1997) made a call for one area in particular to be investigated, this related to franchising and its effect on industry which up until now has remained unanswered. Moreover, much of the franchising research has previously looked at the franchising system without considering the macro-environment within which it operates. However, one of the main contributions of this research is to address the fundamental gap in terms of research and literature relating to franchising and its impact on industry or indeed the evolution of franchising over time. Furthermore, the impact of franchising on industry evolution remains the most understudied aspect of franchising research. The findings of this research suggest that through its emergence and impact, franchising was able to alter the structure of both industries and played an important role in determining the evolutionary path of each industry. Moreover, the impact of franchising varied over time, and firm's strategies were often aimed at protecting and defending their own and industries' interests, thus increasing their (industries') stability and facilitating the continued wellbeing of the incumbents. Franchising also facilitated learning and the dissemination of important information, thus helping franchisors and franchisees deal with changing contexts. In both industries the franchise systems also engaged in training and information dissemination activities, developed codes of conduct and practice thereby promoting shared understandings, socialisation, and new norms and understandings. Absent from the literature but addressed in this research is the effect of franchising and indeed the evolution of franchise systems over time as they co-evolve with the changing strategies of the firm and the subsequent industry effects. Furthermore, by expanding into more industry segments, franchise systems created new variations, including the strengthening and legitimisation of their organisations and reduced competitive pressures on their franchisees. These are all the firm level and industry-level consequences that occurred once franchising was adopted and changed the structural dynamics of both industries in this research.

Most of the franchising research focuses on the competitive advantage which franchising offers organisations and this research supports this viewpoint. Franchising as an organisational structure offers many benefits, enabling firms to achieve a competitive advantage. In both industries the firms who adopted franchising became the most successful in their respective industries and in both cases became the dominating industry leaders. Thus, franchising enabled firms to develop capabilities which led to competitive advantage. The benefits of being part of a franchise system are the ability to draw on the strength of the group and the inter-organisational relationships. Traditionally these strengths were seen to centre on the marketing, branding, and training aspects of the business. However, increasingly it is becoming clear that such offerings are common place among franchisors and given the increased competition for new franchisees, new forms of competitive advantage are required to attract and acquire high quality franchisees. The evolution of strategies developed and implemented in both industries exhibited similar cost and focus patterns. Thus, over time strategies generally evolved from low-cost marketing campaigns to high-cost expensive media campaigns and branding initiatives. The findings of this research support the literature relating to the competitive advantage that the adoption of franchising can offer organisations. There is a definite connection between the role of firms who adopt franchising and their success and therefore their impact on their industry. There is evidence from both cases that once franchising was adopted its effects were so great that those firms who did not adopt franchising ended up joining co-operative organisations to ward off the competition, for example, in the real estate industry with the formation of Property Partners and other such groups or in the fast food/QSR industry the Irish Traditional Italian Chipper Association (ITICA) was formed as a collective organisation representing the independent chippers. Again this specific aspect of competitive advantage is under researched using franchising as a central tenet. There is some work (Collis & Montgomery, 1995) on competitive advantage and how franchising can increase organisational success of firms but this is limited and only from the firm level perspective unlike the approach of this research which relates to a broader macro-environmental and industry-level context as well as agency effects at firm level.

Porter (1980) while looking at industries made the connection between franchising and its ability to overcome industry fragmentation which to date still remains unexplored. The findings of this research reveal that the structural changes once franchising was adopted were profound. In both industries the firms who adopted franchising went on to dominate the industry and in both cases after the adoption of franchising the industries in terms of structure went from fragmentation to consolidation. The findings of this research suggest that once franchising is adopted the structures of industries are altered and the consolidation of industry occurs. Therefore, franchising has played an important role in determining the evolutionary paths of both industries. The impact of franchising varied over time, and the adoption of franchising was often to protect and defend firm's interests, thereby increasing their industries' stability and facilitating the continued survival and success of incumbents.

This research hopes to advance the view that an organisational form such as franchising needs to be understood and researched in the context of the adaptation and choices of the firm over time. Franchising research to date has looked at the franchising system without considering the macro-environment within which it operates. This research seeks to address this shortfall and the findings of this research show that the macro-environmental context is extremely important in terms of the impact of franchising on the industry structure and is affected by macro-environmental changes over time. In addition, franchising has usually been addressed from the firm level and not from the industry level a further gap this research has sought to address. Furthermore, entrepreneurship has an important role in the adoption and the subsequent impact of franchising according to the findings of this research. In both cases entrepreneurs played a role in the adoption and diffusion of franchising and the effects of agency on industry which have not been adequately explored. The franchising literature demonstrates that a competitive advantage can be gained by organisations who adopt franchising. The data from this research have shown that franchising can be viewed as a hybrid structure that can help organisations achieve competitive advantage in hyper competitive and changing external environments. This research supports what the franchising literature promotes (Shane, 2008) that franchising leads to franchisors gaining competitive advantage.

Finally another important observation to note relates to the most debated topic in the franchising research which is the reason a firm chooses to franchise rather than expand through company-owned units. Oxenfeldt and Kelly (1968–1969) proposed a life cycle model of franchising, in which a young company with a limited supply of capital becomes a franchisor in order to use the franchisee's capital to expand. Then as it acquires sufficient capital, the franchisor will later take over the larger units from franchisees. This view has become known as—resource scarcity (Carney & Gedajlovic, 1991). Initial empirical support for this view was provided by Hunt and Nevin (1974), who found an aggregate trend towards company-owned units in the fast food industry. Caves and Murphy (1976) also observed a similar trend towards company ownership in restaurants, hotels, and motels. However, this research has shown that in both industries once firms adopt franchising they tended to reduce the number of company-owned units and increase the number of franchised units over time. In the fast food/QSR industry AIL, McDonalds, O'Briens, and Supermacs did this and in the real estate industry SherryFitzgerald, RE/MAX, and DNG followed suit. Thus, traditional franchising theories such as resource scarcity and AT cannot alone explain the adoption, selection, and retention of a variation such as franchising.

Industry Evolution

This section will explore the relevant industry evolution perspective and will assess the viewpoint taken from the literature and how the findings of this research compare. To begin with the relevance of co-evolution theory as well as industry architecture will be addressed. Moreover, Porter (1980) will be further examined as he has noted that fragmented industries are characterised as being intensely competitive and that 'industry fragmentation has been overcome by franchising' (Porter, 1980). However, apart from this one mention the relationship between franchising and its impact on industry structure has not been previously addressed. This research aims to generate a deeper understanding of the presence of franchising in Ireland's service driven market economy and its effect on industry evolution. It is important to understand the gaps in the literature and to assess possible research contributions of this research. As detailed in the literature review in Chap. 2, Malerba and Orsenigo (1996) observe that there are many gaps in our understanding of industry evolution, particularly in respect of empirical research in the field, as well as theoretical explanations for it. The gaps include a lack of exploration of structural dynamics or structural evolution, a lack of focus on the service or distributive industries. There is also a lack of a dynamic model of industry evolution, a lack of a historical perspective. There is a need to assess the role of institutions in industry evolution, a need to explore the relationship between firm level activity and industry evolution, and the need for finer grained empirical studies. This research supports these observations and it addresses these shortfalls.

Furthermore, recent research on co-evolution and franchising confirms what the findings of this research have shown. At the firm level establishing expectations for creating and distributing a hybrid organisational form such as franchising, the co-evolution of direction, structure, and practices within the context of the evolution of the constituent firms/agents, industry, and institutional environment are all of equal importance. According to the data the choice to franchise, within this view, is embedded within the firm's history and its strategic portfolio and co-evolves with the firm's strategy, the institutional, organisational, and competitive environment, together with management strategic intent for the creation of the franchise system. The research on co-evolution can be drawn on to assess why franchising is selected as an organisational variation. Many firms therefore adopt a franchising model to help them achieve a competitive advantage in their industry. This would lead to firms' legitimisation, the further strengthening and continued adoption of franchising, and to the development of this organisational structure across many industry incumbents. The co-evolutionary lens is receiving more attention from scholars of industry evolution and it is of value to this research. Poole and Van de Ven (2004) explain that co-evolution is viewing the organisation as part of an inter-organisational community, industry or population which fits with the research on franchising in terms of franchise systems being made up of a network of franchisors and franchisees (within a franchise system) at industry level the relationship between competing franchise systems. The seminal paper by Lewin and Volberda (1999) focused on how firms co-evolve with each other and with a changing organisational environment.

Moreover, Lewin et al. (1998) have advanced a theory of the evolution of new organisational forms as an outcome of the co-evolution of the competitive environment, firm intentionality and the institutional environment of the firm under conditions of stochastic or chaotic environmental uncertainty. The findings of this research and the data support the proposition that firms and industries co-evolve and specifically when franchising is adopted at firm level it has a huge impact on the evolution of an industry. In both cases franchising changed each industry's structure from fragmentation to consolidation. In both cases firms and their industry have co-evolved with each other in a changing environment. Therefore, this research validates the propositions upheld by co-evolution theory. Furthermore, one issue that may need further research with a central focus on competencies in relation to the intra-firm dynamic which this research has not fully investigated. As such McKelvey (1997) suggests that the focus of macro co-evolutionary theory is on firms existing in a co-evolutionary competitive context, while micro co-evolutionary considers co-evolution of intra-firm resources, dynamic capabilities and competencies in an intra-firm, competitive context (McKelvey, 1997), and this area could do with further investigation.

In recent years, two other theoretical perspectives, industry architectures and platforms, have attempted to explicitly address the issue of how value is created as well as captured in the context of interdependent systems of firms and institutions. Industry platforms are technological building blocks that act as a foundation upon which an array of firms, organised in a set of interdependent firms (sometimes called industry 'eco-system'), develop a set of interrelated products, technologies, and services (Gawer, 2009a, 2009b). 'Industry architecture' (Jacobides et al., 2006) has emerged. It explores the rules and roles of inter-firm relationships and focuses on the ways in which activities along the value chain get divided among industry participants, paying particular attention to firm roles, interdependencies, and the ways in which organisations attempt to shape the industry's division of labour. Industry architecture is another more recent stream of industry evolution research and its applicability to the context of this research is valid. The literature on industry eco-systems which is linked to research on industry platforms Tee and Gawer (2009) describe platform leaders and how they drive industry-wide innovation. The findings from this research reveal that in both industries the platform leaders (the early adopters of franchising) drove the emergence of franchising and enabled franchising to become the dominant design. Developing this further the business models that 'win' are often championed and copied linking to the concept of dominant design. As such changing business models affect the industry structure (Gambardella & McGahan, 2010). Within the industry, these models compete and through the sequence of VSR, success or failure is determined by the competitive process. The industry then restructures around the new dominant business model leading to new industry architecture (Jacobides et al., 2006) which occurred in both the fast food/QSR and real estate industries once franchising emerged and impacted each industry. One thing to note that was not investigated in the initial literature review was the area of firm competences which links into the development of firm and industry-level capabilities witnessed in both cases as a result of the impact of franchising (competences including branding and the dominant design of franchising). Tae and Jacobides (2011) look at competences within the industry architecture field and build on this. This 'architectural' approach brings together components of existing studies to show how profit gravitates towards a set of firms engaged in one particular activity. The intuition here is that superior capabilities in one activity enable a firm to change the competitive conditions of the segment it belongs to—which also could change the industry architecture to its advantage. This is different from the resource based view (RBV) in that the competition of capabilities takes place not only at market/segment level (e.g. among franchise systems) but also at the value-chain level (e.g. among franchisor and franchisees). Therefore, the issues of competences and how they relate to firm and industry capabilities are concepts evident in this research that were not addressed in the literature review and could be further explored as a main focus in future research.

Finally as suggested by the industry evolution literature on the VSR (Aldrich, 1999) approach once franchising was adopted it was selected and retained. As evidenced by both cases the firms who adopted franchising were the ones who ultimately became industry leaders. Therefore at industry level, selection encouraged continued expansion of profitable firms and a decrease in unprofitable firms. Thus, the 'phenomena of search and selection' are simultaneous, interacting aspects of the evolutionary process. The findings of this research indicate that in both industries structural changes were implemented if firms saw the opportunity to adopt a new variation such as a new organisational structure like franchising. In addition to further retain the newly selected variation of franchising; industry self-regulation is evident in the data extracted from both cases. The threat of external variation imposed by the government and/or government agencies and increasing competition has always been the most significant motivation for self-regulation in both industries. Finally, self-regulation created new variation, an opportunity for new variation, and became a source of new variation within both industries.

Common Themes Between Franchising and Industry Evolution

This section looks at possible common themes between the franchising and industry evolution literatures and thus has implications for the empirical findings of this research. There is an overlap in the research on fragmented industries which is important when addressing a study on franchising and industry evolution. The relationship between industry fragmentation, franchising, and industry evolution is important as Porter (1980) stated that franchising overcomes industry fragmentation, this indicates that franchising might have the potential to alter an industry structure and this suggestion is at the heart of this research. This research reveals that in both industries franchising did impact industry structure as Porter (1980) suggested and helped to overcome industry fragmentation.

An important theoretical connection between the franchising and industry evolution literature is the role of entrepreneurship (Oxenfeldt & Kelly, 1968; Caves & Murphy, 1976; Norton, 1988). The role of entrepreneurs in the emergence and dominance of franchising is hugely important; the area of entrepreneurship pervades the franchising literature as well as the role of entrepreneurs and agency. Even though the area of entrepreneurship and agency is limited in the industry evolution field, there still is some work on dynamic capabilities (Augier & Teece, 2008; Helfat et al., 2007; Teece, 2009; Teece, Pisano, & Shuen, 1997) industry architecture Jacobides (2006) which notes the role of agency and actor in shaping the evolution of an industry. The findings of this research confirm the importance of agency and entrepreneurs in the emergence and impact of franchising on industry structure.

The VSR model (Aldrich, 1999) is a useful meta-theory utilised by this research. This evolutionary perspective adds value to the organisational level theories (TCE, AT, RDT, NIT, and population ecology) and VSR uses these organisational theories to explain organisational change. From the franchising and industry evolution perspectives VSR (Aldrich & Ruef, 2006) incorporates the emergence of a new organisational form, generation/transformation of technologies and dominant design, development and change of industry and firm level capabilities, entrepreneurship and agency, and industry competition. Entrepreneurs and managers alike must try to adapt to the changes occurring within the business environment. Competition is a dynamic process and firms try to obtain a competitive advantage, once gained it can quickly dissipate through imitation and innovation by rivals. The outcome of this process is an industry environment that is continually being altered by the forces of competition. According to the data this research reveals that once franchising emerged and was adopted as an organisational variation two of the most prominent structural effects were: industry consolidation and industry self-regulation. Moreover, variation, the threat of variation, and selection as evolutionary processes drove the adoption of franchising and its subsequent industry restructuring. The findings add to VSR theory by showing how franchising as a new organisational variation is adopted, selected, and retained and becomes the most successful organisational form in both industries. Aldrich and Ruef (2006) suggest that within the context of VSR any organisational theory can be an evolutionary theory and the five competing organisational theories used in this research help to explain franchising and within this VSR acts as a meta-theory and help to explain change at multiple levels both at organisational level, industry level, and macro-environmental level. VSR as a theory helps to explain how a new hybrid organisational form emerges and then becomes the dominant form. As a consequence of franchising emerging (a new variation) and being adopted (selected) and then becoming the industry norm (retained) this research therefore supports VSR as a robust meta-theory which helps to explain how a new variation such as franchising emerges and is selected and retained and the findings of this research empirically show how franchising causes the two industries to go from industry fragmentation to consolidation.

The co-evolution literature McKelvey (1997) and Lewin and Volberda (2011) is also relevant in the context of franchising and industry evolution which promotes that firms and the environment co-evolve. Franchising in the context of this research has displayed co-evolutionary tendencies both in terms of it as an inter-organisational community between franchisors and franchisees and at an industry or population level. The analysis from the cases informs us that in both industries firms have co-evolved with each other in a changing environment. There is evidence of both macro and micro co-evolution in both industries albeit at different stages and different rates of time. Furthermore, the cross-case data affirm what McKelvey (1997) has argued that evolution of organisations cannot be understood independently from the simultaneous evolution of the environment. This thesis supports the propositions made by McKelvey (1997), Lewin and Volberda (2011) and demonstrates empirically that the concept of co-evolution between a firm and its environment is an important one in terms of explaining structural change at both the firm and industry level. Indeed, the evidence from the findings show how franchising emerges at firm level and ultimately helps an organisation to evolve which in turn aids in the evolution of an industry. Furthermore, McKelvey (1997) looked at co-evolution from an organisational level and this thesis also engages with the level of the industry thus extending the empirical co-evolution research.

In addition, the body of work by Tee and Gawer (2009) on industry eco-systems and industry architecture (Jacobides, 2005) is important for this research in terms of helping to explain how firms adapt and innovate. Platform leaders tend to drive industry-wide innovation in a trajectory that allows them to exert architectural control over the overall system, as well as derive large profits and erect barriers to entry in their own market. This research shows that a hybrid organisational form such as franchising can be seen as a value creating industry platform with the industry eco-system comprising of the inter-connected firms (franchisor and franchisees) evident in a franchise system and also between franchise systems in competition with each other in an industry. Whereby franchising once it is adopted the firms who promote it become platform leaders and impact the industry eco-system. This thesis and its findings can confirm that franchising in both industries helped firms to create an architectural advantage which in turn helps to explain their success and industry dominance. This area of research acknowledges the agency of firms and individuals with regards to such changes and seeks to understand the processes and circumstances of architectural change. The data from both cases have shown the influence of entrepreneurs in adopting and developing the franchising model at firm level and thus affecting industry architectural change. This supporting empirically the tenants of industry architecture. Indeed, industry architecture is a relatively new concept this research explores and extends the theory by empirically testing what variables of architecture franchising influences and its effect on promoting firms that adopt franchising and ultimately the new pecking order that is creating once franchising emerges.

Finally in relation to assessing the structural effects of franchising this research supports the proposition by Porter (1980) that franchising enables fragmented industries to become consolidated. Porter (1980) states fast food industries have been historically fragmented, with thousands and thousands of small, owner-managed operations. Yet there are significant economies of scale in marketing and purchasing in both these businesses, particularly if national saturation can be achieved which allows the use of national advertising media. Porter (1980) also states that fragmentation in this industry was overcome by franchising the individual locations to owner-managers, who operated under the mantle of a national organisation which marketed the brand name and provided central purchasing and other services. Close control and maintenance of service are insured, as well as the benefits of economies of scale. Again Porter (1980) cites 'another industry in which franchising is unlocking fragmentation today is real estate brokerage. Century 21 is rapidly expanding share in this highly fragmented industry by franchising local firms, allowing them to operate autonomously with their local names but doing so under the umbrella of the nationally advertised Century 21 name' (Porter, 1980). However, Porter does not offer an explanation of how or why franchising overcomes fragmentation. This thesis offers a unique contribution in addressing both the emergence of franchising and its structural impact and through the data and findings can offer an explanation as to how and why franchising overcomes industry fragmentation. Indeed, after franchising emerged it became the new dominant design in both industries, the findings show that franchising reduced the need for legislation and thus promoted industry self-regulation, franchising helped firms achieve competitive advantage in their industry. Franchising also offered legitimacy to firms in terms of branding and increased capabilities as well as increased industry capabilities. The developments over time as explored in the analysis chapter show that until the late 1970s franchising had not entered either industry. Franchising emerged in the fast food/QSR industry in 1977 and in the real estate industry in 1999. From the 1980s and 1990s onwards in light of increasing competition from international competitors, firms within each industry began erecting barriers to entry and strengthening their position by increasing their capabilities. Since the late 1990s franchising has influenced both industries by securing and strengthening the existing industry level power relationships through the increasing capabilities of franchisors and leading to industry consolidation in both cases. In addition, the findings show that the macro-environmental factors as well as agency influence were extremely important in promoting the emergence of franchising.

The Five Theories and Case Examples Relating to the Emergence and the Impact of Franchising on Industry Structure

The multiplicity of theoretical propositions on what drives industry-level change—seen by many as problematic—was addressed in this research by using multiple theoretical approaches (TCE andAT, RDT, NIT, and population ecology). The review of the literature showed that franchising has mainly been researched from the economics and sociology perspectives. The economics perspective focused on efficiency and self-interest issues, costs, and wealth redistribution issues. From the TCE perspective a firm may choose to introduce franchising following the threat of variation imposed by other agents, or the firm itself. This variation might threaten the efficiency and cost levels of the firm. Similarly, ATsuggests that franchising is driven by the possibility of shirking and control issues and franchisors use the model of franchising to reduce these issues. Therefore, economic theories proved to be more limited in their explanation of the impact of franchising on industries. While their explanatory power captured the initial adoption of franchising they often failed to account for the subsequent impact of franchising on industries.

Sociology theories complement the economic perspectives by offering more behavioural, power, and dependency explanations. They also offered the legitimisation explanations with regards to the impact of franchising in the later stages of industry evolution; however, the sociology approaches often failed to deal with the initial adoption of franchising. Thus, RDT talks about variation, which can cause changes in the power and dependency equilibrium, and NIT emphasises the threat of departures from norms and legitimisation caused by variation. Moreover, NIT also suggests that a firm may choose to deal with existing selective pressures, to amend them or to act as a source of new ones. The complexity of this research revealed five theories dealt with in Table 7.1 (TCE and AT and the sociological theories of RDT, NIT, and population ecology) that are shared by both literature streams. The findings of this research generally support the conceptual and theoretical propositions found in the five competing organisational theories.

In terms of the franchising literature expansion, growth and survival are all explanations for the emergence of franchising, and looking at the five theories they addressed the issues of efficiency (TCE, AT), power (RDT, NIT), survival (population ecology), and therefore the conditions for the variation of a new organisational form such as franchising to emerge. Therefore, the adoption of franchising is mostly driven by transaction costs (TCE) opportunism and AT self-interest. The other three organisational theories address the growth and survival of such organisations such as RDT which explains how organisations reduce environmental interdependence and uncertainty, NIT looks at the need for legitimacy, and population ecology addresses the issue of survival. However, it does appear that TCE, AT, and RDT are best suited to explain the emergence of franchising. As such franchising emerges in response to contextual issues as theory describes and the environmental factors are more prevalent.

Once franchising has emerged in terms of how it impacts on industry structural change perhaps TCE is important as it can offer some explanation in terms of efficiency considerations and transaction cost reduction. AT which has never been used in relation to industry evolution also has a part to play in explaining the self-interest alignment of both parties in the evolving franchising relationship. However, perhaps more appropriate in explanation of the impact of franchising on industry evolution is RDT, NIT, and population ecology which offer more insights into the behavioural and power considerations over time. Thus in both cases once franchising emerged, franchisors increased the dependence of franchisees on their franchisor (RDT), and accordingly, increased the power of the franchisors (RDT). Moreover, market activities increased similarities across franchisors (NIT) and increased the legitimisation of these firms (NIT). In addition, franchise systems also diminished selective pressures by influencing industry level selection processes, thus exhibiting the advantage of expanding their franchisee network.

In summary the keys proponents and theoretical perspectives of the five competing organisational theories and their relevance to VSR and differentiates between the firm level approaches such as TCE, AT, and

RDT and the industry level approaches such as NIT and population ecology. As mentioned previously the model of VSR uses other approaches to explain organisational change and considers how the chosen perspectives deal with the issues of VSR. The evolutionary perspective adds value to each of the approaches and offers hope for a holistic understanding—not an integrated theory—of organisations and change. The diversity of perspectives is necessary given the subject matter and the evolutionary approach serves as an overarching framework within which the other approaches can be recognised and appreciated.

Theoretical Perspectives and VSR

This table (Table 7.1) is a summary of the theoretical perspectives of the five competing organisational theories and VSR adapted from Aldrich and Ruef (2006).

How Does Franchising Impact: Industry Evolution?

Addressing the overarching role that franchising has on industry evolution. This final section will summarise the findings and then present the main contributions of this research. Porter's (1980) work has been central to the purpose of this research; Porter noted that 'industry fragmentation has been overcome by franchising' this is one aspect of Porter's research that this research aimed to assess. It appears from the data that franchising had a major impact on structural change in both industries. In terms of franchising's rate of adoption and emergence both industries differed in terms of the timeframe of the emergence of franchising. Furthermore, it appears that the macro-environmental, industry, and agency context were important factors in the emergence of franchising with macro-environmental and agency influences being the more dominant. The findings show that in the fast food/QSR industry the contextual conditions were evident in the late 1970s and as a result the industry was ready to adopt and diffuse franchising earlier and at a more rapid pace compared to the real estate industry. In the real estate industry franchising emerged nearly 20 years later and its rate of adoption was relatively fast paced but not as rapid as the fast food/QSR industry. In terms of franchising and its effect on industry structure, in both cases prior to the introduction of franchising there was evidence of industry fragmentation and within a short time span industry consolidation was apparent. The analysis helps uncover how firm level adoption of franchising emerged as a result of certain macro-environmental context (government impact, economic and social change, and technology effects), industry conditions (increased competition, international new entrants, branding, and the emergence of industry standards and self-regulation), and agency effects (such as the influence of entrepreneurs) and consequently the impact that these strategies had on the structural evolution of their industries. It appears that from the data the reactions and patterns emerging in both cases once franchising was introduced ultimately led to a degree of industry restructuring. Porter (1980) observed that 'industries evolve because some forces are in motion that create incentives and pressures for change'. There is clear evidence that changes to industry-level relationships, and correspondingly to industrial structures, resulted from the emergence of franchising in both industries.

Addressing the structural change relating to new industry leaders the finding shows that in both cases industry leadership changed once franchising was adopted. The case analysis shows that power-related changes in industrial structures were often caused by increased capabilities, resulting from firms' adoption of franchising. Indeed, both industries exhibit evidence of changing power arrangements and it appears that franchising creates a shift in power towards the franchise systems as they began to dominate their industry and a clear reaction to this is the formation of firm associations or co-operative alliances as witnessed in both case studies. Structural changes such as barriers to entry post franchising adoption were evident. In both cases the impact of franchising has meant that as a consequence industry barriers to entry have increased. Moreover, franchising created firm level advantages in terms of branding and consumer loyalty as well as helping generate cost efficiencies and high levels of operating standards among franchise systems.

Additional consequences of franchising's structural impact on both industries were the development of firm level and industry level capabilities. In both cases franchising helped to create increased firm level capabilities, operating efficiencies, and a fundamental change and improvement in the industry's standards and image thereby raising the bar in terms of the industry's threshold capabilities. Within this branding was a significant capability developed post the emergence of franchising. In both cases franchising has helped to legitimise firms and create a branding differential in the eyes of the consumer. Franchising has helped drive the development of branding in both industries, and became such a threshold capability and business model, that firms who wanted to compete needed a strong brand as an essential component of their strategy. Once franchising was introduced it was selected and retained as a dominant design in both industries. Furthermore, in both cases it appears that once franchising emerged it changed the industry recipe and offered a successful dominant design or a changing business model that other firms would imitate and adopt. In both cases this new dominant design which included standardisation and codes of conduct and practice were developed and implemented by the franchise systems, which in turn altered the structure of both the fast food/QSR and real estate industries. In addition, there was also evidence of the emergence of new industry segments once franchising was adopted.

Another structural change once franchising emerged was the development of networks and relationships. In both cases once franchise systems were established they would hold their own training and development sessions and also disseminate information both internally between franchisees within their franchise system. Franchising as well as promoting the development of networks and relationships throughout the industry both at firm level and at industry level aided the prevention of State regulation by fostering industry self-regulation. Moreover, industry self-regulation was another structural change resulting from the impact of franchising. As well as creating increased firm level branding capabilities and operating efficiencies, franchising has fundamentally changed and improved both industries' threshold standards of operations, branding capabilities, and overall image and led both industries in terms of structure from fragmentation to consolidation.

References

Aldrich, H. (1999). *Organizations evolving.* London; Thousand Oaks, CA: Sage.

Aldrich, H., & Ruef, M. (2006). *Organizations evolving* (2nd ed.). London: Sage.

Augier, M., & Teece, D. J. (2008). Strategy as evolution with design: The foundations of dynamic capabilities and the role of managers in the economic system. *Organization Studies, 29*(8/9), 1185.

Barthélemy, J. (2011). Agency and institutional influences on franchising decisions. *Journal of Business Venturing, 26*(1), 93–103.

Bradach, J. L. (1997). Using the plural form in the management of restaurant chains. *Administrative Science Quarterly, 42*, 276–303.

Brown, S., & Eisenhardt, K. (1998). *Competing on the edge: Strategy as structured chaos.* Boston, MA: Harvard Business Press.

Carney, M., & Gedajlovic, E. (1991). Vertical integration in franchise systems: Agency theory and resource explanations. *Strategic Management Journal, 12*, 607–629.

Caves, R. E., & Murphy, W. R. (1976). Franchising: Firms, markets, and intangible assets. *Southern Economic Journal, 42*, 572–586.

Chirico, F., Ireland, R. D., & Sirmon, D. G. (2011). Franchising and the family firm: Creating unique sources of advantage, with F. Chirico and R.D. Ireland. *Entrepreneurship Theory & Practice, 35*(3), 83–501.

Collis, D. J., & Montgomery, C. A. (1995). Competing on resources: Strategy on the 1990. *Harvard Business Review, 73*(July/August), 118–128.

Dant, R. P. (2008). A futuristic research agenda for the field of franchising. *Journal of Small Business Management, 46*(1), 91–98.

Darr, E. D., Argote, L., & Epple, D. (1995). The acquisition, transfer, and depreciation of knowledge in service organizations: Productivity in franchises. *Management Science, 41*, 1750–1762.

Elango, B., & Freid, V. H. (1997). Franchising research: A literature review and synthesis. *Journal of Small Business Management, 35*, 68–81.

Gambardella, A., & McGahan, A. (2010). Business-model innovation, general purpose technologies, specialization and industry change. *Long Range Planning, 43*, 262–271.

Gawer, A. (2009a). Platforms, markets and innovation: An introduction. In A. Gawer (Ed.), *Platforms, markets and innovation*. Cheltenham, UK and Northampton, MA: Edward Elgar.

Gawer, A. (2009b). Platform dynamics and strategies: From products to services. In A. Gawer (Ed.), *Platforms, markets and innovation*. Cheltenham, UK and Northampton, MA: Edward Elgar.

Hunt, S. D., & Nevin, J. R. (1974). Power in a channel of distribution: Sources and consequences. *Journal of Marketing Research, 11, 186–193*.

Inma, C. (2005). Purposeful franchising: Rethinking of the franchising rationale. *Singapore Management Review, 27*(1), 27–48.

Jacobides, M. G. (2005). Industry change through vertical disintegration: How and why markets emerged in mortgage banking. *Academy of Management Journal, 48*(3), 465–498.

Jacobides, M. G., & Billinger, S. (2006). Designing the boundaries of the firm: From "Make, Buy, or Ally" to the dynamic benefits of vertical architecture. *Organization Science, 17*(2), 249–261.

Jacobides, M. G., Knudsen, T., & Augier, M. (2006). Benefiting from innovation: Value creation, value appropriation and the role of industry architectures. *Research Policy, 35*(8), 1200–1221.

Justis, R., Castrogiovanni, G., & Chan, P. (1992). Examination of franchise failure rates. In *Franchising: Passport for growth and world of opportunity*. Palm Springs, CA: Society of Franchising.

Lafontaine, F., & Shaw, K. L. (1998). Franchising growth and franchisor entry and exit in the US market: Myth and reality. *Journal of Business Venturing, 13*, 95–112.

Lafontaine, F., & Shaw, K. L. (1999). The dynamics of franchise contracting: Evidence from panel data. *Journal of Political Economy, 107*, 1041–1080.

Lewin, A. Y., & Volberda, H. W. (1999). Co-evolution of global sourcing: The need to understand the underlying mechanisms of firm-decisions to offshore. *International Business Review, 20*, 241–251.

Lewin, A. Y., & Volberda, H. W. (2011). Co-evolution of global sourcing: The need to understand the underlying mechanisms of firm-decisions of offshore. *International Business Review, 20*, 241–251.

Lewin, A. Y., Weigelt, C. B., & Emery, J. D. (2004). Adaptation in strategy and change: Perspectives on strategic change in organizations. In M. S. Poole &

A. H. Van de Ven (Eds.), *Handbook of organizational change and innovation* (pp. 108–160). Oxford: Oxford University Press.

Malerba, F., & Orsenigo, L. (1996). The dynamics and evolution of industries. *Industrial Corporate Change, 5*(1), 51–87.

March, J. G., & Simon, H. A. (1958). *Organizations.* New York, NY: John Wiley.

Martin, R. E. (1988). Franchising and risk management. *American Economic Review, 78,* 954–968.

McKelvey, B. (1997). Quasi-natural organization science. *Organization Science, 8*(4), 352–380.

Nelson, R. R., & Winter, S. G. (1982). *An evolutionary theory of economic change.* Cambridge: Harvard University Press.

Nelson, R., & Winter, S. (2002). Evolutionary theorizing in economics. *The Journal of Economic Perspectives, 16*(2), 23–46.

Norton, S. W. (1988). Franchising, brand name capital, and the entrepreneurial capacity problem. *Strategic Management Journal, 9,* 105–114.

Oxenfeldt, A. R., & Kelly, A. O. (1968). Will successful franchise systems ultimately become wholly-owned chains? *Journal of Retailing, 44,* 69–83.

Poole, M. S. (2004). Cental issues in the study of change and innovation. In M. S. Poole & A. H. Van de Ven (Eds.), *Handbook of organizational change and innovation* (pp. 3–31). Oxford: Oxford University Press.

Poole, M. S., & Van de Ven, A. H. (2004). *Handbook of organizational change and innovation.* Oxford: Oxford University Press.

Porter, M. E. (1980). *Competitive strategy.* New York: Free Press.

Shane, S., & Foo, M.-D. (1999). New firm survival: Institutional explanations for new franchisor mortality. *Management Science, 45,* 142–159.

Shane, S. (2008). *From ice-cream to the internet, using Franchising to drive the growth and profits of your company.* Upper Side River, NJ: Prentice Hall.

Tae, C. J., & Jacobides, M. G. (2011). How value migrates within an industry architecture: Kingpins, bottlenecks, and evolutionary dynamics.

Teece, D. J., Pisano, G., & Shuen, A. (1997). Dynamic capabilities and strategic fit. *Strategic Management Journal, 18*(5), 510–533.

Tee, R., & Gawer, A. (2009). Industry architecture as a determinant of successful platform strategies: A case study of the i-mode mobile internet service. *European Management Review, 6*(4), 217–232.

Volberda, H. W. (1998). *Building the flexible firm.* Oxford: Oxford University Press.

8

Conclusion

This chapter offers a summary of the main findings of this research and future research recommendations. In order to understand the role of franchising in industry evolution, we must look to understand why it emerges in the first place and then understand the impact it has on industry, which will allow us to draw some conclusions.

Why Does Franchising Emerge?

The following section conducts a comparative analysis of the two industry cases to understand why franchising emerges, beginning with the macro-environmental context, the industry context, and the actor/agent role, and from this evaluating the emergence and then the impact of franchising on the structural evolution of both industries and assessing the similarities and differences.

© The Author(s) 2017
R. Beere, *The Role of Franchising on Industry Evolution*,
DOI 10.1007/978-3-319-49064-9_8

The Macro-Environmental Context

Changes in both the macro-environment and industry were driven by the forces of technology, consumer preferences, economic growth, and a host of other influences. Change was both the result of external forces and the competitive strategies of the firms within each industry. Competition within the two industries was a dynamic process in which firms were vying for competitive advantage, only to see it erode through imitation and innovation by rivals.

In both cases the entry by an international franchise chain spurred a radical change in strategy for incumbents profoundly affecting both industries for the coming decades and prompting the emergence of franchising for the first time. However, there was a 20 year lag in terms of the time of the threat of entry or entry of the international competitor with regards to the fast food/QSR and real estate industry; however, the effects of these new entrants were the same in both cases.

The impact of government directly influenced the introduction of franchising to both industries but was more immediate and directly influential with regards to the emergence of franchising in the fast food/QSR industry and 20 years later in the real estate industry. In addition both industries displayed other variations at times of dramatic economic change caused by economic recessions and economic booms. In terms of similarities between the two cases both industries have been affected by economic change which ultimately helped to promote greater efficiency, but also impacted the structural shaping of each industry, prompting new competitor entry during periods of industry growth, and firm exits and consolidations during periods of industrial contraction. Thus economic change has had a major effect on both industries and has helped to drive the emergence of franchising. In the fast food/QSR industry franchising emerged in a recessionary period. In direct contrast franchising emerged in the real estate industry during a boom period. However, there appears to be a more dramatic and negative effect on the real estate industry with regards to economic change and economic recessionary periods whereas the fast food/QSR industry appears to be more robust and less vulnerable to these influences. Economic change meant that both industries became more competitive and firms within each industry had to develop strategies to survive. In both cases franchising was a means to overcome economic change at firm and industry level.

The cases reveal several dimensions to the increase in international competition. However, it is evident that the direct impact of increased international competition is different for each industry and has not been uniform over the period studied and perhaps the influence has been more direct and timely with regards to the fast food/QSR industry which happened 20 years earlier than it did in the real estate industry. Furthermore the emergence and adoption of franchising in Ireland was a result of the entry of international competitor McDonald's in the late 1970s. McDonald's brought into Ireland for the first time the fully formed concept of fast food/QSRs and the franchising model. Other international competitors entered into the market from 1980s onwards but McDonald's remained the true initiator of industry change and inspired indigenous fast food/QSR start-ups such as Abrakebabra and Supermac's who would drive the industry forward and adopt the franchising model. In contrast the real estate industry was not affected as quickly or as directly by the increase in international competition; however, 20 years later when the same threat occurred the consequences were similar. From late 1990s the real estate industry experienced increased entry of international competitors and in turn the demand for property (commercial and residential) and real estate services increased. In the late 1990s as a result of the threat of the US RE/MAX franchise system entering the Irish market Sherry FitzGerald in 1999 quickly adopted the franchise format and began to expand nationally. RE/MAX entered the Irish market shortly after and both of these companies helped to create major industry change, as a result of their success DNG followed suit and adopted franchising in 2004. Indeed the government's outward reaching policies of the 1950s, 1960s, and the free trade initiatives of the 1970s had a lasting impact on both industries allowing new international entrants to set up in Ireland. These new competitors brought new ways of doing business (such as franchising) and created increased international competition. Economic development would therefore sow the seeds for the prosperous Celtic Tiger years. Subsequent government influence since the 2008 recession has been once again to try and stimulate economic demand and international trade and foster industrial development and economic growth for the future. The threat and the inevitable introduction of international competition encouraged the emergence and adoption of franchising into both industries at different points in time but will similar consequences.

Social change has also had a great influence on the adoption of franchising in both cases. Comparatively social change has probably had a slightly greater impact on the fast food/QSR industry in terms of the immediate and swift emergence of franchising in the late 1970s when compared to the emergence of franchising 20 years later in the real estate industry. Furthermore, in both industries franchising can be seen as a new technology in itself and has had a major influence on the emergence of many now standardised practices promoted initially by the larger franchise systems. In addition new technologies adopted by firms also enabled the rapid adoption of a dominant design in both industries of which became widely imitated once shown to work. This technology played a significant role in the evolution of the two industries studied. While the evidence suggests that the benefit sought was usually increased efficiency, technology also helped give franchisors more power and control over their franchisees, as well as allowing online presence of firms and business to business communications. Therefore, technology has had a great influence on the emergence of franchising in both industries but there is significant evidence to suggest that the rapid adoption of information technology has had the greatest effect on the real estate industry. However, there is evidence that the adoption of technology as a dominant design was more intense and swift and happened 20 years earlier in the fast food/QSR industry.

The Industry Context

Analysis of the contexts of the Irish fast food/QSR and real estate industries and the subsequent emergence of franchising suggests that these industries exhibited the features of comparative cases. Therefore, both cases also showed evidence of structural differences across a range of factors. First, in terms of longevity, the Irish real estate industry was established before the fast food/QSR industry; however, franchising emerged in the fast food/QSR industry 20 years before it was introduced into the real estate industry. Second, there is a considerable difference between the industries' demographic characteristics, roles, experiences, capabilities, and the power of their players. However, both industries were fragmented prior to the introduction of franchising. For example, in the real estate industry until the introduction of franchising there were very few dominant real estate agents. Most industry competitors were small and economically insignificant. In the fast food/QSR industry the industry demographics were also characterised by a large number of small independent firms, which also exhibited industry fragmentation. Both industries were affected by increased international competition and prior to this both were highly fragmented. In the fast food/QSR industry McDonald's entered the Irish market in 1977, and in the real estate industry RE/MAX entered in 1999. In terms of the fast food/QSR industry, McDonald's, perhaps, was the most influential international competitor entered the Irish market. McDonald's entry was pivotal to bringing change to the Irish fast food/QSR industry at the time as the company was the first to introduce the franchising concept to Ireland. The evidence from the fast food/QSR industry shows immediate and direct correlation between the outward looking policies of the 1970s, the increased competition and international new entrants of the late 1970s and early 1980s. From the 1980s onwards there was an influx of international competitors into the Irish marketplace. During this period there was also a distinct expansion of food segments within the fast food/QSR industry. Entry of international competition into the Irish market has continued to the present day. In contrast in the real estate industry the outward looking economic policies and free trade initiatives of the 1970s, which were meant to attract overseas investment into Ireland, had no great impact on the industry directly. However, that changed 20 years later in the late 1990s when international competition became an issue with the threat of the international competitor RE/MAX entering the market. In 1999 Sherry FitzGerald adopted the franchise model and in doing so changed the rules of the game in terms of competing in the industry. Once these changes occurred in the late 1990s a change in industry concentration was apparent. RE/MAX has been the one international competitor to have an influence on the industry and prompted the emergence of franchising. Thus increased international competition was a driver in the emergence and adoption of franchising in the real estate industry.

The adoption of franchising was preceded by increased competition and international new entrants in both cases. In addition the increasing competitive demands of the industry with the need for high levels of service, brand development, and cost efficiencies encouraged many firms to adopt the organisational structure of franchising. Overall, following changes in the macro-environment and the subsequent increased international competition, both industries saw the emergence of franchising. Moreover, following these changes franchising as an organisational structure helped firms to expand into new industry segments propagating its norms and values, and increasing firm's potential for success. However, in balance it appears that international competition has affected the fast food/QSR industry more profoundly and earlier than the real estate industry. Indeed without the international entrant RE/MAX the real estate industry may not have adopted the franchising model so both industries were affected in a similar way but at different points in time.

In both cases from the 1990s onwards, most franchise systems began to engage in brand building as well as knowledge dissemination activities. Throughout the 1990s and 2000s the increased demand for business transparency, full information, and ethical practices forced firms to develop Public relations (PR) and information campaigns aimed specifically at their end customers. For example, most firms developed websites for promoting their activities. In both industries some firms believed that unfavourable changes in their macro-environments and industry could be ameliorated by adopting franchising and both industries witnessed the correlation between the emergence of franchising and brand building and development. Brand building was equally important in the two industries and it was of particular necessity in the fast food/QSR industry when differentiation was needed across the industry's generic product and service offerings. In relation to real estate services brand building helped to impart much needed consumer confidence in the industry.

In both industries there is evidence of industry self-regulation. However, ultimately the real estate industry exhibited greater evidence of industry self-regulation activity than the fast food/QSR industry. The contextual factors that triggered this varied across each industry. The influence of self-regulation and trade associations differs greatly between the two industry cases. These differences were consistent with contextual differences at industry level. In summary the emergence of franchising enabled both industries to further develop self-regulation strategies but the effects were more profound in the real estate industry when compared to that of the fast food/QSR industry.

Actor/Agent

In both cases entrepreneurial activity at firm level has been seen to promote greater efficiency, in particular entrepreneurial firms who quickly adapted to new business models such as franchising, brought about firm level efficiencies, branding dominance, investments in technology, high organisational standards, and organisational growth and expansion.

The influence of entrepreneurship in the identification and emergence of franchising as an organisational model is equally relevant to both industries and is as important as a factor in the emergence of franchising as the macro-environmental context. The firms who adopted franchising were clearly entrepreneurial, with a vision and focus for strategic growth and increasing market share, acting as innovators and drivers of change in their industries. Each case demonstrates how individual entrepreneurs served as archetypes for others, raising standards and expectations throughout their industry, and setting new performance criteria primarily through innovation and sheer determination. All of the entrepreneurs mentioned have given a sense of strategic direction and vision to their firms, with ambitions to grow, which led them to become some of the most successful in their industry, enabling their companies to continually innovate, and develop new products and new markets. Clearly key individuals and firms act as drivers of change, though often in ways linked to both efficiency and power considerations. Thus the role of agency and entrepreneurship appears to affect both industries equally.

Overall the macro-environmental and agency contextual factors were more powerful than the contextual factors. However, the time lag of 20 years from when franchising emerged in the fast food/QSR industry compared to the real estate could be justified by the differing macro-environmental context and as such the threat of entry of an international competitor and also the industry contextual factors prominent at the time of the emergence of franchising.

What Impact Does Franchising Have on Industry Structure?

Analysis of the data shows that reactions and patterns are emerging in the fast food/QSR and real estate industries, once franchising emerged ultimately led to a degree of industry restructuring. This is of particular relevance to this research which explores the impact of franchising on the structural evolution of industry as its main research question. The emergence of franchising is taken in the context of macro-environmental change and can be seen to benefit multiple industry stakeholders including; customers (by improving product and services), the firm level (with benefits of efficiency gains and branding benefits), and at an industry level (as protection from increased competition). For both industries the adoption of franchising helped increase firm sales, operating efficiencies, and brand development. This adoption also provided a level of standardisation in terms of operations and on-going economies of scale, as well as providing set up services, advisory services, standard setting, R&D, training services, and marketing and PR activities. Once franchising emerged at industry level some of the benefits seen in both industries included: the standardisation of products and services, marketing campaigns to increase customer loyalty, and the development of training programmes to increase franchisees' operational capabilities. Ultimately franchising aided firm level organisational efficiency, branding, and growth strategies—as well as speed to market—all essential in tackling increased industry competition.

Franchising as an organisational structure emerged and evolved within the Irish real estate and fast food/QSR industries, and exhibited dramatically different characteristics in terms of timeline and rate of adoption. Structural franchising has had a substantial impact on both industries albeit at different points in time. However, it appears that in the fast food/QSR industry franchise adoption and diffusion took immediate effect and the key industry leaders were franchise systems (with large numbers of outlets per franchisor) and the rest of the industry comprised independent operators. Franchising emerged early in the fast food/QSR industry in 1977 with the entrance of the US chain, McDonald's, resulting in both international and indigenous firms quickly embracing the model. Within a few short years other industry competitors quickly adopted the franchising model and expanded by opening multiple franchisee outlets which ultimately changed the industry makeup. Once franchising was introduced in the fast food/QSR industry the rate of adoption was swift with individual franchisors opening up multiple franchisee outlets. In contrast franchising as an organisational structure emerged and evolved within the Irish real estate industry, 20 years later in 1999. From that time onwards only three firms have successfully adopted franchising and become franchise systems (each with their own network of franchisees and expansion of outlets) and two of these franchisors are indigenous and one international. In 2012 the two industry leaders franchise systems and the third biggest competitor is a co-op—all three competitors share 60 per cent of the market. The majority of firms in the industry remain small independent real estate agents.

There appears to be major industry changes once firms adopt franchising, they began to gain organisational capabilities and organisational power, which resulted in changes in industry-level relationships, and eventually in industry structural change as well as adjustment to industry concentration. Therefore in both cases key franchise systems became dominant players and opened up multiple outlets nationally which ultimately led to industry consolidation among a few franchisors. The analysis helps uncover how firm level adoption of franchising emerged as a result of certain macro-environmental conditions, industry factors, and agency influences and consequently the impact that franchising strategies had on structural evolution of both industries. It appears from the data that reactions and patterns emerging from the two industries once franchising emerged which ultimately led to a degree of industry restructuring. Franchising aided firm level organisational efficiency, branding, and growth strategies—as well as speed to market—all essential in tackling increased industry competition. The fact that important structural changes across the two industries took place at different times suggests divergent contextual pressures occurred at different points in time prompting the adoption of franchising. However, there is clear evidence in both industries that the impact of franchising created changes to industry-level relationships, and correspondingly industrial structures, all of which resulted from the emergence of franchising.

Franchising has also influenced power arrangements within both industries. The main franchise systems became the dominant operators. The case analysis shows that power-related changes in industrial structures were often caused by increased capabilities, resulting from firms' adoption of franchising. Moreover, both industries exhibit evidence of changing power arrangements and it appears that franchising created a shift in power towards the franchise systems as they began to dominate their industry and a clear reaction to this was the formation of firm associations or co-operative alliances as witnessed in both cases.

Once franchising was adopted, there is evidence that an emergence of new segments occurred. In the fast food/QSR industry during the early 1990s convenience and fast food began to be offered in pubs and petrol stations and not just in fast food/QSR outlets. Franchising, once it took hold in the industry, enabled the emergence of new segments, as well as changing the boundaries of the industry. In the real estate industry once franchising was adopted, there is evidence that new segments also emerged. In the real estate industry prior to the introduction of franchising the majority of real estate agents were qualified and usually members of a trade association. However, RE/MAXs franchising model did not require that their real estate agents be qualified or even full time, and so unqualified franchisees could purchase a 'desk' from a RE/MAX office and begin selling properties. Other changes that affected the industry were the influence of technology and the establishment of Daft.ie (and myhome.ie), an online property listings company which revolutionised the advertisement of properties for sale or rent. In both cases, after the adoption of franchising, there has been a definite shift and emergence of new segments across both industries albeit at different periods of time.

Franchising in both industries helped to create increased firm level capabilities, operating efficiencies, and a fundamental change and improvement in the industry's standards and image thus raising the bar in terms of the industry's threshold capabilities. In both cases franchising has helped to legitimise firms and create a branding differential in the eyes of the consumer. It has also helped drive the development of branding in both industries, and became such a threshold capability, that firms who wanted to compete needed a strong brand as an essential component of their strategy. In both cases it appears that once franchising was adopted it changed the industry recipe and offered a successful dominant design that other firms would imitate and adopt. In both cases a dominant design which included standardisation and codes of conduct and practice was developed and implemented by the franchise systems, and altered structures of both the fast food/QSR and real estate industries. Franchising has helped create a dominant design in terms of best practice in the industry and gave competitive advantage to the franchise systems over independent operators. It also helped improve firm's operational efficiencies, reduce costs, and increase profits. The operating model of the business format franchising promotes a dominant design and standardisation across a franchise chain—with franchisees following a pre-determined operations manual and approved methods of business operations to achieve the highest levels of efficiency and high quality service and product offering which in both cases became the industry benchmark or best practice.

Franchising has also helped to promote the development of networks and relationships in both industries and particularly among franchisees within their franchise systems and it has even helped to prevent state regulation by encouraging industry self-regulation and cooperation. It helped promote the development of networks and relationships throughout the industry both at firm and industry level.

However, once it emerged franchising has helped to set best practice and industry standards in both industries. The fast food/QSR industry has been successful at self-regulation and avoiding government regulation. In the fast food/QSR once franchising was adopted it enabled industry wide improvements in the quality of food and service, thus raising the bar in terms of the industry's threshold capabilities. In contrast the real estate industry prior to the emergence of franchising had the two trade associations help the industry to self-regulate and after franchising emerged the franchise systems helped to set standards and ward off regulation. However, in recent years due to some questionable operating practices the government in 2004 stepped in and carried out a formal review of the industry and set some regulatory guidelines. Since then the franchise systems have adhered to the new industry guidelines with little changes needed and therefore have maintained a level of industry self-regulation. Indeed franchising has still had a profound effect on helping to set high standards in terms of best practice, branding, and operations and thus enabled a degree of industry self-regulation in both cases.

The next section will look at the contribution of this research and suggested future research.

Contribution of the Research

The literature reviewed in the first few chapters of this book suggested that there has been a shortage of studies on how industries evolve over time in terms of structure, and on what drives these industry-level changes. By exploring the impact of franchising on the evolution of industries over time, this research contributes towards filling a gap in the literature and makes a valuable contribution to knowledge of industry evolution and franchising. The multi-modal design of this research, which utilises five theories common to both fields, and the innovative application of the evolutionary approach to the individual case analysis make theoretical and conceptual contributions. Two substantial case studies constructed to answer the research question became the first comprehensive accounts of the evolution of the two Irish industries: the fast food/QSR and the real estate industries. These cases not only offer great historical data, but also provide great sources of information for practitioners, franchisors, government, and academics, thus making a unique contribution to practice. Finally, the longitudinal processual comparative case study approach used in this research required a well-built methodological base and well-constructed data collection and analysis methods.

Contribution to Knowledge

The role of franchising as a driver of industry-level change has not been previously explored. The comparative analysis of the impact of franchising on industry evolution contributes a number of valuable insights into the two understudied bodies of literature. The empirical contribution to the industry evolution literature stems from the comprehensive accounts of the two case studies that reveal common evolutionary phase patterns across the two industries discussed in the comparative case analysis chapter. This research also offers an insight into the types of structural changes that take place at the industry level. Literature on franchising benefits from the analysis of the contextual drivers relating to the adoption of franchising, and the impact that franchising makes on the two industries. The research supports much of the empirical evidence found in the literature. At the same time it puts forward several propositions that have not emerged from previous work on franchising. For example, this research found that the macro-environmental contextual drivers are much more powerful triggers of the introduction of franchising, than the industry ones and that agency (entrepreneurs) was an important factor in the emergence of franchising. This research also found that earlier in the century the adoption of franchising was mostly driven by threats, while towards the end of the twentieth century—by opportunities and possibilities. Franchising, its drivers, its impact across the two industries demonstrated increasing similarities over time and differences across the two industries and the impact of franchising was often shaped by the structural properties of the franchise systems and their leadership.

Conceptual Contribution

The use of a multi-modal approach in the theoretical framework of this research makes a two-fold contribution. First, multi-modal study designs have been often recommended but rarely employed. Therefore, this research is one of the few to explore the usage and implications of such an approach. Second, the conceptual findings of this research prove the usefulness of the usage of a multi-modal framework. No single theory is able to fully explain the impact of franchising on structures of industries. Economics-based approaches work best with the drivers of franchising adoption. Sociological theories, on the other hand, offer comprehensive explanations of the franchising development, such as entrepreneurship, and the relationship with franchisor and franchisees. The analysis of the data highlights that the transaction cost economics and agency theory better explains the motivational factors and the impact of franchising during the earlier stages, while the resource dependency theory, Neo Institutional Theory (NIT), and population ecology better account for the processes and actions at the later stages of industrial development, when issues like branding, transparency, and power prevail over transaction costs and efficiency considerations. Another contribution of this research is the innovative application of agency theory, which was rarely applied in the strategy field, and which has not been generally viewed through an evolutionary approach. The application of agency theory to the analysis of the contextual drivers and the impact of franchising on the structures of their industries proved valuable. This theory offered useful explanations of the motivations and outcomes of franchising, in preventing new variations or resulted in the creation of new variations. In addition neo-institutional theory has been useful in understanding the behavioural, power, and institutional considerations of franchising activities within each industry. Finally, the population ecology model has implications for franchise network survival and success.

Contribution for Practitioners

This research produced two original and comprehensive case studies of industry evolution with an emphasis on the origins, establishment, and evolution of both industries. The evolution of the Irish real estate and fast food/QSR industries in general, and the introduction of franchising have never been explored and documented. This research is of great interest to representatives of the franchising industry, policy-makers, and other stakeholders—a sentiment that was repeatedly expressed in the interviews for this research. The fact that this research is the first in-depth exploratory and descriptive account of the emergence and impact of franchising in Ireland makes it a solid contribution to academia and practitioners. The account of industry evolution offers an insightful description of the contexts, adoption, and impact of franchising. Over time the essence of franchising generally remains unchanged, its application and success rates within different contexts can be studied for strategic purposes. This should prove useful for franchising policy and strategic management theory. This knowledge becomes especially valuable in light of the recent financial crises, which initiated much debate on the optimal balance between industry self-regulation and the degree of government involvement. Finally, while this research achieved its research objectives, the contextual nature of the two cases offers a great pool of historical and industry data that can be used for primary or secondary analysis by the franchising industry, and scholars of strategy and history.

Methodological Contribution

As discussed previously, very few longitudinal studies have been undertaken in the field of strategy because of the complexity of this type of research. Accessibility of data, complexity of coding, and data reduction are among the concerns that prevent researchers from conducting this type of investigation. This research addresses some of these complications and makes a strong methodological contribution to the future research on industry evolution. First, the conceptual framework incorporates an innovative approach to the analysis of the impact of franchising on industry evolution. This thesis provides a contribution to methodology and practitioner use by extending the model developed by Pettigrew (1985) and Quinn (2002). Second, this research employed the archival and document methods of data collection that have been underused in the strategy field.

Future Research Agenda

This research has provided an important base line from which future research can further explore the implications of franchising and its impact on the evolution of other industries in Ireland and in other countries. The unique design of this research can be applied to other settings thus expanding the general understanding of franchising as one of the driving forces of industry. Increasing the number of settings being explored also increases the capacity to draw generalisations about what drives franchising, what strategies are the most successful, and what the impacts of these strategies are. There remain a number of gaps in franchising research. Namely if researchers want to study the evolutionary, developmental stages of franchising in completely new contexts, they need to go beyond the North American domain of enquiry. Qualitative studies have complemented the portfolio of research approaches in the past few years (Doherty & Alexander, 2006; Grunhagen et al., 2011), however, in an effort to gain richer insights into the rationale of key decision makers, such as franchisees, system managers, or franchise customers. Further research needs to be conducted using finer grained approaches. Moreover, some major gaps in the franchising literature still remain and are suggested by Dant (2008) who highlights that much of what we know about franchising is based on investigations of the franchisors to the virtual exclusion of research focused on the franchisee perspective. Dant (2008) also concludes by suggesting that while a handful of franchisee-based studies exist; there is a virtual absence of examining the franchising phenomenon from the perspective of the customer.

Entrepreneurship has a huge impact on the adoption and the subsequent impact of franchising and again this research has highlighted the importance of entrepreneurs as agents in the adoption and diffusion of franchising and thus their effects on industry evolution. Again Dant (2008) highlights the lack of research focused on the franchisee perspective. Emerging from the literature and data collected perhaps future research could focus on the role of entrepreneurship (both from a franchisor and franchisee perspective) as a central influencing factor in industry evolution with regards to the emergence of franchising and its evolution. Indeed the author has begun work on a paper relating to this particular area. Absent from the literature and empirical studies of franchising are the evolution of franchise systems over time as they coevolve with the changing strategies of the firm. Future research could therefore address the evolution of franchise systems, alliances, and networks over time, as they coevolve with the changing strategies of the firm, evolving industry strategic practices, and the changing regulatory and institutional environment and extend the initial findings of this research further.

Finally, in relation to industry evolution the progress demonstrated over the last 15 years is encouraging, but some significant gaps persist.

This may be explained by the complexity of the research that would be required to fill these gaps and recognition of the theoretical limitations that may have existed in the past. The theoretical foundations of industry dynamics and evolution are not frozen and new spheres of influence have emerged to combine with the traditional paradigms to progress the research agenda. In addition the importance of competences has been acknowledged by Tae and Jacobides (2011) who look at competences within the industry architecture field and build on this. The issues of competences and how they relate to firm and industry capabilities are concepts evident in this research that were not addressed in the literature review and could be further explored as a main focus in future research. The area of trade associations or industry collective grouping could also be explored in more detail as these were evident in both cases once franchising emerged as a way for independent operators to join force against the franchise systems. Some of the industry evolution and theoretical combinations are giving researchers stronger and more robust vehicles for enquiry than ever before, and enabling them to dig deeper into the questions of the field and the mystery of industry evolution. Through such approaches, mindful of multiple theoretical perspectives, different levels of analysis, and temporal aspects of influence, research can take up this challenge and uncover the mystery of industry evolution. Then a more enriched understanding of industries and their incumbent firms can be provided for the betterment of practice and of theory as a whole.

The chapter then offered a discussion of the contribution of this research to knowledge as well as the theoretical, conceptual, practitioner, and methodological contributions of this research. Finally, it concluded with an overview of a possible future research agenda.

The main contributions of this research are that it offers a focused assessment of franchising over time. There has been a lack of research on the relationship between franchising and its industry setting and this research addressed this gap. This research therefore explored why franchising emerges in an industry as well as its impact over time. It also enables the use of industry evolution material to explain this and therefore addresses the gap in the evolutionary literature in understanding the emergence of a new organisational form such as franchising. This research also makes an empirical contribution by providing evidence on how the

Irish fast food/QSR and real estate industries evolved over time, particularly in terms of structure as research in service sectors still suffers from the 'lack of empirical evidence' (Malerba & Orsenigo, 1996). By exploring franchising and its impact on the structural evolution of industry, this research enhances the literature and research in both the franchising and industry evolution fields.

References

Dant, R. P. (2008). A futuristic research agenda for the field of franchising. *Journal of Small Business Management, 46*(1), 91–98.

Doherty, A. M., & Alexander, N. (2006). Power and control in international retail franchising. *European Journal of Marketing, 40*(11/12), 1292–1316.

Malerba, F., & Orsenigo, L. (1996). The dynamics and evolution of industries. *Industrial Corporate Change, 5*(1), 51–87.

Pettigrew, A. M. (1985). *The awakening giant: Continuity and change in imperial chemical industries.* Oxford: Blackwell.

Quinn, J. (2002). *Industry evolution: A comparative study of Irish wholesaling.* Unpublished doctoral dissertation, Dublin City University, Dublin.

Tae, C. J., & Jacobides, M. G. (2011). How value migrates within an industry architecture: Kingpins, bottlenecks, and evolutionary dynamics.

Index

© The Author(s) 2017   **219**
R. Beere, *The Role of Franchising on Industry Evolution*,
DOI 10.1007/978-3-319-49064-9

Druck:
Customized Business Services GmbH
im Auftrag der KNV-Gruppe
Ferdinand-Jühlke-Str. 7
99095 Erfurt